Praise for *Tears Are Holy Water*

Picture something that comforts you the most, such as a heat-ed blanket, a hot cup of cocoa, or a warm embrace. Reading this book gives the same sense of well-being and safety as those comfort items. Readers will be moved by the personal stories of growth and the easy-to-understand concepts and applicable strategies in each chapter. Whether or not one has a psychological diagnosis, it is safe to say that everyone in general has struggled at some point mentally and emotionally. Therefore, anyone in the age bracket of teenagers to older adults would be positively influenced by this book, which I strongly endorse. The tone, voice, and style of this book exude comfort, safety, and validation. As someone who works as a school counselor with high school–age students and who is always seeking new strategies for myself personally, I strongly endorse this book.

—Meagan Crandall, MA

This book is a poetic and science-informed invitation to healing, grounded in rhythm, relationship, and remembering. Through stories, somatic rituals, and reflection prompts, it offers not solutions, but mirrors—gentle pathways back to self. It honors the cultural roots of healing practices with care and respect, weaving wisdom and science into something both beautiful and deeply human.

Chapter 13 shifted something in me—it reminded me that healing isn't just personal; it's also relational. I felt a deep desire to become that grounded, calming presence for others, especially in my work. The idea that our own regulation can ripple outward as medicine was both humbling and empowering.

The tone of the book is gentle, poetic, and deeply compassionate. The voice is knowledgeable, yet warm. The style weaves science with storytelling, ritual with reflection, offering both clarity and comfort in equal measure.

This book is a beautiful blend of science and soul—grounded, poetic, and deeply wise. It offers not quick fixes, but lasting resonance, guiding readers gently back to their bodies, their creativity, and their sense of safety. A vital companion for anyone on a healing path.

—Dail Williams, MA

Rose Rita writes with poetic clarity, offering meaningful insight into how our nervous system responds to stress and trauma. Her book serves as a beautifully written accessible manual for self-exploration and healing. As she reminds us, "Healing is not about erasing the past, but about creating new living experiences that tell the body another story."

Having explored a variety of transformative modalities—including psilocybin, ayahuasca, ketamine-assisted therapy, and holotropic breathwork—I find this book to be an ideal companion before or after such journeys. It also serves as a supportive tool for integration. Rita includes practical exercises and step-by-step guidance to assist in the healing process.

She writes with both gentleness and precision. Her words feel like a warm velvet weighted blanket to the soul. I plan to recommend this book to participants as essential reading prior to upcoming retreats and to anyone interested in emotional healing.

– DG, NP-C

This is the most wonderful book I have read on somatic healing—on healing, for that matter—and I have read many. Rose Rita writes clearly, concisely, and poetically while combining research, knowledge, therapeutic experiences, insight, and practical exercises—all with so much care and compassion and while honoring the ancient traditions and peoples who have been practicing somatic healing for centuries. *Tears Are Holy Water* is thorough and well organized, offers helpful exercises at the end of every chapter, and is written with such a caring, compassionate voice! Did I mention that? LOL. I know I did because I have read extensively about healing and have never before encountered such care and compassion within the text. I am filled with excitement and hope and cannot wait to share this book with my sisters, mother, children, nieces and nephews, and so many friends! I am so grateful to Rose Rita for writing this book.

Everything in this book resonated with me, probably partially because I've been reading a lot about somatic healing over the past year while integrating some intense somatic experiences from a retreat in the Peruvian rainforest last September to October. The things that stood out most against the backdrop of all my other readings are probably the clear, concise poetic language; the thoughtfulness, care, and compassion of the author's voice; and the care and honor given to ancient healers across the earth who have been practicing somatic healing and honoring our connection to earth/nature for centuries. This is very distinctive among the other books I've read.

While reading this book, I have been able to clarify a number of things about my healing journey, including my on-again-off-again-on-again artistic practice throughout my lifetime (including many years of dance as well as visual arts), which has been moving me toward reclaiming and reinhabiting my body. I am thrilled to finally (at sixty-six years of age) be coming home to myself in this way. I feel renewed and excited and so happy and grateful to continue on this path.

It is truly a gentle, compassionate invitation to pay attention to the senses, to reconnect with the self and with the natural world and all who inhabit it. The tone itself gently invites openness and healing.

—Dawn Liddicoatt, MSEd

This is a book about somatic healing that couples scientific knowledge with traditional and intuitive practices. It includes actionable steps to take toward regulation and healing.

This book includes a number of passages that use strong figurative language to describe emotional processes. I find it very useful to have the vocabulary to describe feelings and emotional processes. I am, by nature, a very visual person; and I found that the author's descriptions resonate with my own experiences.

The idea of practicing feeling my big feelings in small doses and then quickly coming back to a place of calmer, safer feelings spoke to me. I will definitely be using this practice.

Through reading this book, particularly the portions that include actionable steps, healing feels more attainable to me.

Amid my own journey toward healing, I have learned a number of things:

I need to actually feel my feelings.

I need to find a way to calm my nervous system.

I need to learn to regulate my emotions.

I need to feel safe.

I know I need to do these things, but I keep finding myself asking the same question: "How?"

This book works as a guide, offering concrete actionable suggestions for how to move toward feeling my feelings, calming my nervous system, regulating my emotions, and, hopefully, eventually feeling safe.

—APB

This book offers insights into the disconnect between the way our bodies and selves are programmed to process our experiences and the way the modern world tells us we should. It offers a clear understanding of how multiple and varied cultures had similar understandings and practices that allowed processing and how we can return to that today.

Aligning the physical with the emotional and their effects on one another provided clarity and understanding. The best way to describe it is that I felt one with myself and my experiences as if reading validated something I knew to be true.

Warm and enveloping, it reads as a personal conversation from the author to the reader, with insights, allowances, and suggestions rather than an academic solution or directive.

—Morgan Mudron, MA

This book is a beautiful and heartfelt invitation into coming home to yourself. Rose Rita guides the reader with an empathetic touch through both the research and the felt experience of developing a deeper relationship with your own nervous system.

All the moments of people starting to feel again and realizing there was nothing wrong with them to begin with—what powerful medicine!

I would recommend this book to anyone who is interested in becoming happier and more in tune with the rhythms of their felt sense in life.

Warm and wise.

—Christina Sedlmaier

It's a great read for someone who is trying to understand what it means to heal, how to process emotions, and why this matters today, tomorrow, and in the past. I will continue reading it.

Rose Rita's style of writing stands out. It's well written for sure, but it connects science and history in a way that helps understanding and gives the everyday person a perspective on understanding the healing journey and its importance.

I would recommend this book to anyone that is trying to make sense of therapy. It answers my questions and helps me have greater appreciation for therapy—this coming from a guy raised in a way that discouraged conversations about feelings and emotions.

Engaging, intellectual, fun, and informative.

—Julio Paz

A book grounded in scientific and cultural knowledge. A book that introduces embodiment and somatic exercises in approachable ways. A book to savor slowly.

The reflections and rituals at the end of each chapter were so lovely. I found myself lingering over them. Honestly, I lingered over this entire book, picking up each lesson carefully and living with it for a time.

I was particularly interested in learning more about glimmers, terminology I had only heard but now fully understood. I find myself looking for and savoring the glimmers more as a tool to keep me present in my body. There are so many out there, and I'm loving naming them more directly!

Honestly, I think [reading this book] feels like a hug from a great emotionally reliable friend.

—Brekke Bounds, MSFS, BCHN

I'm inspired to share a positive experience that I think was enabled in part by the work I'm doing because of the prompts you provide. I've been in therapy for years and have long believed in the power of somatic healing through Reiki/acupuncture, but your prompts seem to be the thing that is helping me put this knowledge into practice in my own body. For me, therapy often serves as an opportunity for a pressure release, but not much reflection, if that makes sense. I go. I dump. I feel a little catharsis because I'm not complaining to a friend/family member. I try to hold the recommended practices in mind when moving through the world. Rinse/wash/repeat. It seems your book is an unlock!

—Ellen Gladish

In her lyrical prose, Rose Rita performs the very guidance her work recommends for anyone who seeks to find inner equilibrium and to glimpse the ineffable joy available for those who have experienced trauma, which, in some way or another, includes all of us. Her poetic and figurative language works, in itself, to provide a balm for the soul.

Time and again, I was struck by the resonant power of the evocative images or examples offered repeatedly in this work, such as the sensation of cradling a baby for comfort, or of the "glimmers" available when we are open to recognizing them, which encouraged me to head to my porch at firefly time as darkness falls.

Having experienced some trauma, what this book left me with was a deepened sense of hope. I appreciated the concrete and practical methods of recognizing the "body" of knowledge that Rose Rita offers to unbind my body, lift my spirit, and shift my thinking.

I consider this an important book for anyone, whether a seeker of self-healing and wholeness or a professional therapist.

The tone of the book is deeply respectful and kind, creating a space for safe self-explorations. The voice is warm and welcoming. The style is well organized and comprehensive. The language is often gorgeous.

—Mary Ann Ryan, PhD

Tears
Are
Holy
Water

Tears Are Holy Water

Somatic Wisdom & Rituals
for Feeling and Aliveness

Rose Rita James, LCSW

Grá Mór Books
Chicago, IL, 60643
www.roseritajames.com

Publisher's Cataloging-in-Publication Data

Names: James, Rose Rita, author.
Title: Tears are holy water : somatic wisdom & rituals for feeling and aliveness / Rose Rita James.
Description: Includes bibliographical references. | Chicago, IL: Grá Mór Books, 2025.
Identifiers: LCCN: 2025920461 | ISBN: 979-8-9932443-0-3 (hardcover) | 979-8-218-77759-3 (paperback) | 979-8-9932443-1-0 (ebook)
Subjects: LCSH Mind and body therapies. | Psychic trauma--Alternative treatment. | Post-traumatic stress disorder--Alternative treatment. | Healing. | Self-actualization (Psychology) | Self help. | BISAC BODY, MIND & SPIRIT / Healing / General | SELF-HELP / Emotions
Classification: LCC RC489.M53 .J36 2025 | DDC616.85210651--dc23

Printed in the United States of America

First edition

For the family I came from and the family I created:
This book exists because of you.
This book exists for you.

"Ar scáth a chéile a mhaireann na daoine."
(We live in the shelter of each other.)

—Irish proverb

Contents

Preface

This book began as a whisper. Not a plan or a deadline, but a low hum inside my body that said, "There is an important story here. Lean in, listen, learn, and be curious about it before you tell about it."

At the time, I did not know the story would only partially reveal itself through the pulse of my own nervous system, shaped as it was by love, rupture, and repair. I sensed an important thread running through the cycles of birthing, grieving, and living I had both done and witnessed in my forty-five years, though I could not yet see where it would lead. Open and curious, I leaned into the voices of my ancestors, the wisdom of my clients, and the experiences of students that passed through my eyes and ears. The moments that caught my breath and stilled my heart. What came back was not a single narrative, but a constellation of stories—woven from theirs, mine, and ours.

Over the years, that deep listening grew into a practice of recording words and ideas, first privately and then shared with clients and colleagues, as a way of processing and remembering. That practice became a burgeoning personal language of healing—clinical and poetic all at once—weaving together the rigor of science, the tenderness of somatic therapy, the vitality of art, and the grounding of ritual. It evolved into how I came to understand not only my own repair but also how we might begin to mend what is frayed in our families, our communities, and our world. Our nervous systems showed me they were not only records of what we had endured but also guides, mapping the way toward repair. They reminded me that what we carry is never only our own. It belongs to our lineages, our communities, and the larger field we inhabit together. After decades of listening, the story wanting to be told had finally and fully revealed itself.

These pages are not here to tell you who to be or how to live every moment of your life. They are here to remind you that your body knows how to return to itself when asked and given safety. They are here to remind you that your nervous system is not a machine to manage, but a living intelligence that has always been protecting you. They are here to remind you that the tears you shed are not your weakness, but your own fount of holy water—clearing, blessing, and opening space for what is yet to come.

I offer this book in the hope that it meets you wherever you are. In grief, may it hold you. In overwhelm, may it steady you. In joy, may it mirror your aliveness and whisper, "Stay here and bask as fully and as long as you can."

May you find your own way of listening deep inside yourself and translating what you hear. May you trust what you find there.

Acknowledgments

I wrote the book I needed and the book I wanted everyone I love to read. Every page carries the fingerprints of those who have poured into me: mentors, friends, family, clients, teachers, guides, and fellow travelers. There is no me without them. This book is the culmination of my adulthood, my healing, and my professional life. It is my offering back.

To my ancestors in America and Ireland, who whispered stories of resilience through my bloodline, who kept rhythm in my bones when I needed to sing and dance and wit between my ears when I needed to learn and laugh, and who bore heavy stories of hunger, war, and loss in silence so that I might one day be born to speak of their impact aloud, this work is for you and because of you.

To my children—Josephine, Vivienne, and Rowan—you are my greatest teachers in aliveness and my most powerful daily glimmers. Thank you for being the heartbeat beneath every day I live. Any striving I've ever done was to pave the path for your unique creative contributions to this world. There is nothing more important to me in this world than preserving and protecting your vitality. A chlann, is sibh cuisle mo chroí. Sláinte, go deo. Beannachtaí.

To my husband and partner of twenty-five years, Jason, thank you for seeing my heart through every transformation and for your relentless commitment to showing up in service to our family, always doing your fair share and more. Thank you for walking beside me even when the path got rambling, brambly, and weary—believing in me that the journey and the view would be worth it. I became an adult alongside you, and I love you beyond any tools of language I have to communicate the enduring commitment of that love.

To my parents—Mary Ann Ryan, PhD; Ed Walsh; and Margaret Walsh, DVM—thank you for instilling in me a reverence for education, for modeling lifelong learning, and for helping to raise my children as I changed careers, pursued advanced degrees, and found my way into the work that became this book. Your own ambition and exploration provided a map for me on what is possible to commit to and achieve in this short life. Your steadfast support of my family made every chapter of my professional transformation possible as a working mother of three children.

To my siblings—Sam Walsh, Fran Walsh, Andrew Toan, and Nathan Toan—and to all my aunts, uncles, cousins, sisters-in-law, nieces, nephews, fairy godchildren, and extended kinfolk by blood and heart, thank you for teaching me complexity, devotion, and resilience in the most intimate ways. Our family circle's ethos—rooted in fiercely direct dialogue, adaptability, creativity, resourcefulness, loyalty, and an unmistakably felt vitality—has shaped the way I live, love, and lead. Your unique brilliance and presence have been both mirror and catalyst—reminding me that love, even when messy or hard and especially when it is hilarious, is our most enduring inheritance.

To my lifelong sister friends and soul family—Muffie Delgado Connelly, SEP; Corina Favia Fitzpatrick; Keelin Mayer, MAT;

Janelle Favia Fitzpatrick; Caitlin Broderick, MSW; Annie Novotny, LCPC; and Colleen O'Sullivan, MSW—thank you for over forty years of shared life. Our fiercely honest conversations, tear-inducing laughter, foot-stomping dance parties, old-timey song circles, and spontaneous altars, rituals, and extravagant adventures in adornment have been steady nourishment since I was small. Together, we've shared late-night memes, breathtaking journeys near and far, and the kind of desperately needed vacations that restore the soul. You helped me write this book simply by being living proof that love regulates. We have friendships that transcend category, platonic romances marked by fierce loyalty, creative devotion, willingness to repair, and an expansive tenderness that makes room for the whole self. Your love is sacred, not secondary. You are enduring nervous system medicine.

To my village of fairy godparents—Pam Holt; Jan Favia, MFA; Peggy Malone; Patrice Ceisel; Patsy Walsh; Kate Ryan, MFA; Jim Green; Kevin Fitzpatrick; Jim Battistoni; Tomas Kaysen; Kathleen McInerney, PhD (RIP); Barb Malone (RIP); Deb Cole (RIP); and Virginia Delgado Connelly (RIP)—you have supported me in ways seen and unseen for the entirety of my existence. Thank you for committing to and holding space for my becoming.

To my recent clinical consultants and guides: Jackie Smith, LCSW; Cris Avila, LMFT, SEP; Rhonda Kelloway, LCSW, SEP; Mark Vecchio, LP, SEP; Margaret Crowley, LCSW, SEP; Suzanne Mikkelson, PhD; and others not named here, thank you for your brilliance, generosity, and the quiet clarity of your presence.

To the therapists who have supported my growth, my self and family system inquiry, and my larger personal expansion where it meets my professional passions—Carol Locasio, LCSW; Thomas Goforth, MDiv; Kelly Dineen, PhD; Carrie Cherep, LCPC; Dan O'Grady, PhD; and Jenny Korotko, LCPC, SEP—and the several high school and college counselors who supported me during years of transition and flux, thank you for routing me back to myself.

To the instructors who shaped my recent clinical and somatic work—Arielle Giaretto, LMFT, SEP; Francine Kelley, LCPC, SEP; Dave Berger, LMFT, PT, SEP; Raja Selvam, SEP, PhD; Marina Toledo; and the Thrive EMDR training faculty—thank you for modeling precision with compassion. To my professors and academic mentors—Phyllis West, MSW, MPH, PhD; Giesela Grumbach, MSW, PhD; Kim Boland-Prom, MSW, PhD; Lydia Falconnier, MSW, PhD; Elizabeth Essex, MSW, PhD; Robin Wucherer, PhD; Janet Lorch, MAT; Kamau Rashid, PhD; Sophie Degener, PhD; Sharon Rak; Todd Price, PhD; Lt. Michael Schlosser, EdD; Yan Searcy, MSW, PhD; Mary McCay, PhD; John Biguenet, MFA; Susanne Dietzel, PhD; Catherine Wessinger, PhD; Katherine Adams, PhD; Melanie McKay, PhD; John Mosier, PhD; Christopher Chambers, MFA; Constance Miu, PhD; Jim Thomas, PhD; Doris Perry, MSW, PhD; Nadine Harris-Clark, MSW; Kelly Norman Ellis, PhD; and Jan Pinkerton, PhD—and the other luminous minds who shaped my emerging understanding of systems, self, and spirit, thank you.

To my supervisors, mentors, and former fellow field wizened clinicians and educators—Tammy Rohan Bobel, EdD, LCPC;

Lindsay Ortman, LCSW; Nicole Saunoris, MA; Patrick Mellin, MA; Steve St. Jean, MA; Tricia Weber; Roger Schnitzler; Kyle Flanigan; RJ Haines; Andy Furbee; Crisel Andrade, LCSW; Jose Baltazar, LCSW; Margaret Black, MEd; Amy Youngman Weglarz, MEd; Lindsey Girard; and Lt. Paul Connolly—and the many unnamed school leaders, clinicians, and officers who taught me what safety, leadership, and integrity look like in motion, thank you.

To my past colleagues and collaborators at Criú de Sheela, Beverly Area Arts Alliance, Edna White Community Garden, Manteno High School, CICS Longwood, the Center for Self Actualization, Chicago Public Schools, and the Metropolitan Water Reclamation District, you have helped weave healing into institutions and communities. You made the systems we toiled in feel human and the work sacred.

To my fellow Reiki learners and energetic travelers, thank you for being there when I needed to remember that the body will tell you what it needs and the soul will reveal its secrets if you can slow yourself down enough to listen.

To every client and student who has trusted me with their story, this book is for and because of you. You have been some of my most profoundly humbling and benevolent teachers.

To the early readers and reviewers, your generous feedback and clear support were necessary medicine. Thank you for reflecting the soul of this book back to me.

To the Potawatomi, Ojibwe, and Odawa peoples—the original and enduring stewards of the land where I write, live, and heal—I honor your legacy. The breath and spirit of this work hope to be in conversation with yours.

And to the many unnamed, remembered in my bones but not yet typed here, thank you. I carry your wisdom in the margins, your voice in the rhythm, and your hand in the spine of this book.

Grá mór,

Rose Rita

INTRODUCTION

A Soft Place to Land

Welcome.

There comes a moment in every healing journey when something inside whispers, "I want to feel alive."

Not just survive the things that took you nearly down, but feel aliveness after them.

In the body.

In the moment.

In yourself.

This book was written for that moment and for all the ones that come before it and after it.

You do not need to be "fixed" once and for all.

You need only to be more fully felt, moment to moment, day by day.

Our culture often tells us that healing is a destination, one more thing to achieve. But your nervous system is not a problem to solve and be done with. It is a living intelligence, electric and ancient, shaped by every instinct you've ever had to protect yourself, to seek connection, to survive what was never meant to be survived alone.

If you have struggled to rest, to cry, to speak up, to laugh, to play, to soften, to create, this book is a map back to the place where those capacities live.

If your body has felt like a battlefield or your emotions too much, too fast, too often, this is your invitation to return gently. To feel your way home.

This book is not a step-by-step manual. It is not a one-and-done fix. It is a field guide for your back pocket.

An important conversation held over soft candle glow.

A calm boat in unpredictable waters.

A poetic collection of stories, studies, practices, and quotes to accompany you as you remember what your body has always known: Healing is possible.

It lives in rhythm. In repetition. In rest. In relationship.

Each chapter offers a new doorway into the nervous system—mapping its design, learning its language, rooting in to breath and ground, and opening to creative expression and ritual. Along the way, you'll meet clients whose stories echo your own, and you'll find questions and practices to help you land more deeply in your body.

Like many of those I serve, I came to this work years ago because I wanted to feel again. I found myself numb after a series of traumatic events and several years working as a first responder. As a trauma therapist and educator, I've sat with fellow artists, performers, parents, children, teachers, healers, and seekers—many of them brilliant at showing up for others, but unsure how to show up for themselves. In walking with them daily, I was reminded to be sure to walk myself home as well. While I found there were no shortcuts, walking the terrain so frequently did reveal some well-worn paths—quiet evidence that others had made this journey too.

Daily reminders that I was not alone.

Let this book show you *you are not alone.*

Long before neuroscience gave language to nervous system regulation and trauma responses, ancestral and Indigenous cultures held deep embodied practices for restoring balance. The Hawaiian tradition of Ho'oponopono used synchronized breathwork for communal reconciliation, resolving conflict through presence and intention. Jewish mystical teachings of Sitra Achra explored the emotional shadow not to fix it, but to integrate it. The Māori practice of whakapapa wove personal emotion into ancestral lineage, linking one person's healing to the health of their entire community. These traditions did not treat emotions as symptoms to suppress, but as sacred energies to be moved, witnessed, and metabolized (Kimmerer, 2013).

As we move deeper into these pages, you'll encounter tools and insights inspired by both modern neuroscience and ancient traditions. This is intentional. Healing is not owned by any one system. It is a birthright shared across time, culture, and spirit. It is also essential to name and honor the lineages from which many of these practices come. Breathwork as regulation draws from yogic traditions in India. The use of drumming, movement, song, and story can be traced through the Indigenous Americas, Africa, the Pacific Islands, Asia, and pre-Christian Ireland, among countless other earth-based cultures. Somatic awareness, though often claimed by Western psychology, is not a new discovery. It is a remembered knowing.

These traditions were not created in laboratories. They were born in ceremony. In survival. In land-based belonging. In communities that treated the body as sacred and healing as collective.

To honor this truth, this book will cite origins when known, avoid appropriation and reduction, elevate voices from within the cultures whose wisdom is being shared, and encourage you to explore with reverence, not extraction. At the end of the book, you'll find a further reading and exploring appendix that invites you to delve into the published work of writers, thinkers, activists, and artists who carry forward ancestral and Indigenous somatic and liberatory practices.

Before using a specific and unique ancestral or Indigenous practice, readers are encouraged to pause and ask the following: Who does this belong to? Have I been invited into it, or am I taking it? Am I contributing to the culture that created it or just collecting tools? How can I honor its roots with integrity?

May your healing deepen your respect for others' paths, not eclipse them. Let it be an act of remembrance, not erasure. Let it be a homecoming that makes room for many homes. Because nervous system healing is not just personal. It is also historical. It is cultural. It is communal. The nervous system does not heal in isolation. And neither should we.

With that in heart, this book follows no rigid formula, but it does have a rhythm. Each chapter begins with a quote or line from a poem—words meant to open your heart before your mind. What follows is a narrative exploration, weaving together somatic wisdom, neuroscience, trauma-informed practices, and cultural memory. You'll encounter stories from therapy, metaphors for embodiment, research that speaks your body's language, and reminders that your pain is not pathology; it is adaptation.

You'll find client vignettes throughout, drawn from years of therapeutic work. All are composites, ethically crafted from shared patterns of human experience to protect the sacredness of individual stories. Details have been changed, identities protected, and multiple truths gently held inside each case vignette. No story belongs to one person; each belongs to many. This choice is both ethical and sacred. Trauma therapy requires a covenant of deep trust, and that trust continues here. By using composite characters, I honor the privacy of those who've entrusted me with their most vulnerable moments while offering you glimpses into the archetypal terrain of healing. These vignettes are not here to diagnose you, but to be a point of recognition. To say you are not alone in this.

You may see yourself or someone you love in these stories. You may recognize not the exact experience, but the familiar emotional echo. Let that recognition be an invitation, not a comparison. These stories are not offered as solutions. They are offered as mirrors. You are not alone in your tenderness, your complexity, your longing to come home.

At the end of each chapter, you'll find two anchoring sections: "Journal and Reflection Prompts," a set of questions to help you pause, turn inward, and notice what is shifting. And "Somatic Ritual," a gentle invitation into your body's knowing through breath, touch, movement, or sensory attention. You are encouraged to engage with these slowly, again and again. This is not homework. It is homecoming.

You may read this book front to back or skip to the chapter that calls to you. You may underline or weep or close it halfway through to take a walk. All ways of moving through are welcome. If some of the early chapters feel research-heavy, know this: Grounding in science is only one strand of this work. The rest live in your cells, your stories, your communities. Come back to the denser chapters when they begin to feel more accessible for you, if that supports your path toward aliveness. Healing has never been linear. Nor has knowledge.

Thoughts are the language of the brain. Emotion is the language of the body. Knowing this, words may fall short to communicate soul-to-soul understanding; and still, we try nonetheless. The language of healing shared in this book is tender, powerful, and evolving. In these pages, you'll find terms drawn from neuroscience, somatic psychology, trauma theory, and poetic metaphor. Some are clinical, others intuitive. All are chosen with care. We as clinicians, researchers, and theorists try to name what it means to come home to ourselves, even when homecoming is something felt more than understood. Allow your own somatic language to rise to meet you as you read, write, weep, dance, and remember. The words in this book are fertile ground to grow from, not a strict blueprint for your reconstruction.

Let this book be your companion, not your taskmaster. A rhythm to sway to, not a rule book to follow. It offers you an invitation, not an obligation. You do not have to rush through this book and its exercises. Your nervous system will meet the work in its own right timing. Go as fast or as slow as you need.

Take a breath. We're here together now.

I am writing to you not only as a therapist but also as a fellow traveler on this path. Like many of you, I have had to relearn how to listen to my body. To slow down. To feel safe. To cry in the middle of the day. To rest without guilt. To let joy in. To prioritize pleasure. To make time to create. I have known the weight of silence and the freedom of a full breath. This book was written from that place.

I believe in the intelligence of your body. I believe in its desire to heal. I believe in the sacredness of tears, the wisdom of sensation, and the courage it takes to stay with yourself when everything in you wants to run. If there is one message I want this book to leave with you, it is this: *You are not broken. Your body is trying to bring you home to safety.*

This work is deeply personal to me. And yet I offer it to you with open hands. May it be a lantern for your journey, a companion in the dark, a gentle reminder in the light. May you come to know the sound of your own nervous system's *yes.*

With reverence,

Rose Rita James, LCSW, MSW, MAT

1

Your Nervous System Is You

I shall gather myself into myself again,
I shall take my scattered selves and make them one,
Fusing them into a polished crystal ball
Where I can see the moon and the flashing sun.

—Sara Teasdale, "The Crystal Gazer"

There are parts of you that have never stopped bracing. Not because you are broken, but because you adapted to survive. Beneath the tension in your shoulders, the holding in your breath, the way your body braces before love or shrinks from rest, there is something ancient, intelligent, and alive.

All of it is your nervous system in motion.

Your nervous system is not a machine to be fine-tuned or silenced. It is not a problem to solve. *It is you.* A living intelligence, electric and fluid, shaped by every sigh, every instinct, every moment you learned to protect yourself by pulling away or leaning in. It is the wordless memory of your becoming. And it is also the path home.

In a world increasingly disembodied, where human connection is mediated by screens and digital and artificial intelligences

1

encroach on the terrain of human emotion and creativity, turning toward the body is a revolutionary act. Our culture rewards us for staying in our heads. We are taught that intellect is superior to intuition, that productivity is more valuable than presence, and that emotional discomfort is something to be medicated, numbed, or avoided. We are seduced by technology's promise of quick fixes and digital escapes, but these only deepen the distance from our own flesh and breath.

To work somatically is to refuse this drift into disconnection. It is a curative for these times: a way of remembering our humanity in the face of forces that would have us dissociate from pain, from joy, and from our very aliveness. Each moment you return to your breath, your sensation, your inner knowing, you participate in a quiet, but potent counterbalance. You reclaim something ancient and essential: your right to feel, to heal, and to be fully here.

This work is not indulgent. It is necessary. In choosing to stay with yourself, you are not only healing personal wounds; you are also participating in a broader act of resistance. You are saying, "I will not abandon myself. I will not hand over my humanity to a world that tries to flatten and fragment it. I will be here, fully, in this body that is mine. And from this place of embodied presence, I will reach out and connect to others."

From the moment you were formed in the womb, your nervous system has been in relationship with the outer world, attuning to the sounds of your mother's voice, to the rhythms of safety or threat, to the presence or absence of comfort, to her stillness and movements. Long before you had words, you had a body that knew how to reach, to brace, to freeze, to rest. These responses are not psychological quirks. They are biological miracles of survival, encoded deep within.

This is an invitation to get to know the language of your body's intelligence. In this book, we will explore how the nervous system functions, how it responds to stress, and why it plays such a central role in emotional and physical health. States of dysregulation—like anxiety, shutdown, anger, and chronic tension—arise not because something is wrong with you, but because something was once too much. The same system that learned how to brace to protect you can also learn how to soften, to trust, to rest, to play, and to dance to its own rhythms.

Understanding your nervous system is not just a scientific endeavor; it is also an act of deep self-compassion. It's how you begin to make sense of why you feel the way you do and, more importantly, how to meet those feelings with care instead of criticism. Healing isn't about reaching a perfect, peaceful state. It's about increasing our capacity to move fluidly between states, with awareness, choice, and communication.

This work lays the groundwork for tools that help you increase that capacity. Through breath, movement, sensation, mindful awareness, creativity, and pleasure seeking, you'll begin to form a new relationship with your inner world—one that honors both your pain and your strength. Because here's the truth: Your nervous system isn't just a biological system. It is also your body's love letter to life. It is the evidence that you adapted, endured, and persisted. And it is capable, beautifully and profoundly capable, of transformation.

So take a breath.

Drop your jaw.

Let your shoulders soften.

Feel your feet and your seat.

Take another breath, this time with a long exhale.

You are not starting from scratch.

You are coming home.

We currently live in a world that prizes doing over being, distraction over depth. Amid this modern paradox, we are more connected to others through technology, yet profoundly disconnected from our own inner worlds. This estrangement is palpable, physically echoing in our bodies: Shoulders carry unspoken tensions, bellies tighten with hidden anxieties, and our breaths become shallow—betraying the relentless pursuit of endless demands.

This chronic disconnection is not merely philosophical; it is also physiological. Neuroscience underscores a profound truth: The brain does not clearly distinguish between physical and emotional threats (Sapolsky, 2004). A critical email can ignite a stress response nearly identical to being chased by a predator, flooding the body with survival hormones. Yet workplace norms dictate that we stay seated and composed, even as our nervous system sounds the internal alarm. We suppress our reactions, send a polite reply, and then mindlessly dissociate on our phones for hours, rarely connecting the emotional aftermath to the moment that triggered it. Without adequate emotional processing, we remain trapped in a cycle of unacknowledged stress, locked in perpetual survival mode, and disconnected from the possibility of living with intention and fullness (van der Kolk, 2014).

Our nervous system acts like a sensitive ancient tuning fork, delicately attuned to each nuance of experience. According to the polyvagal theory of Stephen Porges (2011), our emotional terrain consists of three dynamic states: dorsal vagal shutdown, sympathetic mobilization, and ventral vagal connection. These states are fluid; we shift unconsciously among them throughout the day. Somatic healing provides tools for consciously noticing and inhabiting these states, developing self-awareness by recognizing shifts in our internal landscapes. The gentle oscillation between states, known as "pendulation," gradually restores our body's natural rhythm, creating pathways for profound healing (Levine, 2010).

The nervous system is not a single structure, but a vast constellation of connections including the brain, spine, nerves, hormones, and tissues. Together, they form the electrical and chemical network of your *aliveness*. It governs how you sense the world, how you move through it, and how you respond to what you meet along the way. It is the system that alerts you to danger, signals safety, and allows you to connect, feel, rest, and grow.

At its core, the nervous system is organized around one central question: *Am I safe?* This question is asked and answered thousands of times a day—not with words, but through sensation. A tone of voice. A shift in light. A gut feeling. A silence that lingers too long. These subtle cues are read by your body before your conscious mind ever catches up. In this way, the nervous system operates beneath your thoughts, creating the physiological foundation of your moods, impulses, and relational patterns.

Stephen Porges (2011), originator of polyvagal theory, describes the autonomic nervous system as a hierarchy of survival strategies.

At the base is the dorsal vagal system, responsible for states of shutdown, freeze, collapse, and dissociation—the body's last-resort strategy when a situation feels too overwhelming or inescapable. Above it lies the sympathetic nervous system, the domain of fight or flight, fueled by adrenaline and cortisol. Here, we also see the fawn response: an appeasement strategy that mobilizes the body's social engagement cues in an effort to maintain safety through compliance, people-pleasing, or overaccommodation. While it can look calm on the outside, fawning is still driven by survival energy. At the top of the hierarchy is the ventral vagal system, a branch of the parasympathetic system that allows us to feel safe, connected, and present. This is the state of coregulation, play, intimacy, and joy (Porges, 2011). All three states are intelligent. All three are necessary. The goal is not to avoid them, but to recognize them and expand our capacity to move between them with greater ease.

Dan Siegel (1999), MD, a renowned interpersonal neurobiologist, describes this range of distress tolerance as the "window of tolerance." When we are within this window, we can think clearly, respond flexibly, and stay connected to ourselves and others. When we fall outside of it, into hyperarousal (fight/flight/fawn) or hypoarousal (freeze/collapse), our ability to feel safe and connected diminishes. The good news is that the window can be widened. Not all at once. But gently. Repeatedly. Through practice, care, and curiosity. Your nervous system can learn that it is no longer in the past. It can learn how to stay present.

Many people begin this journey with a mistaken idea that healing means becoming perpetually calm. But nervous system regulation is not about maintaining a constant state of peace. It is about being able to move through life's inevitable stressors without becoming stuck in overwhelm or collapse. A regulated nervous system still experiences anxiety, sadness, irritation, even rage. But these emotions are able to flow rather than flood. They rise and fall, crest and pass—leaving you changed, but not shattered. Regulation means there is enough safety inside your body to hold discomfort without drowning in it. Regulation is not perfection; it's flexibility.

The ways your nervous system has responded to life are not moral failings. They are evidence of your body doing exactly what it was designed to do. If you shut down during conflict, it is not because you are weak; it is because your nervous system, long ago, learned that going numb kept you safe. If your body tightens when someone raises their voice, that is not overreacting; it is a response shaped by memory, often older than language. If you find it hard to trust, hard to slow down, or hard to rest, this too is the legacy of a body that has been vigilant. These are not signs of being broken. These are signs of adaptation. Healing begins not by overriding these patterns, but by understanding them and meeting them with deep unshaming compassion.

We are not aiming for perfect control. We are learning to build capacity, the ability to stay present with what is, even when it's hard. It is what allows you to feel anger without becoming destructive. To feel grief without shutting down. To feel joy without fearing it will be taken away. Building nervous system capacity is like learning to lift heavier emotional weights, not all at once, but through titration and practice. You don't start with the heaviest memories. You begin with what's tolerable. You find the edge. You come back. You build resilience slowly, like a tree that bends with the wind but does not break. This work is not linear. You will have days where everything floods back. You will have days when rest feels impossible. But you will also have moments, perhaps more than you expect, when you notice something has shifted. A pause. A choice. A new breath where panic used to live.

That's your nervous system learning.

That's you healing.

Research now confirms what traditional wisdom has long suggested: Our bodies store what our minds suppress. Chronic emotional avoidance disrupts essential physiological pathways, specifically the hypothalamic-pituitary-adrenal (HPA) axis, elevating cortisol levels and undermining overall health (Chrousos, 2009). Physical ailments such as persistent jaw tension, chronic back pain, high blood pressure, or inexplicable fatigue often reflect emotional distress awaiting acknowledgment. A groundbreaking study published in *Psychological Medicine* (2023) discovered that emotional suppression alters gut microbiota, creating a direct physiological feedback loop between gut health and emotional well-being (Ke et al., 2023). Thus, emotions profoundly inhabit our physicality, stubbornly refusing to remain abstract or intangible.

Emotions are intrinsic messengers. Ignored, they distort into suffering; honored, they guide us toward transformation. Consider anger: Left unaddressed, it festers into high blood pressure or chronic bitterness. Externalized impulsively, it becomes aggression, fracturing relationships. However, when mindfully witnessed, anger serves as a compass signaling injustice, prompting necessary boundaries (Lerner, 2014). Pioneering somatic therapist Pat

Ogden, the creator of sensorimotor psychotherapy, emphasizes each emotion's distinct bodily signature: Fear instinctively contracts the body inward, while joy encourages expansive postures and open gestures (Ogden & Fisher, 2015). By permitting these natural physical expressions, we complete the emotional response cycle, reestablishing emotional harmony and bodily integrity. We live in coherence.

Neuroanatomist Dr. Jill Bolte Taylor (2008) reveals that the physiological lifespan of emotions is surprisingly brief, approximately ninety seconds. If we pause, observing emotions without judgment or additional narrative, their intensity naturally rises and falls like ocean waves. What prolongs emotional distress is our resistance, our unwillingness to simply feel. Recognizing and naming our emotions, localizing their presence within the body, and breathing intentionally through them facilitate a recalibration of our nervous system. This attuned response to internal signals, known as "neuroception," enables us to discern safety from danger, reshaping entrenched emotional reactions (Porges, 2011).

The consequences found in modern Western societies of chronic emotional avoidance are far-reaching. Beneath the surface of curated lives and numbed-out routines, an epidemic of disconnection hums. The nervous system, built to move emotion through the body in waves, becomes dysregulated when those waves are chronically suppressed. Short-term numbing through substances, compulsive productivity, screen addiction, or perfectionism may offer momentary relief but extracts significant long-term costs: dopamine depletion, sustained fatigue, immune dysregulation, and a fragmented sense of self (Hari, 2018; Sapolsky, 2004). Emotion, when unexpressed, does not vanish. It lingers in the tissues, alters neurochemical patterns, and compounds stress loads within the body, laying the groundwork for chronic illness and burnout (van der Kolk, 2014).

In Western cultures that prioritize intellectualism over embodiment, autonomy over interdependence, and productivity over presence, this avoidance is often institutionalized. Mental health diagnoses—including depression, anxiety, and substance use disorders—continue to rise sharply. In the United States alone, over 42 million adults experienced a mental illness in a recent year, with suicide now a leading cause of death among youth and middle-aged adults (National Institute of Mental Health, 2022; Centers for Disease Control and Prevention, 2023). The nervous system—overstimulated, yet emotionally starved—begins to interpret everyday life as a threat. We may appear calm on the outside; but inside, the body pulses with suppressed grief, rage, loneliness—all of which long for movement, for witness, for care.

In interpersonal realms, these costs compound dramatically. The Gottman Institute (2015) identifies emotional avoidance as a major predictor of relationship breakdown, revealing an 81 percent higher likelihood of relational dissolution among couples who avoid challenging conversations. Suppressed emotion becomes misdirected reactivity. Silence hardens into resentment. And intimacy—which requires vulnerability, not just proximity—quietly withers. Conversely, emotional openness fosters authentic connection, resilience, and repair. Vulnerability, far from weakness, is the very language of secure attachment and somatic safety

(Brown, 2012). It is how we say to another nervous system, "You can meet me here. I am willing to be seen." In this way, individual healing becomes cultural reclamation, a return to feeling as an act of resilience.

Further illuminating the profound connection between emotional and physical health and the dueling public health crises that arise when this connection is ignored, the adverse childhood experiences (ACEs) study has significantly deepened our understanding of trauma's lasting impact and transformed how we comprehend human suffering. Participants were surveyed about experiences of abuse, neglect, and household dysfunction. Conducted by Dr. Vincent Felitti and Dr. Robert Anda in the late 1990s, this groundbreaking research demonstrated how childhood traumas—such as abuse, neglect, and household misfortune and dysfunction—continue to live on in the body and are deeply correlated with chronic health problems in adulthood, including heart disease, diabetes, and autoimmune disorders (Felitti et al., 1998). Over seventeen thousand participants were surveyed about their experiences of childhood abuse, neglect, and household dysfunction, including witnessing violence, having a caregiver with mental illness, experiencing sexual abuse, or growing up with addiction in the home. The results were staggering. Nearly two-thirds of participants reported at least one adverse childhood experience. More than one in five had experienced three or more (Felitti et al., 1998).

The results showed that the higher a person's ACE score, the more likely they were to suffer from a range of physical and mental health conditions in adulthood, including heart disease, diabetes, cancer, depression, addiction, anxiety, autoimmune illness, and even early death. These findings were not merely statistical. They were also revelatory.

For decades, modern medicine treated the body and mind as separate domains. Emotional pain was often dismissed. Trauma was viewed as a psychological matter, to be talked through or left behind. But the ACEs study told a different story, one that survivors had long known but lacked the language to articulate:

What happens to us emotionally shapes us biologically.
What is unhealed in the heart does not disappear; it lodges in
the tissue, the immune system, the breath, and the cells.

The implications of ACEs extend beyond mere correlation; they reveal how unresolved emotional wounds embed themselves physically, shaping health outcomes across a lifetime. The ACEs study highlights that chronic stress and unresolved trauma alter our neurobiology, leading to persistent inflammation and dysregulated stress responses. Early traumatic experiences, often buried beneath layers of emotional avoidance, profoundly disrupt the body's capacity to regulate itself. Over time, this manifests physically through heightened vulnerability to illness, chronic pain, and mental health conditions such as depression and anxiety (Anda et al., 2006). Recognizing these links underscores the necessity of emotional healing not merely as psychological wellness but also as an essential strategy for holistic health.

Addressing ACEs also means acknowledging the resilience and inherent adaptability of the human nervous system. Even amid significant trauma, the brain and body retain remarkable plasticity. Therapeutic interventions, community support, and compassionate self-care can mitigate the impacts of early adversity, reshaping health trajectories. Somatic practices that engage both mind and body offer particularly potent pathways for healing these deep-seated emotional wounds, fostering a profound sense of safety, reconnection, and embodied presence (van der Kolk, 2014).

The ACEs study gave scientific voice to what so many survivors have always known in their bones: that the hurts of early life echo through the body like distant thunder. It traced the invisible threads between childhood adversity—abuse, neglect, the rupture of unstable homes—and the later emergence of heart disease, anxiety, autoimmune conditions, and depression. Trauma doesn't just reside in memory; it also takes up residence in tissue, breath, and blood pressure. And yet this knowledge isn't a death sentence; it's an aliveness invitation—an invitation to understand the ways that your body has been adapting, surviving, and protecting you all along. Healing begins not in blaming the self, but in listening to the signals and gently responding with care.

To explore your own ACEs score is not to dwell in the past; it is to understand the shape of your nervous system's landscape. It is to ask, "Why do I feel this way?" not with blame, but with curiosity. *Why does my body respond like this? What is it trying to protect me from?* You do not need to remember or recount every detail to heal. Your body remembers enough. In this book, we begin the sacred task of "re-membering"—of bringing fractured parts of you back into connection, back into wholeness, from their state of dismemberment.

As the ACEs study elucidates, childhood is not simply a phase; it is also the foundation of your nervous system, and your parents are its architects. The development of the nervous system begins in the womb. Long before your first breath, before your eyes opened or your lungs filled with air, your nervous system was already forming. In the dark, warm sanctuary of the womb, your body began to encode sensation. Through the rhythm of your mother's heartbeat, the chemical signature of her emotions, the vibration of her voice, you were already learning the world through the language of the body.

The development of the nervous system begins in the earliest weeks of gestation. Around the third week, the neural tube forms, the structure that becomes the brain and spinal cord. From there, an intricate network of neurons, glial cells, and synaptic pathways begins to branch outward like roots searching for water. But this growth is not mechanical. It is relational. The fetus is exquisitely responsive to its environment. If the gestational parent is calm, the fetus receives cues of safety. If they are overwhelmed, chronically stressed, flooded with cortisol or adrenaline, those same signals bathe the developing nervous system in activation.

The fetus learns "This is what the world feels like. Prepare for it accordingly."

This is not to place blame. This is to place reverence on how profoundly interconnected we are, how your first lessons in aliveness were not spoken, but felt in body-to-body relationship.

After birth, the nervous system continues developing at astonishing speed. The infant brain is still under construction, with billions of neural connections forming and pruning every hour based on lived experience. In the first three years alone, an estimated 100 trillion connections take shape (Center on the Developing Child at Harvard University, 2007). The primary teacher in this education is the caregiver as human infants are born neurologically unfinished and cannot self-regulate. Unlike other mammals, we require coregulation with an external nervous system to help us manage our own. Without it, infants may fail to thrive, even die. What builds the foundation for emotional resilience is not independence, but attuned interdependent relationships with caregivers.

Attunement, caregivers consistently tuning in to their infants' needs, teaches the nervous system safety. This is not instinctive; it is earned through repeated acts of noticing, mirroring, and soothing (Bowlby, 1988). When a baby is cold and someone brings warmth, they learn "I am cared for." When they are afraid and someone holds them, "I am not alone." When they cry and someone responds, "My needs matter." These micromoments lay the groundwork for secure attachment, not just a psychological style but also a physiological reality and strategy for survival. The body learns that connection leads to regulation.

It is important to distinguish attunement from attention. Many people grow up believing they did not experience trauma or attachment disruptions because their basic needs were fully met: They were clothed, fed, well educated, given gifts, and even praised for their achievements. But attention, especially performance-based or task-oriented attention, is not the same as attunement. Attention might focus on meeting basic needs or rewarding behavior, success, or compliance. Attunement listens beneath the surface. It responds to the emotional and physiological cues that are often wordless. A child can receive tremendous amounts of attention without being truly seen or felt. They may learn to perform for connection, to silence their discomfort, or to detach from their own internal signals. This disconnect, though invisible to many, leaves lasting imprints in the nervous system. Attunement is what allows a child's body to *feel* safe in a relationship, not just appear well cared for from the outside. When attunement is missing, inconsistent, or chaotic, the nervous system adapts. It may dissociate, brace, or scan for threat. It learns to please, perform, or go numb to maintain safety. These aren't choices; they're protective recalibrations: intelligent responses to a world that felt unsafe or unkind.

Such adaptations often echo into adulthood as anxiety, people-pleasing, chronic tension, emotional distance, self-limiting beliefs, and/or shutdown. If no one came when you cried or, worse, you were chastised, you may now feel unworthy of comfort. If you were raised in chaos, stillness may feel unbearable. If you had to parent a parent, self-care may make you feel guilty. If you were only noticed when you were sickly and needy, health and competence may feel dangerous. These embodied patterns are not personal failings; they are our survival strategies. And understanding their origin helps us move from shame to self-compassion. Your body was not malfunctioning; it was adapting. And now through somatic awareness, that same body can learn a new pattern—one rooted in choice, presence, and care.

ACEs live not just in memory; they live also in the nervous system's default settings: the heart that races too fast, the breath that stays shallow, the stomach that clenches at intimacy, the sleep that won't come easily. What's crucial to understand is this: Your body did not fail you. It protected you as best it could. And now it may need your help learning something new. Neuroplasticity, the brain's ability to rewire itself, offers profound hope. Through repeated experiences of safety, coregulation, and embodied presence, we can rewire the very circuits that once wired us for defense. We can teach our nervous system that the danger has passed. That we no longer have to brace, withdraw, or shut down to survive.

This is the work of healing.

Not to erase the past, but to reinhabit the present.

To slowly, gently reclaim the body as a place of belonging.

Trauma is not destiny. While the ACEs study highlights risk, it does not determine fate. An elevated ACE score is a red flag, but it is not a life sentence. Many people with high ACE scores live healthy and fulfilling lives. What makes the difference? What creates resilience? Support. Connection. Repair. Coregulation. Nervous system capacity. New experiences of safety, especially in the body. This is where resilience lives and somatic healing comes knocking at the door. We cannot simply "think our way" into regulation. The systems shaped by early adversity require felt embodied experiences of safety and connection—repeated, gentle, and trustworthy enough to rewire what once was wired for vigilance.

That might look like the following:

- A therapist who mirrors your pain without trying to fix it
- A walk outside where your breath syncs with the rhythm of wind in the trees
- A hand over your heart when the panic arises
- A moment of surrender to much-needed rest

These experiences, though small, are profound.

They whisper to the body, "It's different now."

Your story matters.

You're not alone.

You're not in danger.

You don't have to run or brace.

Your body's adaptations are not flaws.

They are the sacred architecture of your resilience.

Imagine your nervous system as a wave: rising, peaking, and falling. It constantly adjusts. This movement is not random. It's your body's intelligent response to life.

And when we learn how to notice and influence this wave, to skillfully ride its rise and fall, we begin to participate in our own healing with greater clarity, intention, and care. Two essential tools in this journey are upregulation and downregulation. Upregulation activates the nervous system when we are in freeze or shutdown. Movement, sound, alert gazing, or shaking the limbs can help us reengage. Downregulation calms the system when we're overwhelmed by using breath, grounding, soothing touch, or quiet rhythm to cue safety. There is no better or worse state, only what is needed. Just as a musician tunes their instrument, you learn to tune your nervous system. Some moments call for rising energy, others for softening. The more you practice noticing and adjusting your state, the more you build capacity.

Understanding the nervous system is only the beginning. To truly heal, we must go beyond knowing and into embodied practice. This book will guide you through tools drawn from somatic psychology, neuroscience, breathwork, and ancestral traditions. These tools do not fix you. They help you listen more deeply, more tenderly, more wisely. One of the deepest acts of self-love is to ask your nervous system, "What do you need right now? More energy or more ease? To move or to rest? To speak or to be still?" And then to honor the answer.

Some practices will help you downregulate. Others will up-regulate. Still, others will expand your capacity to feel without becoming flooded. You will learn to orient, anchor, pendulate, titrate, coregulate, and name your states. You will not be asked to dive headfirst into the hardest moments of your past. You will be asked to go gently into what comes up with an observer's mind. To stay curious. To notice what feels too much and to come back to what feels like enough. This is not a race. It is a relationship with your nervous system and with the parts of you that have long been waiting to be seen.

You may have days of clarity, peace, and connection. You may have days of spirals and grief. You may have days where you slip back into old patterns of numbness, reactivity, or doubt. That is not failure; it is the nature of healing. It moves in spirals, in tides, in cycles of return. Each time you pause to notice, to breathe, to respond with care, you are rewiring your inner world. You are saying, "I matter. I am willing to learn a new way. I am choosing not just survival but also wholeness." And your nervous system—wise, ancient, and responsive—is listening. It is not about achieving a permanent state of peace. It is about learning how to respond, with increasing wisdom, to the ever-changing rhythm of being alive.

The wave rises.

The wave crests.

The wave falls.

And with time, you learn to ride it—not with fear, but with grace.

Your nervous system is not the enemy. It is the sacred record of all you've endured. And it is the instrument through which joy, connection, and meaning are still possible. You will meet yourself not as a problem to solve, but as a being to befriend. Let us begin— not with urgency, but with reverence. Let us begin with the truth that your body, even now, is on your side.

Case Study
Alex: The Echo of Absence

Alex is twenty-six. He spends most of his days inside his one-bedroom apartment, with the blackout curtains drawn and his phone on silent. Time slips through his fingers. Some days, he doesn't get out of bed until 2:00 p.m., disoriented and exhausted. He tells himself it's laziness, a lack of discipline. But the truth is deeper than that. The truth is older than that.

Raised in a quiet suburb, Alex's childhood was filled with silence—no dramatic outbursts, no visible chaos, but no warmth either. His parents divorced when he was nine. Afterward, both were too consumed by long work hours and new relationships to offer more than the basics. He remembers his dad's back always turned toward the glow of his computer screen, drawn into chat rooms and internet arguments. His mother often saying, "I'm too tired right now," while texting her latest boyfriend and smiling at her phone. No one ever asked Alex how he was feeling. No one noticed when he stopped trying to be seen.

Screens became his primary caregivers. Video games taught him how to dissociate, how to pass time without feeling it. He became a master at escaping into digital worlds, where needs were simple and goals were clear. But real life remained confusing and unrelenting. He couldn't figure out why jobs never stuck, why he felt such dread just from leaving the house. He ghosted friends—not because he didn't care, but because being around people made him feel like he was underwater: present, but distant, muffled, unreachable.

When Alex began somatic therapy, he was skeptical. He was used to talking *about* his issues, not *feeling* them. But his therapist invited him to begin small: noticing the way his shoulders curled inward, how his chest felt caved in. She named it "collapse": a biological response to chronic emotional starvation.

They began practicing simple things: pressing his feet into the floor, finding a single object in the room to orient to, placing a hand on his own chest while he breathed. At first, it felt absurd. But over time, Alex began to sense small shifts, like less panic in the mornings, more awareness of time passing, a flicker of desire to go outside. It wasn't a straight line. He still slept through alarms, still lost whole afternoons. But now he was noticing the dissociation, naming the numbness, feeling the ache instead of fleeing from it.

In one session, Alex wept for the first time in years—not for what happened, but for what didn't. For the absence of touch, of tenderness, of someone attuning to his breath. It was grief, but it was also the beginning of return. The beginning of being with himself instead of drifting away.

Journal and Reflection Prompts

1. When you reflect on your current nervous system patterns, what state feels most familiar? Fight, flight, fawn, freeze, or collapse? Why do you think that is?
2. What messages did you receive growing up about expressing emotion? How have those messages shaped your body's current responses to stress or connection?
3. Can you recall a moment when your body *knew* something before your mind did? What did it feel like?
4. What is one small practice you can begin this week to signal safety to your nervous system?
5. How do you want to relate to the cultural or ancestral traditions that inform your healing journey?

Somatic Ritual: Listening for Desire

This simple, but powerful somatic ritual invites you to pause and enter into quiet communion with your body. Begin by asking, without judgment, the following:

- What would my body like right now?
- What would feel good to me in this moment?
- What do I desire right now?
- What quiet urges are trying to speak?

Wait and listen. The answers may be subtle. They may arrive as whispers in sensation rather than words. Then if at all possible, honor what your body asks.

Adjust your weight in your chair.

Stretch your arms overhead.

Look up and around the room.

Circle your ankles slowly.

Drink a cool glass of water.

Stand up and walk across the floor.

Whatever small request or longing your body offers, allow it. Let that simple act be enough.

If what your body longs for isn't possible right now, like lounging on a sun-drenched beach, take yourself there via your imagination. Let your senses bring the experience to life:

Feel the warmth of sunlight on your skin.

The sand between your toes.

The rhythmic hush of the waves.

The way your body softens in this imagined space.

Remember, while your thinking brain knows the difference, your nervous system does not. An imaginal embodied journey can offer just as much regulation and nourishment as a real one.

Returning to this ritual regularly allows you to build a bridge to your body's true desires. It trains you to notice, trust, and follow the inner pulse of what you need. Over time, it becomes an act of sacred listening, a way to make your inner world feel safe enough to reveal its truths.

Prepare to meet the radical aliveness within you.

Prepare to welcome pleasure, creativity, and passion.

Prepare to truly, fully, and tenderly meet yourself.

2

Understanding the Nervous System

Not I, nor anyone else can travel that road for you,
You must travel it by yourself.
It is not far, it is within reach,
Perhaps you have been on it since you were born and did not know.

—Walt Whitman, "Song of Myself"

To understand the shape of our emotional lives, we must first understand the system that holds them. The journey to comprehend the nervous system is not merely biological; it is also historical, cultural, and relational. Long before the language of synapses and neurotransmitters entered Western thought, ancient physicians and philosophers observed the body's responsiveness to the environment and described the vitality that coursed through its fibers.

The first documented references to the nervous system in Western medicine appear in ancient Egyptian texts around 1700 BCE, such as in the Edwin Smith surgical papyrus, which identified the brain as a source of bodily function (Breasted, 1930). Greek physician Hippocrates later asserted that the brain was the seat of sensation and intelligence, while his contemporary Galen, a

Roman anatomist, proposed an early understanding of the nervous system as a network of "pneuma," or vital spirit, carried through nerves (Finger, 2001).

It was not until the Renaissance, with Andreas Vesalius's detailed anatomical dissections, that the structure of the central and peripheral nervous systems began to be clearly illustrated in Western thought. By the nineteenth century, Santiago Ramón y Cajal's meticulous drawings and theories introduced the neuron doctrine, the idea that the nervous system was made of individual communicating cells (Shepherd, 1991). These milestones laid the groundwork for our modern understanding of the nervous system as an interconnected network of tissue, electricity, and emotion.

Yet while Western science slowly named and mapped this system, Indigenous cultures across the globe already lived in relationship with its rhythms. In many ancestral traditions, the nervous system was not isolated or mechanistic; it was woven into spirit, community, and land. Among the Quechua peoples of the Andes, the concept of *sumaq kawsay* (harmonious living) included bodily and spiritual coherence. Among the Anishinaabe, the breath and heartbeat were understood as the drumbeat of spirit—not metaphorically, but literally as sources of knowing and emotional attunement (Sefa Dei, 2011).

The Chinese meridian system, developed over two thousand years ago and foundational to traditional Chinese medicine, identified energetic pathways that correlate closely with the paths of major nerve bundles. Qi, the vital life force, was thought to flow through these meridians and become disrupted by trauma or imbalance. This concept resonates with the vagus nerve's role in regulating states of calm and distress (Kaptchuk, 2000). Similarly, in Ayurvedic medicine from India, the *nadis* and chakras mapped the flow of consciousness and emotion, linking bodily experiences to nervous and spiritual health (Frawley, 1997).

The nervous system, in both ancient and modern worldviews, is far more than a clinical structure. It is a relational interface, a medium through which safety, threat, connection, and meaning are felt and expressed. What we now call "neuroception" in polyvagal theory was once called "gut instinct," "the whisper of ancestors," or "the song of the body." This chapter invites us not only to learn the anatomy of the nervous system but also to remember its sacred history. To know it as the source of regulation, yes, but also of intuition, lineage, and longing. To reclaim it as both a site of scientific precision and ancestral reverence. Because the nervous system does not only govern survival. It also holds the memory of how we have survived.

Under modern medical understanding, the nervous system comprises two primary structures: the central nervous system (CNS), including the brain and spinal cord, and the peripheral nervous system (PNS), which relays information between the CNS and the body. Embedded within the PNS is the autonomic nervous system (ANS), responsible for regulating vital involuntary functions, such as heart rate, digestion, and hormonal rhythms (Siegel, 2020). But beyond biology, this system subtly governs how we interpret threat, experience belonging, and return to balance after distress.

The ANS includes the sympathetic nervous system (SNS), which mobilizes us into action when we encounter challenge or danger, and the parasympathetic nervous system (PNS), which helps restore calm and support healing. Polyvagal theory adds a profound refinement: It distinguishes between two branches of the parasympathetic system. The dorsal vagal pathway is responsible for shutdown and collapse. The ventral vagal pathway supports safety, engagement, and connection (Porges, 2011).

We can imagine this system as a river delta, where each branching stream or tributary represents a physiological state. When the waters run calm and connected, we inhabit the ventral vagal state—open to relating, regulating, and reflecting. When the current floods into sympathetic mobilization, we prepare to fight or flee. When the waters recede or stagnate, dorsal vagal stillness settles in; and the body withdraws to conserve energy, to endure. These are not conscious decisions, but fluid shifts shaped by perception and history.

Our ability to navigate these states depends on the width of our internal container. Dr. Dan Siegel (2020) calls this the "window of tolerance," a range of arousal within which we can function with presence and integration. Within this window, we are flexible, responsive, and emotionally available. Outside it, we may become overwhelmed (hyperarousal) or shut down (hypoarousal).

When the window of tolerance narrows, life begins to feel like a tightrope walk above a chasm. Even minor stressors—like a delayed text, a missed appointment, and a raised eyebrow from a loved one—can feel immense, as though the body is preparing for catastrophe. Hyperarousal often takes the form of anxiety and restlessness. For example, Maya, a college student, finds herself spiraling into panic before every class presentation. Her heart pounds, her thoughts blur, and even breathing feels like a struggle. Although the stakes are low, her nervous system sounds the alarm.

Conversely, hypoarousal can mute the world. After a long week of caregiving, Marcus collapses on the couch and finds himself unable to move for hours. He's not resting exactly; he's zoning out and disconnected. His body is present, but his mind is fogged. This is not laziness; it is his nervous system seeking refuge in shutdown.

Even joyful moments can be overwhelming with a narrowed window. Take Ana, who recently entered a healthy romantic relationship after years of emotional neglect. The sweetness of being seen and cared for triggers unexpected discomfort. Her body tenses. She wants to retreat and self-isolate, even though she craved this connection. Safety feels unfamiliar and thus threatening.

Returning to our river metaphor, a narrowed window is like a stream choked by sediment and debris. A small rainfall causes flooding. A dry spell causes drought. The ecosystem is vulnerable to every fluctuation. A widened window, by contrast, is like a clean and steady channel. The water rises and falls with the seasons, but the flow returns. There is room for change without flooding or levee collapse. There is capacity.

Each of us has our own patterned responses to threat: fight, flight, fawn, freeze, or collapse. These are not identities, but learned strategies, shaped by our earliest environments, repeated until they became reflex. The fighter bristles, postures, and lunges to protect. The flight response flees to create space and reach safety. The fawner appeases to defuse tension and curry favor. The freezer disappears in the background to be forgotten and avoid harm. The collapser goes limp to be spared from a fight or chase and conserve vital internal resources. These are creative embodied solutions to stress, not signs of dysfunction (Walker, 2013). The identified threat responses of fight, flight, fawn, freeze, and collapse are not symptoms of brokenness. They are the elegant survival strategies of the nervous system—ancient involuntary mechanisms designed to keep us alive in the face of danger. Each one is biologically intelligent, instinctually fast, and profoundly protective.

When we encounter a threat, whether real or perceived, our autonomic nervous system doesn't wait for logic or language. It acts. It mobilizes us into fight to push danger away, flight to get to safety, fawn to reduce threat through connection or appeasement, freeze to go still and avoid detection, or collapse to conserve energy in the face of helplessness. These are not moral choices. They are embodied reflexes—refined over generations, encoded into our tissues, and passed down through lived experience and lineage.

For many people, especially those who grew up in environments of chronic stress, these responses become habitual. Not because they're wrong, but because they worked. The body doesn't always differentiate between then and now. A raised voice, a closing door, a certain look—these can activate survival reflexes long after the original danger is gone. We begin to rely on one or two dominant strategies—not because they're ideal, but because they became familiar. The fighter may always lead with anger. The freezer may numb before even noticing discomfort. The fawner may lose themselves in meeting others' needs before their own even surface. The collapser may stay in bed, protecting themselves from difficulties real and imagined, missing out on years of living.

And yet these very responses, when no longer hijacked by trauma, can be transformed into strengths.

- **Fight**, when integrated, becomes healthy aggression: the ability to set boundaries, speak up, protect, and assert. It can look like advocacy, bold creativity, or the discipline of martial arts. In a nonthreatening context, someone who once fought to survive may become a fierce guardian or protector of others or a passionate truth teller.

- **Flight**, when not rooted in panic, becomes discernment and clarity. It supports leaving harmful environments, creating and communicating relational safety by providing spaciousness, seeking new perspectives, and physically moving the body through dance, distance running, or intentional travel. What was once escapism can become agility and forward momentum.

- **Fawn**, also known as "appease," is often misunderstood. It is a relational strategy, part of what researchers call the "*tend-and-befriend* response" (Taylor et al., 2000). This strategy—often activated alongside or instead of fight or flight, especially in those socialized as female—draws on affiliation and care to reduce threat and soften conflict. Fawn isn't about weakness, people-pleasing, or seducing. It's about surviving through attunement and coregulation. In healing, this becomes the gift of relational intelligence—the community builder, the connector, the bridge between worlds.

- **Freeze** teaches the value of stillness and observation. In healing, this can become deep meditation, mindful pausing, and the capacity to wait and sense before acting. Freeze becomes the wisdom of the watcher, the mystic, the contemplative.

- **Collapse**, the most profound form of dorsal withdrawal, is the body's last-ditch effort to endure when all else fails. But even collapse has a sacred shadow. With support, it can be transmuted into surrender, rest, and a return to the earth. Collapse holds the doorway to deep restoration, like the body's natural impulse to sleep after trauma. It is the nervous system asking to begin again.

In healing, we learn not to discard these responses, but to reclaim them. We ask the following: What was this part of me protecting? What strength is hidden inside this reflex? What happens when I bring choice into the moment?

Instead of shaming ourselves for "overreacting", we begin to see the legacy of our nervous system's brilliance. We learn to pendulate, to move with intention and awareness between survival strategies and embodied presence. And in doing so, we widen our window of tolerance. We build capacity to choose rather than react. Your fawn response might transmute into leadership through displays of emotional fluency that engender trust. Your fight instinct might forge boundaries where none existed. Your freeze might reveal the wisdom of stillness. Your flight instinct may initiate world travel. Each response, once born of necessity, can become a sacred gift.

This is not bypass. This is integration. Not rejecting what kept us alive, but learning how to live fully, from the inside out.

Regulation helps us soften the grip of our conditioned responses by offering new experiences of safety. Two essential pathways are upregulation and downregulation, tools that help us meet our state with choice rather than reactivity. These practices aren't about forcing ourselves into calm or energy, but about listening for what the body needs and responding with care.

Upregulation helps activate and mobilize us when we're hypoaroused and stuck in shutdown, numbness, or depressive states. For example, when Jordan wakes up feeling heavy and disconnected, he turns on a favorite upbeat playlist and lets himself dance around the room, even half-heartedly. Within minutes, his breath deepens, his heart rate rises, and the fog begins to lift. Movement, especially when rhythmic or vigorous, is one of the most accessible upregulation tools. Others include jumping jacks, shaking out the limbs, splashing cold water on the face, singing loudly, drumming, or even playful yelling in a private space like a car.

For some, touch-based stimulation works better, like rolling the feet over a textured ball, engaging with cool stones, or holding ice. It can provide just enough intensity to bring awareness back to the body. Visual cues can also be powerful: Gazing out a window at bright daylight or focusing on a vibrant color can gently nudge a hypoaroused system into alertness.

Downregulation, on the other hand, is used when we are hyperaroused and overstimulated or anxious, when the sympathetic nervous system has pulled us into fight or flight. In these moments, we need cues of safety and containment. Rosa, a high school teacher, knows her stress levels spike after work. Rather than diving straight into more obligations, she steps into her garden, removes her shoes, and stands barefoot in the grass, face turned toward the sun. The earth becomes her anchor, and the sun gently replenishes her energy into a calm focus. She breathes slowly, feeling each exhale drop her a little deeper into calmed settling.

Downregulation can take many forms: diaphragmatic breathing, placing a hand over the heart or belly, gentle swaying, weighted blankets, warm herbal tea, or even placing one's forehead against a cool surface. Some people benefit from listening to slow instrumental music or chanting low tones. Others find it helpful to orient visually by looking around the room and naming objects or by following the edges of a safe contained space with their eyes.

More importantly, regulation is deeply personal. What soothes one nervous system may overwhelm another. What energizes one person may feel too intense for someone else. It's a process of discovery: What brings you back into relationship with your body? What helps you stay with discomfort instead of fleeing from it? These tools are not the destination. They are the bridge.

And though early life shapes the nervous system profoundly, it does not seal its fate. The nervous system is not static; it is alive, dynamic, and capable of renewal. This capacity for change is known as "neuroplasticity," the brain's remarkable ability to rewire itself in response to new experiences. It is the underlying science that gives somatic healing its power.

Imagine a forest trail. When a path is walked again and again, it becomes clear, worn, familiar. This is how neural pathways work. Our reactions, habits, even our emotions follow well-trodden roads carved by experience. Some of these trails were formed in childhood, shaped by safety or by pain. But just as new paths can be cleared in the woods, new neural connections can form in the brain. At first, they may feel uncertain or overgrown. But with time and repetition, they grow strong. With care, they become the new default, the new worn path.

This is where somatics comes in. Somatic healing doesn't just ask us to think differently. It also invites us to move differently, breathe differently, relate to sensation with curiosity instead of fear. Every time we pause to notice a tight jaw and soften it, every time we choose to breathe through discomfort instead of flee it, we lay a new path. Somatic practices are the embodied repetition that makes neuroplasticity and therapeutic integration real.

Consider Julia, who used to dissociate during conflict. Her body would go numb, and her voice would disappear. In therapy, she began a simple practice: placing a hand on her chest and breathing when tension arose. At first, it changed nothing. But slowly, something shifted. Her heart rate slowed. Her voice returned. Her presence held. These were not dramatic transformations; they were microadjustments, each one forging a new connection between safety and embodiment.

This is how biology bends toward possibility: not in grand gestures, but in small sustained acts of choosing presence. Reaching for warmth when we used to reach for distraction. Holding our ground when we used to disappear. Breathing through the moment instead of bracing against it. Over time, these moments accumulate. The body learns that the world is not always dangerous. That the past is not always now. That change, while slow, is possible. And that healing is not about becoming someone new; it's about remembering who we were before we had to adapt.

What science now confirms, many ancestral cultures have always known: The body remembers what the mind forgets; and healing is a communal, rhythmic, and embodied act. Across continents and generations, Indigenous and ancestral peoples developed deeply relational practices that honored the nervous system long before there was a name for it.

In the Yoruba tradition of West Africa, communal drumming circles offered not only ceremony but also regulation. The polyrhythmic beats created coherence in the brain, stimulating the vagus nerve and fostering both personal and collective equilibrium (Thompson, 2005). Drumming was not performance; it was medicine. Participants could entrain their breath and heartbeat to the rhythm of the drums, recalibrating their nervous systems in real time.

The Diné (Navajo) people engage in Blessingway ceremonies, which emphasize beauty, harmony, and restoration. These rituals use sandpainting, chanting, and story to reconnect individuals to the web of life and to the natural order, reinforcing ventral vagal states of safety and belonging. Through these rituals, the nervous system is invited to rejoin the rhythm of the community and cosmos (Wyman, 2017; Kahn-John (Diné) & Koithan, 2015).

In the Sufi tradition, the whirling dance known as the Sema ritual invites a trancelike state through spinning. This movement, paired with breath and sacred music, facilitates both emotional release and spiritual regulation. The body, through repetition, finds stillness inside the swirl—a metaphor for the nervous system's return to centeredness amid chaos (Helminski, 2000).

Māori healing traditions include whakapapa, the genealogy that links all beings across time. Telling one's story within this sacred framework is not simply an act of memory; it is also an act of restoration. By naming their lineage and ancestors, individuals locate themselves within a living, breathing system of connection and continuity. This reaffirms identity and safety, foundational elements of nervous system resilience (Mead, 2003).

Even within European ancestral traditions, we find echoes of this embodied wisdom. In pre-Christian Celtic Irish communities, keening—the communal wailing of grief—was a structured, vocal, and movement-based ritual used to metabolize sorrow and trauma. The keening woman helped the community process what could not be spoken in ordinary language, creating somatic release and emotional coherence (Ó Madagáin, 1985).

Each of these practices—whether breath, movement, chant, or narrative—understood something essential: that the nervous system is not an isolated mechanism, but a relational instrument. It must be tuned through presence, through rhythm, through connection. These traditions were not decorative. They were essential technologies of survival and repair.

When we engage with these ancestral practices today, we are not adopting tools. We are remembering relationships, with land, with lineage, with the nervous systems of those who came before us. Somatic therapy and neuroscience now affirm what these communities carried intuitively: that healing happens in rhythm, in witness, and in belonging.

This chapter honors both the maps of neuroscience and the wisdom traditions that first guided us. It invites us into a deeper understanding of the nervous system not merely as tissue and impulse but also as a site of memory, connection, and identity. Our nervous systems are living archives of all we have endured, all we have inherited, and all we might yet become. They carry the imprints not only of early experiences but also of ancient rituals, ancestral songs, and collective survival.

To study the nervous system today is to hold the paradox of science and story. It is to know that neurons fire in patterns and also that the heartbeat of a drum can restore order to chaos. It is to learn about vagal tone and to feel how a grandmother's lullaby soothes the infant's trembling body. It is to grasp the language of stress hormones and also to bow to the knowledge of elders who never named cortisol but who understood how to call the spirit home through touch, breath, and sacred rhythm.

We are not the first to tend to nervous system health. We are part of a lineage of caretakers and healers, dancers and storytellers who understood that the body cannot be separated from the soul, that the health of the nervous system is inseparable from the health of the community and the land. In relearning how to regulate, we are rejoining a great current of remembering.

Let this chapter serve not only as an education in biology but also as an invitation into belonging. May it help us understand our personal responses, yes, but also place them within the vast and holy story of human resilience. Because healing is not just about restoring function. It is also about restoring relationship.

Case Study
Tara's River Within

Tara had always been a high-functioning storm: sharp, capable, and endlessly productive. At thirty-three, she had built a career she was proud of, maintained friendships others admired, and showed up for every obligation with practiced precision. But inside, something felt misaligned. She often found herself riding waves of intense anxiety, followed by sudden numbness. Bursts of energy would carry her through long workdays. But by evening, she collapsed into detachment. She was surviving, but not inhabiting her life.

When Tara began therapy, she described herself as "broken in cycles"—at once energized, then flattened; open, then withdrawn. Her therapist gently introduced her to a new possibility: These weren't character flaws. They were the imprints of her nervous system doing its best to protect her. Together, they explored the language of polyvagal theory and began mapping Tara's emotional patterns onto her body's physiology. What Tara thought of as inconsistency was, in fact, intelligent adaptation.

Using the metaphor of a river system, Tara began to imagine her nervous system as a vast and flowing landscape. Her central nervous system—brain and spine—was the main river, carving her internal world. Her peripheral nervous system, like branching tributaries, sent signals out to her limbs and organs. But it was the hidden waters, the autonomic nervous system, that held the key. This unseen aquifer of breath, heartbeat, and gut feeling revealed the source of her inner turbulence.

She learned how her body cycled between ventral vagal safety with close friends, sympathetic mobilization during tense work moments, and dorsal vagal shutdown on weekends, when exhaustion overtook her. She could now name what once felt like chaos: *This is fight. This is flight. This is fawn. This is freeze.*

Tara recalled how, as a child, she had tiptoed around a volatile parent, her body coiling at the sound of slammed doors. Her nervous system had learned early to scan for danger, to react before thinking. Even in adulthood, her boss's disapproving tone would spike her heart rate. She became argumentative and defensive, entering fight mode. Later, she'd spiral into shame, shut down emotionally, and avoid social interaction, falling into freeze.

She also recognized a fawn response in her personal relationships. With romantic partners, she overaccommodated, anticipating needs before they were voiced. She believed if she could be perfect, she could prevent abandonment. This wasn't people-pleasing. It was her nervous system's survival strategy, rooted in years of needing to regulate others' emotions to maintain safety at home.

With this somatic map in place, Tara's work turned to regulation. When she felt herself slipping into collapse, she practiced upregulation: brisk walks on chilly mornings, singing loudly in her car, shaking out her limbs to music with a heavy beat. At first, the movements felt silly. But over time, they woke something in her—a spark, a pulse, a returning aliveness. Her fog began to clear.

When the panic rose, during emails marked urgent or tense conversations with her partner, she turned to downregulation: a hand over her heart, exhaling twice as long as she inhaled, or lying flat on the floor to feel the weight of her body supported. She learned to orient to safety by naming five objects in the room or rubbing a smooth stone between her palms. These practices became her anchors.

Her therapist also invited her to explore touchstones of joy: the smell of cedar, the sound of ocean waves, the comfort of soft cotton against her skin. These sensory cues became part of her personalized nervous system tool kit, reminders that regulation was about not just managing distress but also expanding capacity for pleasure and rest.

As Tara's window of tolerance widened, she stopped bracing for collapse after every peak. She became more attuned to the subtle signs her body offered: the way her breath shortened during conflict, the tightening of her jaw before a deadline, the flutter of joy when a friend made her laugh. She learned to pendulate, to move between intensity and ease without losing herself.

And perhaps most importantly, she stopped pathologizing her patterns. What once felt like emotional whiplash now made sense as survival brilliance. Her body wasn't betraying her; it was trying to keep her safe.

In one session, Tara said softly, "I used to think my nervous system was the problem. Now I see it as a partner I never learned how to listen to."

That shift, from enemy to ally, marked the beginning of her true healing. Tara wasn't erasing her history. She was reclaiming her rhythm.

Tara's story is a reminder: Healing is not about becoming someone else. It is about remembering how to live from the inside out. About rediscovering that your nervous system, with all its currents and curves, was never broken. Only waiting for a chance to flow again.

Journal and Reflection Prompts

1. Which part of your nervous system's story feels most surprising or validating?

2. What is your go-to survival response in moments of stress? How does it show up in your body?

3. Reflect on a time when you were within your window of tolerance. What helped you stay there?

4. Which somatic practice (upregulating or downregulating) feels most accessible to try this week?

5. How do the ancestral examples shared involving drumming, storytelling, and movement resonate with your own lineage or practices?

Somatic Ritual: Mapping the Waters Within

This ritual invites you to connect with the river of your nervous system—not as something to fix, but as something to befriend. Through attention, breath, and remembrance, you'll begin to trace the shape of your unique emotional landscape and offer your body the safety of presence.

Time required: 20–25 minutes

Optional items: blanket or shawl, small bowl of water, candle, journal, ancestral object or photograph

---

1. Create a threshold of arrival.

Choose a quiet space where you can remain undisturbed. Place a blanket or shawl around your shoulders or waist to signal the beginning of something sacred. If you have an ancestral object, photograph, or natural item (like a stone, feather, or flower), place it nearby.

Light a candle, and if available, place a small bowl of water in front of you as a symbol of the nervous system's river. Say silently or aloud the following:

I am here to listen. I am here to feel. I am here to remember.

2. **Orient to safety.**

Turn your head slowly to take in your surroundings. Let your eyes land on *three objects*. Say them aloud or to yourself:

> *I see the window.*
>
> *I see the book.*
>
> *I see the plant.*

Let your body feel the *nowness* of this space. You are not in the past. You are not in the future. You are here.

3. **Sense your stream.**

Close your eyes (if safe) and bring awareness to your breath. Without changing it, simply observe.

Now scan your body gently from head to toe, asking the following:

- Where in my system is there stillness?
- Where in my system is there movement?
- Where in my system is there constriction? Or flow and ease?
- What temperatures live in different parts of me?

Let one area draw your attention. Stay with it. Place your hand there if it feels right.

Ask the following: *What is this part of me trying to say?*

You do not need to answer. Just listen.

4. **Locate your nervous system state.**

   With kindness and curiosity, ask the following:

   - Am I in *sympathetic mobilization*? (tense, fast, alert, agitated)
   - Am I in *dorsal vagal freeze*? (numb, distant, heavy, flat)
   - Am I in *ventral vagal safety*? (connected, calm, curious)

     There is no wrong answer. Simply name what is true. Let

   yourself *know* where you are in this moment.

   If helpful, speak aloud the following:

   I am in sympathetic energy, and I'm staying with it gently.

   I am feeling dorsal stillness, and I am meeting it with care.

   I am in ventral safety, and I am savoring it.

5. **Respond with resonance.**

   Now choose one small gesture in response.

   If you're in *sympathetic charge*, try the following:

   - A long, slow exhale
   - Placing a cool cloth on your forehead
   - Pressing your feet firmly into the ground

   If you're in *dorsal stillness*, try the following:

   - Humming or sighing
   - Lightly tapping your chest or legs
   - Rolling your shoulders or stretching your spine

   If you're in *ventral regulation*, try the following:

   - Smiling gently at yourself
   - Swaying, rocking, or cradling your arms
   - Placing a hand over your heart and saying, "Thank you for this moment."

6. Honor your lineage.

Gaze at your bowl of water. Let it represent the river of nervous system wisdom belonging to you and your ancestors. Say aloud or in silence the following:

This body remembers.

This system has survived.

I carry the strength and wisdom of those who came before me.

Dip your fingertips into the water and touch your forehead, chest or sternum, and belly. This is your ritual anointing. Simple, sacred, and sufficient.

7. Return and integrate.

Orient again to your room. Name three more objects. Find and feel your feet and your seat. Blow out the candle or close the ritual in your own way.

Optional: Journal for 5–10 minutes using the following prompt:

What did I feel today, and what did I offer myself in response?

Closing Blessing

May you trust the river that flows within you—even when it runs wild, even when it runs quiet.

May you know that your nervous system is not a problem to be managed, but a compass to be honored.

And may each breath bring you closer to home.

3

The Body as Compass, Emotions as Guides

I measure every Grief I meet
With narrow, probing eyes—
I wonder if It weighs like Mine—
Or has an Easier size.

—Emily Dickinson, "I measure every Grief I meet"

In a capitalist culture that prizes pace, productivity, and performance, many of us have drifted far from the wisdom of our own bodies. We are praised for our minds, applauded for our output, and taught to seek answers in logic and external validation. Many of us move through life speaking the language of thoughts, but not of feelings. We can explain our calendars, our opinions, our goals. But we struggle to name what we are actually feeling. We say, "I'm fine," when we are anything but. We name everything "stress" because the finer hues of emotion have faded from memory. This is not because we lack depth. It is because we were taught to look away.

From an early age, many of us were trained to minimize emotion: Don't cry. Calm down. Be strong. These messages, offered in moments of distress, taught us that emotion was inconvenient.

47

Over time, we internalize a more subtle story: that feelings are liabilities. That tears make us weak. That anger makes us bad. That vulnerability makes us unlovable. To survive, we learn to numb, to mask, to perform. And in the process, we become strangers to our own inner worlds, when we learn to hide our truth, not just from others but also from ourselves.

Beneath all the external noise and distraction lives a quiet, yet insistent voice—ancient and wordless. It speaks in the language of sensation. It stirs in the breath, the skin, the gut, the ache behind the eyes. That voice is your body, and it has always known the way. To live from the body is not indulgent; it is essential. Your body is not just a container for your thoughts and actions; it is also a compass, forged through evolution, tuned by experience, and pulsing with the intelligence of survival and connection. It holds the truth of what you've felt, feared, longed for, and endured. And it holds the map back to yourself.

This chapter invites you into a relationship with that compass—not to control it, but to listen. To ask "What is this tension saying?" or "Why does my chest feel tight right now?" is to begin to orient to the truth beneath the surface. The body doesn't lie. It can't. In its curative honesty, it tells us what the mind has learned to overlook. And when we learn to listen, we begin to move not from reaction, but from rootedness. Listening to the body in these times is no small thing. We are living through an era that encourages us to fragment and to live from the neck up, to dismiss sensation, and to trust data over intuition. In a world that celebrates productivity and speed, the body's pace can feel inconvenient. Its pain can feel like failure. Its wisdom can feel like rebellion.

And in many ways, it is. To reclaim your body as a compass is an act of defiance. It is a refusal to be flattened into mere output or intellectual performance. It is a way of saying, "My lived experience matters. My gut feelings, my grief, my joy, my trembling hands—they are all part of my intelligence." In a culture that would have us outsource our knowing to AI, algorithms, experts, and institutions, learning to trust your own inner signals becomes revolutionary. Each time you pause to feel before deciding, before acting, you are engaging in an act of liberation. You are recentering your own humanity in a world that is increasingly disembodied.

And something else happens too. As we reconnect with the felt sense of our own experience, we expand our capacity for empathy. We cannot fully attune to the pain or joy of others if we are exiled from our own. Empathy is not just a mental exercise; it is also a bodily resonance, a shared pulse of knowing. When you honor your own sorrow, your own fear, your own delight, you strengthen the muscle that allows you to honor those same experiences in others. This is the quiet revolution of somatic work: Not only does it heal us, but it also ripples outward, softening the spaces between us. In restoring relationship with our own bodies, we restore the possibility of deeper, truer connection, with each other and with the world we share.

In the sections ahead, we will explore how emotions express themselves through the body, how interoception builds emotional fluency, and how the act of naming and feeling our inner states can restore connection and clarity. We'll consider the neuroscience behind why embodiment matters and why, for so many, it has been so difficult to access. We will also name the forces of trauma, shame, and disconnection, which have trained us to turn away from ourselves, and the practices that gently bring us back. Because your body is not broken. It is broadcasting. And when you learn its language and how to adjust the volume of your channels, you begin to find your way again, not just through crisis but also in dancing toward joy.

To be embodied is not merely to have a body but also to live in relationship with it and to sense, to feel, to respond. It is the radical practice of staying *with* yourself, in real time, rather than observing from a distance or retreating into abstraction. In a world that elevates intellect and detachment, embodiment becomes an act of individual uprising. It insists that what happens *inside* you matters, that sensation is not an inconvenience, but a source of truth. To be *em-bodied* is to be rooted and grounded in your *em-otional body*.

Most of us have learned, consciously or not, to override our nervous system's cues. We drink coffee instead of sleeping, smile when we want to cry, say *yes* when our bodies are screaming *no*. This habit of override is not a personal flaw; it's a survival strategy—one many of us inherited from caregivers who were also disconnected from their own needs. But over time, chronic override trains the nervous system to distrust its own signals. We begin to live in contradiction: exhausted, but unable to rest; lonely, but afraid to connect; overwhelmed, but pretending we're fine. Part of returning to ourselves is noticing where override lives and learning to honor what the body is asking for before it has to scream.

There is a secret language your body speaks—one that does not use words, but pulses, currents, shivers, and heat. It is the language of interoception, your sixth sense, the subtle and sacred ability to perceive what is happening within you. The thrum of your heartbeat. The flutter of breath beneath your ribs. The heaviness behind your eyes after a long day. The tightening in your gut when something feels off. This inner perception forms the foundation of all feeling. It is the birthplace of emotion, the compass of aliveness, the guide that whispers before words arrive. It is the sensory foundation of emotional intelligence. Without it, we are disoriented, disassociated, and emotionally mute. With it, we begin to recognize emotion not just as thought but also as presence, alive in muscle, breath, and blood (Craig, 2002; Mehling et al., 2012). Through this sixth sense, you can recognize joy before it smiles, grief before it cries, and anxiety before it speaks its trembling name.

But trauma, ever the disruptor of truth and tenderness, can dull this inner sense or twist its messages into sirens of alarm. Trauma, chronic stress, and emotional suppression all interfere with our ability to feel ourselves. This is not a failure; it is adaptation. When the body becomes a battlefield or a burden, interoception often becomes distorted or silenced. Survivors of chronic stress may find themselves caught between two extremes: feeling too much (as in panic that boils from a flicker of sensation) or feeling too little (as in numbness so vast even pleasure cannot break through). Both are common. Both are wise adaptations.

This fun house mirror of emotional distortion is not imagined. It is neurobiological. Interoception is rooted in a complex network of brain-body communication, primarily governed by the vagus nerve, which acts as the body's information superhighway. This vast nerve system transmits signals from the internal organs to the brain, where they are interpreted by a region called the "insula," the seat of bodily awareness. When this system is functioning well, the body and brain are in dialogue: a two-way conversation of breath and sensation. But in the aftermath of trauma, this connection may become either severed or flooded.

In states of depression, the insula often shows reduced activity, contributing to a sense of internal deadness, disconnection, and emotional flatness (Leech et al., 2024). People may feel as if they are underwater, watching life unfold behind a pane of glass. Their body becomes not a home, but an echo. An abandoned place.

Conversely, anxiety may heighten interoceptive awareness, but in acutely distorted ways. A small change in heart rate may be misread by the insula as a life-threatening event. A flutter becomes a warning. A whisper becomes a scream. Trauma research shows this is not imagined fear, but the result of increased connectivity between the insula and the brain's fear circuitry, particularly the amygdala, following traumatic stress (Garfinkel et al., 2015). Sensation becomes overwhelming, misinterpreted, and unbearable. Whether your system numbs you out or floods you in, the result is often a painful phenomenon we might call an "inner vagrancy." You are evicted and exiled from the very body meant to anchor you. Split. Disoriented. Unmoored. Disassociated. This is the lived reality of dysregulation, and it is more common than we know.

But here lies the invitation: Interoception is not fixed. It is a sense, and senses can be retrained.

Like regaining balance after a fall or speech after a stroke, the skill of tuning in to your body's signals can be rebuilt. With gentle attention and steady practice, the vagus nerve can be soothed, the insula reactivated, and the once-fractured communication restored. Over time, this becomes a form of neural rehabilitation—a way of mending the signal between brain and body so that the messages of the inner world become clear, accurate, and trustworthy again.

This process is not only restorative; it is also a personal revolution. As you begin to reclaim interoceptive awareness, a quiet agency awakens within you. You stop ricocheting between panic and shutdown. You catch the wave before it crests. You learn to stay with the sensations of the present moment rather than being dragged by echoes of the past.

And more than that, you begin to feel joy again because interoception is not only the key to recognizing pain; it is also the gateway to pleasure. The warmth of sunlight on skin. The softness of a favorite blanket. The heartbeat of a loved one against your chest. These are not luxuries. They are lifelines. Yet many trauma survivors find pleasure just as difficult to access as pain. The same mechanisms that numbed the suffering also dulled the sweetness. Rebuilding interoception opens the doors to the full emotional spectrum, not just what wounds but also what heals. To hear the sweetness of a loved one's voice or a songbird on a spring day, to feel tingling from our lover's kiss or soft grass on the backs of our legs, these are not frivolous sensations. They are pleasure anchors to time and space, to the moment. Pleasure is what anchors us to our aliveness.

Research shows that individuals with higher interoceptive awareness tend to have greater emotional clarity, resilience, and social attunement (Füstös et al., 2013; Mehling et al., 2012; Pollatos & Schandry, 2008). They can distinguish subtle emotional states—grief from exhaustion, anger from fear, excitement from panic—and respond accordingly (Füstös et al., 2013; Pollatos & Schandry, 2008). Interoception allows us to intervene early, to adjust course before being swept away. This nuance allows us to respond with care rather than react from confusion. Interoception gives us the early warning system we need to intervene before distress becomes dysregulation—if we can remember emotion is not an enemy invader. Emotion is a messenger. It is body language in its most honest form. Anxiety may be the body's plea for rest. Anger may be a boundary flaring into view. Grief, a measure of how deeply we loved. These sensations are not problems to solve. They are thresholds to cross.

The first step in crossing them is deceptively simple: Notice. Pause. Breathe. Ask, "What do I notice? What am I feeling? Where do I feel it?" And then deeply listen without judgment or intellectualized explanation. Not for words, but for pulses, tension, warmth, quivers. The sensate body speaks in rhythm and metaphor.

Practices that cultivate interoception—like mindful breathing, body scans, gentle movement, and somatic tracking—are not just wellness trends. They are also forms of neural rehabilitation. They are tools of reconnection with the felt sense. Each time you notice your breath or feel the pulse in your hands, you are strengthening the neural pathways between your brain and your body. Every time you feel your breath or place your attention on your beating heart, you strengthen the circuitry of self-awareness. You are building the capacity to stay with what's here. Over time, this becomes less effort and more instinct. You rebuild trust with your body. And from that trust, wholeness grows.

You begin to inhabit yourself again. You become someone who knows when to rest. When to speak. When to soften. When to protect. You begin to feel like yourself again—not the version molded by survival, but the one rooted in presence, belonging, and sensation.

You learn not just how to be in your body.

You learn how to be *with* your body.

And from that sacred reuniting, you learn how to be in and with the flow of your life.

After noticing comes naming. Neuroscience shows that naming an emotion engages the brain's prefrontal cortex, calming the amygdala, the emotional alarm system (Lieberman et al., 2007). This process, called "affect labeling," helps shift us from reactivity to regulation. Saying "I feel overwhelmed" may seem small, but it is a powerful act of self-contact. It is a way of saying "I see you" to the feeling within so it doesn't have to keep screaming for our attention.

To name emotions effectively, we need a richer emotional vocabulary. Too often, we reduce a kaleidoscope of feelings into three or four familiar colors: happy, sad, mad, stressed. But what if we expanded the palette? What if instead of just "angry," we tried "irritated," "resentful," "indignant," "betrayed," "righteously enraged"? Each word carries a different charge, a different direction for healing. Emotional granularity, the ability to distinguish and label emotions precisely, is linked to improved mental health and emotional resilience (Kashdan et al., 2015). Tools like emotion wheels or feelings charts are not childish; they are profound. They remind us that every hue and shade of emotion has a slightly different name and that every name is a kind of permission to be seen and witnessed.

For many, the act of naming emotions brings up not clarity, but shame. The moment a feeling rises through a lump in the throat, a flash of rage, or a well of sadness, an inner voice responds, "You're too much. You're too sensitive. You shouldn't feel this way." Shame is not the emotion itself; it is the judgment of the emotion. It says, "Not only do I feel something . . . but I shouldn't." It is a secondary wound layered atop the first. And it is one of the most insidious barriers to emotional embodiment.

Where does this shame come from? Often, it is inherited. From caregivers who themselves were shamed. From a culture that equates stoicism with strength. From systems that reward control and punish expression, especially in those marginalized by race, gender, class, or neurodivergence. Over time, the nervous system learns the following: *Emotion is dangerous. It leads to rejection.* And so we disconnect. But suppressing emotion doesn't make it disappear. It drives it underground, where it becomes diffuse and distorted. Unnamed sadness becomes irritation. Suppressed fear becomes avoidance. Hidden grief becomes fatigue. The feelings leak through in ways that sabotage relationships, health, and self-worth.

The antidote to this emotional shame is not more self-discipline; it is self-compassion. This is not indulgence. It is repair. Dr. Kristin Neff (2003) defines self-compassion as a practice of three elements: mindfulness (noticing without judgment), common humanity (remembering we are not alone), and self-kindness (responding with care). Each element directly counteracts the isolation and inner violence of shame.

Somatically, self-compassion is a *felt* experience. It might mean placing a warm hand over your heart. Softening your belly. Speaking to yourself like you would to a frightened child. These gestures, however small, send powerful signals to the nervous system: *It's safe to feel. You are not bad. You are worthy of care.* This activates the ventral vagal pathway, the neural circuit associated with safety, connection, and presence (Porges, 2011). To practice self-compassion is to reclaim the emotional territory that shame tried to colonize. It is to say, "This feeling belongs. I can feel it and still be good. I can feel it and still be loved."

Emotions are transient lived experiences, not permanent identities. In the Irish language (Gaeilge), there is a gentler way of naming them. Instead of saying "I am sad," one might say "Tá brón orm," which translates to "Sadness is upon me." This phrasing suggests that emotions are not who we are, but visitors, weather systems passing through. They arrive, they linger, and they eventually move on. When we meet them with tenderness rather than terror, they pass through us with more grace and less destruction. We stop clinging. We stop resisting. We simply notice and allow.

And yet what if these emotional weather patterns are not hardwired and fixed storms that we are destined to ride out the same way every time they show up, but stories, crafted by the brain in real time? Emotions may feel sudden and overwhelming. But neuroscience tells us they are interpretations, shaped by sensation, memory, and meaning. We do not just *have* emotions—we also *make* them, moment by moment, in dialogue with our bodies and our histories. This is the revolutionary insight offered by Dr. Lisa Feldman Barrett and her theory of constructed emotion. According to her research, emotions are not universal packages stored in the brain, waiting to be activated. Instead, they are predictions—stories your brain tells about the meaning of bodily sensations, shaped by memory, language, and culture (Barrett, 2017).

Your brain is a story- and meaning-making organ. At every moment, it is receiving interoceptive data—your heart rate, temperature, muscle tension, breath—and it is trying to make sense of that data based on past experience. What we call "emotion" is the result of this interpretive process. A racing heart might mean fear in one context, excitement in another, grief in another still. The sensation is the same; the story changes everything. This means emotions are not just responses to the world; they are also guesses about what is happening inside and outside of you. They are constructed through pattern recognition. And the more aware we become of our internal signals and the stories we attach to them, the more flexibility we gain. We can begin to ask the following: *What else could this mean? Can I write a new story for this old feeling?*

This is not to say emotions are imaginary. Quite the opposite. They are deeply real, felt, and consequential. But they are also malleable and temporary. And in that malleability and temporality lie enormous possibilities. If emotions are constructed, they can be reconstructed. Reframed. Reinterpreted.

Anxiety can become readiness, a call to prepare for what matters. Anger can become clarity, a signal that a boundary has been crossed. Grief can become testament, a sign of how deeply we have loved. This isn't spiritual bypassing or toxic positivity. It's the neuroscience of perspective. It's the practice of reclaiming authorship over your emotional life. And because emotions are shaped by culture, language, and context, part of healing is expanding our inner landscape by learning new words for what we feel, unlearning the silences we were taught, and naming experiences our more recent ancestors never had space to name. This is how we reclaim emotional agency: by noticing the feeling, naming it with care, and offering it a more generous interpretation.

The brain is not fixed. Its predictions can change. Its stories can soften. Your inner narrator can learn a new vocabulary—not of shame and suppression, but of curiosity and compassion. Every emotion is a story told not just in the mind but also in the tissue. Once a feeling takes shape in the brain, it doesn't stay there; it travels. It is translated into heart rate, breath pattern, muscle tension, posture, voice tone. It becomes *you* in motion. *Our issues are*, quite literally, *in our tissues.*

This is the realm of the autonomic nervous system, which governs the body's unconscious responses to emotion and threat. When your nervous system perceives danger, whether real or remembered, it mobilizes. The sympathetic branch ignites, flooding the body with adrenaline and cortisol. Heart pounding. Pupils dilating. Breath shallow. Muscles coiled to strike or flee.

If danger is overwhelming or inescapable, the body may shift into dorsal vagal shutdown, a branch of the parasympathetic system. This is the freeze response: numbing, dissociating, and, finally, collapsing. A kind of energetic invisibility. The body, unable to fight or run, goes still to survive.

These shifts aren't conscious. They are ancient. They are what kept our ancestors alive in the face of lions, war, and starvation. And they still govern how we respond to a tense conversation, a slammed door, a partner's silence, a traumatic memory. Your nervous system doesn't wait for your rational mind to weigh in; it acts. Its loyalty is to survival, not subtlety. But not all responses are rooted in present danger. Often, the nervous system is reacting to *memory*, to something that once was true but is no longer happening. This is the legacy of trauma: a body that cannot distinguish past from present. A system that stays braced long after the threat has passed. Dr. Bessel van der Kolk (2014) writes, "Trauma is not the story of something that happened back then. It is the current imprint of that pain on the body, mind, and soul."

Dr. Stephen Porges's polyvagal theory adds vital nuance. He describes the nervous system not as a binary on/off switch, but as a hierarchy of states. At the top is the ventral vagal state—calm, curious, socially engaged. In the middle is sympathetic arousal—mobilized, alert, ready to defend. At the base is dorsal vagal collapse—shut down, numb, withdrawn. We cycle through these states all day long, influenced by cues of safety and threat, connection and isolation. These states are not wrong. They are intelligent responses shaped by context and history.

Yet when trauma traps the body in sympathetic fight or dorsal freeze, we lose flexibility. We can't return to ventral calm. The body stays caught in reflex; and the mind interprets this as anxiety, fatigue, rage, shame. Healing then is not just about talking through trauma. It is also about completing the nervous system's interrupted responses, what Peter Levine (2010) calls our "unfinished survival energy." Animals in the wild, after escaping danger, shake or tremble to release adrenaline. They reset their systems through instinct. Humans, conditioned to "keep it together," often override this process. We don't shake. We tighten. We swallow the scream. We distract from the ache. We keep calm and carry on. We survive, but the charge stays trapped.

Somatic healing helps us finish what our bodies started. Sometimes it looks like trembling. Sometimes like weeping. Sometimes like dancing or curling up or punching into a pillow as we slow down time and feel all our nerves, muscles, and tendons in motion. Sometimes it's just a breath, a long exhale that says "You are safe now. You can come home." When we complete our interrupted survival responses via discharge, *shift happens* toward regulation.

Before we ever had language, we had sensation. Before we learned to name our feelings, we lived inside them. A baby's cry, a startle at a loud noise, a gaze reaching for warmth—these were our first conversations with the world. Our earliest experiences of safety or threat, of love or neglect were encoded in memory not as stories, but as states—bodily imprints in the architecture of the nervous system. This is where the concept of the inner child emerges, not merely as a metaphor but also as a *somatic state*. The inner child is the part of us still wired to those early impressions: to the sound of footsteps that meant fear, to the stillness that meant abandonment, to the smile that meant safety. The body doesn't forget what it once had to endure to belong and seek connection. It remembers through muscle tone, breath patterns, and instinctive reactions. What psychology frames as "attachment style," the body simply registers as "my preferred safety strategy."

When those early needs went unmet—our needs for comfort, for mirroring, for repair—the body adapted. It braced. It became small or loud, invisible or perfect. These adaptations helped us survive, but they also formed grooves that we still move through unconsciously. Healing requires that we meet the inner child not with logic, but with presence, with the very kind of attunement that was once missing. This is the heart of somatic reparenting: offering your nervous system new experiences of safety, coregulation, and care. A hand on your own chest during a wave of shame. Whispering words of reassurance to yourself in the tone you once longed to hear. Rocking gently when tears come. These are not childish gestures. They are acts of *neural repair*.

Neuroscience confirms that the nervous system is capable of earning secure attachment—that is, developing a felt sense of safety and trust even if our early caregivers did not provide it (Siegel, 2010). Each moment of self-soothing, each embodied act of kindness, each experience of being with your feeling instead of rejecting it creates a new imprint. You are not too late.

Inner child work may bring up waves of grief, like grief for what was never given or grief for how long you've carried certain burdens. This grief too is somatic. It lives in the body as tightness, as tears that won't come, as restlessness or fatigue. Making space for this grief is not regressive; it is liberating. The body can finally stop pretending. It can start telling the truth. And within this grief is a doorway: the possibility of becoming the caregiver you needed. You can offer yourself what was absent. You can choose softness where there once was silence, compassion where there once was confusion. This is not bypassing the past. It is rewriting the nervous system's conclusion about what is possible now.

You do not need to become someone else to heal. You need to become someone who can stay with yourself, especially when that younger part of you shows up trembling, raging, or fawning for love. And slowly, as trust builds, the child within stops crying out. Because they know you're finally listening.

Please know staying with yourself doesn't mean staying only inside yourself, away from others, isolated from outside triggers. To live in a feeling body is to live in constant contact—with the self, with others, with the world. Sensitivity is not a flaw; it is a finely tuned antenna. And the more deeply we connect with our own internal signals, the more clearly we begin to hear the noise that is not ours. Healing the inner child gives us a center, a sanctuary within. From that rooted place, we can begin to notice the following: *What is mine to hold? And what is not?*

Without discernment, emotional sensitivity becomes saturation. We absorb what isn't ours. We carry what doesn't belong. We mistake the emotional weather around us for the weather within us. This is especially true for those who are empathic, people whose nervous systems are exquisitely responsive to emotional shifts in others. You walk into a room and feel the tension before a word is spoken. You comfort someone and leave with their sadness lodged in your chest. You confuse intuition with overidentification, compassion with self-erasure. Discernment begins in the body. The nervous system is constantly scanning for cues: *Is this safe? Is this familiar? Is this mine?* But if we've never been taught to attune to our internal signals, we may override them. We think boundaries are just rules or phrases. In truth, boundaries are sensory experiences that are felt as constriction, expansion, alertness, or fatigue. They show up in the body long before they're spoken aloud.

To practice discernment, start by learning your baseline. What does your body feel like when you're alone, regulated, at rest? Let that become your reference point. Then when a new emotional current enters, like a partner's frustration or a colleague's urgency, you can ask, "Did something change in me, or did I just pick something up?"

This isn't about blaming others. It's about staying rooted in your own center. You can care without collapsing. You can witness without absorbing. And you can learn to discharge what's not yours. Sometimes that means shaking out your limbs after a tense interaction. Sometimes it means stepping outside, placing your feet on the earth, and breathing deeply until your energy returns.

Somatic practices can support this differentiation and individuation. Body scans help track sensation shifts. Orienting practices—like naming what you see, hear, or feel—can help bring you back to the present moment. Even vocalizing can help: saying "I release what's not mine" while exhaling fully. These rituals are not magical thinking; they are neural recalibrations. They remind the body that it can return to itself.

Over time, this practice of discernment becomes a kind of emotional and somatic hygiene. You stop confusing other people's storms for your own climate. You stop shrinking to make others more comfortable. And you begin to trust that your own feelings, even the inconvenient ones, are worth honoring. As we grow in awareness, we begin to track the difference. We learn to ask the following: *Is this activation mine or someone else's? Is this sorrow ancestral, collective, or current?* This kind of discernment is not just cognitive; it's also somatic. It lives in the body's subtle shifts: a tightening in the gut, a pressure behind the eyes, a sudden quickening of breath. To tell what is yours and what is not is an act of self-trust, built through daily embodied listening.

And sometimes what we discover cannot be named in words, only felt and honored through creative processing. The body, at its core, is not merely a container for emotion; it is also a crucible of alchemy. A place where raw experience is metabolized into wisdom. But this transformation does not always happen through logic or language. Sometimes the emotions we carry—grief, rage, joy, longing—are too vast, too nuanced, or too early to be spoken. The body finds a way to communicate its experience through creativity, in image, in rhythm, in sound. Do not be surprised or alarmed if, after working somatically, you feel an unexpected urge to create. It is the body's way of speaking what cannot be said, of weaving sensation into shape and experience into expression.

When you dance your sorrow, you are giving movement to what has become frozen. When you paint your joy, you are making visible what once lived only as sensation. When you sing your rage, you are letting the vibration of your voice carry what your nervous system can no longer hold in silence. These acts are not indulgent. They are sacred acts of emotional alchemy.

Neuroscience shows us that creativity engages the default mode network of the brain, a circuit associated with introspection, empathy, memory, and emotional processing (Andrews-Hanna et al., 2014). Engaging this network allows us to integrate disparate experiences, to make meaning of what once felt chaotic. In other words, art doesn't just express; it also reorganizes.

Somatic therapy encourages this kind of expression not for performance, but for presence. You don't need to be a trained artist to benefit. Scribbling on a page, humming while you walk, molding clay, making sound—these are all acts of regulation. They help your body say, "This is how I feel. This is what's true. This is me coming into coherence."

When you create, you offer the inner child a safe playground. You offer the adult self a place to rest. You offer the nervous system a new pattern: one in which emotion is not suppressed or shamed but welcomed. Witnessed. Given shape or sound. Over time, this creates a rhythm, one where emotion no longer floods or disappears but flows. You learn to trust your waves. To ride them. To let them shape you without capsizing you. This is embodied integration—not the erasure of pain, but the inclusion of it. Not the elimination of vulnerability, but the capacity to hold it with grace.

You become someone who can feel. Who can move through grief without drowning, anger without destruction, joy without fear. You become someone whose emotions are not liabilities, but guides. And your body? It becomes the map, the compass, the home. You don't need to understand every feeling to honor it. You don't need to heal all at once. You need only to stay curious. To stay with. To offer yourself, again and again, the gift of attention. Because in the end, every time you feel and stay, you build a bridge. From mind to body. From wound to wisdom. From reaction to choice.

That is what healing looks like: not perfection, but presence. Not closure, but continuity. Not escape, but embodiment.

Case Study
Elias's Return to Feeling

Elias was the kind of man others called "steady." He showed up on time. He paid his bills early or on time. He answered questions with nods or silence more often than words. In meetings, he was reliable. In friendships, he was generous, but hard to read. He had mastered the art of being present without ever quite being seen.

At forty-two, Elias had never cried in front of another person. Not at his father's funeral. Not during his divorce. Not even when he held his stillborn son. He felt things, he supposed, in the way a distant thunder rumbled without rain. But mostly, he had learned to hold it in. He carried his emotions like stones in his coat pockets—weighty, but quiet.

When Elias finally came to therapy, it wasn't because he was in crisis. It was because he couldn't feel anything at all. His partner had ended things, saying she never knew where he was emotionally. His body ached with tension he couldn't explain. He slept in short fitful hours, and even laughter with his nephews felt like something he was observing through glass.

He wasn't sure what he hoped therapy would do. "I'm not the emotional type," he said on the first day. "I just want to get back to normal." But "normal," he would soon learn, was a lifelong pattern of shutdown. Of sympathetic bracing and dorsal collapse. Of silence in place of sorrow.

Over time, Elias's therapist introduced the concept of interoception. At first, Elias laughed, saying, "You want me to talk to my spleen?" But slowly, through the practice of body scans, he began to notice things: the tension in his shoulders that never eased, the shallow breath that barely reached his belly, the way his jaw ached each morning from clenching all night long. These weren't just aches. They were also unspoken stories.

Polyvagal theory provided a frame. His therapist explained how the body moves through ventral vagal safety, sympathetic arousal, and dorsal vagal shutdown (Porges, 2011). Elias realized that he had spent most of his life hovering between mobilization and collapse. He was hyperfunctional at work and utterly disconnected in his personal life. He was all the way tuned in or all the way tuned out. His default state wasn't peace. It was survival.

In one session, the therapist invited him to place a hand on his chest and breathe. It was a simple thing. But Elias couldn't do it. "It feels . . . stupid," he muttered. Underneath that word was shame, a belief that softness was weakness. That to feel was to fail. His childhood had taught him this: Boys who cried were ridiculed and called "sissies." Boys who felt and expressed their feelings were told to toughen up. Over the years, Elias had become excellent at suppressing what came up and disappearing inside his own body.

But something in him was curious. He began practicing alone. He sat with his hand on his chest in the early morning, when the house was still. He breathed into the space beneath his ribs, sometimes imagining he was softening the tissue around a stone lodged deep in his throat.

A memory emerged: ten years old, being told to "man up" at his grandfather's funeral. The lump and tightness in his throat had never left.

Weeks passed. In one session, Elias shared that a song on the radio had made his eyes sting. It was about a father and son. "I didn't cry," he said quickly, apologetically. But his therapist simply nodded. "Your body is gaining capacity and remembering feeling and sensation," she said. Elias began to name sensations: heat in the face, a heaviness behind the eyes, the flutter in his chest when someone looked at him kindly. These were emotions as sensations, not stories. And through naming them, he found a language he never knew he spoke.

Somatic tools became bridges: orienting to the room when he felt overwhelmed, pressing his feet into the floor during hard conversations, using slow exhalations to stay with his own discomfort. His therapist guided him in visualizations—returning to the boy inside him who had been silenced, placing a warm hand on his back in the imaginal realm, whispering, "You don't have to hold it all alone anymore."

One night, sitting alone after journaling, Elias cried. It wasn't loud. It wasn't cinematic. It was quiet, cleansing, holy, and utterly without apology. His breath shuddered. His body shook. And afterward, he felt . . . lighter. Not happy. But more whole. Clearer.

Over the months, Elias's stoicism softened into strength. He could say "I feel angry" without exploding. He could admit "I don't know what I feel" and stay curious instead of shutting down. He practiced emotional discernment by asking himself, "Is this mine? Is this old? What do I need?"

One day, when his nephew fell and burst into tears, Elias didn't say, "You're fine. Get up." He knelt down, held the child close, and said, "That was scary, huh?" He didn't rush the boy out of his feelings. He made space for them. The boy stopped crying faster than usual, but not because he was told to. Because he was held.

Elias was learning to do the same for himself.

The work wasn't linear. Sometimes the fog returned. Sometimes he still felt like he was faking it. But now he knew how to come home. He had a map. A breath. A body. A name for what he felt. And in that, there was shelter.

Elias's story is one of transformation not through force, but through softening. Through the quiet and radical act of feeling. In learning to let his body speak, he finally began to hear his life calling back.

Journal and Reflection Prompts

1. What emotions do you tend to suppress or avoid, and how does your body signal their presence?
2. How were emotions expressed (or silenced) in your family or culture of origin?
3. In moments of overwhelm, can you sense your body's early signals? What do they feel like?
4. What is one creative or nonverbal way you could begin expressing emotion more freely?
5. What might it mean to treat your emotional body not as a problem to fix, but as a compass to follow?

Somatic Ritual: Returning to the Compass Within

This ritual is an invitation to come home to your emotional body by honoring its signals and feeling without judgment and to listen for the wisdom underneath the sensation.

Time required: 15–20 minutes

Suggested props: a quiet space, journal, a warm blanket or shawl, optional candle or object of comfort

---

1. **Create sacred space.**

   Find a quiet, undisturbed place to land. Sit or lie down in a position that feels both restful and alert. Light a candle, hold a grounding object, or wrap yourself in something soft to signal to your body that this is sacred time.

2. **Orient to the present.**

   Turn your head gently and look around your space. Let your eyes find and name *three objects* that feel familiar or comforting. Say them aloud or silently: "I see the plant. I see the window. I see the candle." This tells your nervous system, "I am here. I am safe. I am in the now."

3. **Ground into sensation.**

   Bring your awareness to the points where your body meets the ground or chair. Feel the weight of your seat, your back, your feet. Inhale slowly through your nose. Exhale through the mouth with a soft sigh. Repeat 3–5 times. Feel yourself arriving.

4. **Drop in and track.**

   Close your eyes (if safe) and scan your body slowly from head to toe. Ask the following:

   • What sensations are present?

- Where is there tension? Softness?
- Is there a pulse, a flutter, a holding?

Choose one sensation to stay with without trying to change it. Just notice it. Ask gently the following:

- What does this part of me want me to know?
- What might this feeling be pointing to?

Allow any emotion, memory, or image to arise. You don't need to understand it fully. Just be with it as a companion.

5. **Name the emotion.**

    If an emotion becomes clear, name it quietly: "This is sadness" or "This is anger" or "This is tenderness." Say, "This is here, and I am here with it."

    Let the naming be a form of welcoming, not analysis. This is not about fixing. We are just noticing and witnessing.

6. **Express and move.**

    Ask your body, "How would you like to express this?"
    You might do the following:

    - Place a hand over the area of strongest sensation
    - Hum, sigh, or whisper what you feel
    - Write a few words in a journal
    - Draw an image of what the emotion feels like
    - Gently sway, stretch, rock, or shake
    - Slowly push, pull, or kick—feeling every tendon and muscle being called upon

    Let the body shape its truth. Let sensation find form.

7. **Return to the room.**

    When you feel complete, orient once more to your surroundings. Find the same *three objects* with your eyes and name them again. Feel your feet on the floor, your seat on the chair. Wiggle your fingers. Take a few cleansing breaths to mark the return.

8. **Seal the practice.**

Place both hands over your heart or belly and say aloud or silently the following:

I am allowed to feel. My emotions are valid. My body is wise. I am learning to listen.

Blow out the candle or gently close the ritual in any way that feels meaningful.

4

Merging vs. Joining:
What's Yours, Mine, and Ours?

Trust thyself: every heart vibrates to that iron string. . . .
Nothing is at last sacred but the integrity of your own mind.

—Ralph Waldo Emerson, *Self-Reliance*

There is a subtle and sacred difference between dissolving into another and standing beside them in sovereign connection. Many of us were never taught how to remain rooted within ourselves while loving another. Instead, we learned to disappear by folding ourselves into the moods of our parents, the heartbreaks of our partners, the electric weather of a crowded room until we no longer knew what belonged to us and what did not. This is the shape of merging: a nervous system strategy masquerading as love.

Merging is not empathy. It is not attunement. It is a survival reflex born of relational danger, where our safety once depended on absorbing the pain or volatility of others. As children, we scanned our caregivers' faces before we spoke. We learned to tiptoe through emotional minefields, to flatten our joy, or to intensify our care, believing that if we merged deeply enough, we might avoid rupture and secure connection. This kind of fusion feels like closeness. But it is not connection; it is self-abandonment in disguise.

To merge is to lose the felt sense of your own edges. The body forgets its perimeter. Your chest tightens with someone else's borrowed grief. Your breath disappears when their anxiety rises. You ache with the echo of a pain that is not yours to hold. In polyvagal terms, this state reflects a collapse of boundary clarity in the social engagement system, pulling the nervous system toward sympathetic vigilance or dorsal withdrawal (Porges, 2011). The cost is cumulative: emotional fatigue, burnout, a chronic low-grade sense of disorientation in your own life.

But there is another way.

Joining is the somatic art of standing inside yourself while reaching toward another. It is not a wall. It is not detachment. It is presence without absorption, love without losing your breath. When we join rather than merge, we stay connected to our own nervous system while offering space for someone else's. This is not selfishness. It is sacred boundary. And it is essential for sustainable empathy.

To truly join another, we must be willing to feel without fusing. We must be willing to say, "I see you, and I am still here in me." This is the practice of emotional differentiation, the ability to be with another's suffering without disappearing into it. In the body, joining feels like anchored openness: the spine tall, the breath steady, the heart available. It is not that we don't feel. It's that we don't become one with their emotional state. Joining becomes possible when we begin to recognize our internal warning signs, the subtle somatic cues that tell us we're slipping out of ourselves. A sudden weight behind the eyes. A fog that rolls in during conversation. A hollowing of our chest and solar plexus. A familiar almost-invisible tightening in the lower gut when someone unloads their pain. These sensations are not trivial. They are the nervous system whispering, "You've left yourself again."

The first act of reclamation is noticing. When we ask "Is this mine?" we create a pause, a break in the reflex to merge. This pause is sacred. It is the moment where choice reenters. And in that moment, we begin to shift from automatic empathy into embodied discernment. According to somatic and expressive arts researcher and practitioner, Cathy Malchiodi (2007), trauma-informed embodiment starts not with fixing what we feel, but with noticing where we begin and end.

Joining asks that we develop a kind of interoceptive fluency. It's the ability to notice our own breathing while in conversation, to feel our feet on the floor even as someone cries in front of us. This is the gateway to sustainable connection: staying attuned to your internal signals while responding to external need. Neurobiologically, this allows the prefrontal cortex, the center of executive function and compassion, to stay online, even in the presence of emotional intensity (Siegel, 2020). When we embody this distinction, our relationships begin to change. We find that we can be present for a partner's grief without drowning in it. We can listen to a friend's rage without becoming reactive. We can sit with sorrow, frustration, or disappointment and still feel our own pulse beneath it all. And in doing so, we become steadier. Truer. More trustworthy, both to ourselves and to those we love.

Merging is a nervous system strategy forged in the fires of survival. But joining is a nervous system skill forged in the light of awareness. It is a practice we build one breath, one boundary, one small moment at a time.

This capacity for discernment, for staying with oneself in the presence of another, is ancient. Long before psychology had words like "emotional boundaries" or "self-regulation," communities across the world created rituals to hold collective emotion without personal collapse. In both the West African tradition (where we find the griot) and the Irish tradition (where we find the *seanachi*), there was a keeper of oral history who would share grief, joy, and communal memory through story and song, allowing listeners to feel deeply without losing themselves. Listeners could momentarily hold the story in their head or their heart without becoming wholly consumed by the story. Among the Dagara people of Burkina Faso, grief rituals were not private burdens, but public ceremonies, designed to move emotional energy communally, preventing any one person from absorbing too much (Somé, 1994).

These practices were wise to the body. They gave emotion a place to land, a rhythm to follow, a communal container. And they honored boundaries—not as division, but as necessary architecture for collective healing. When we engage in similar practices today, whether through ritual, therapy, journaling, or movement, we are continuing this lineage. We are saying, "I can feel with you without becoming you. I can love you without leaving myself."

This is the essence of relational safety: to be with another in their pain while also being with ourselves in our own truth. To offer empathy without rescue. To offer care without collapse. And to do so again and again, in small ways, until the body no longer fears that presence will cost it everything.

For many, especially those shaped by familial trauma or cultural messages equating love with sacrifice, setting such boundaries can feel unnatural or even abandoning and cruel. But boundaries are not a rejection of others; they are an honoring of ourselves. They are an invitation to sustainable closeness. True boundaries make space for both our needs to matter, yours and mine.

Learning this takes time. It asks us to rewire not just our behaviors but also our biology. Each time we notice we're merging and gently return to ourselves, we are reshaping our nervous system. Each time we speak a boundary with kindness, we are building neural pathways of self-trust and relational integrity. Each time we breathe and say, "This is not mine," we are softening old patterns of survival into new patterns of belonging.

Let the body lead. It knows the difference between collapse and connection. Between sacrifice and sovereignty. Between merging and joining.

To choose joining over merging is to choose presence over performance. It is to live from a regulated body rather than a reactive one. This choice does not make us cold or distant; rather, it roots us in clarity. From that place, we become safer to ourselves and to others. We learn to say yes when we mean yes and no when we mean no—not from defensiveness, but from alignment. This alignment is everything. It tells the nervous system, "You are allowed to have needs." It tells the inner child, "You do not have to carry everyone else to be loved." It tells the lineage of caretakers and sacrificers behind us, "We are learning a new way, one that honors selfhood without abandoning community."

This work is not linear. There will be days we slip back into old patterns, moments when guilt or fear pulls us toward merging. But each time we return, each time we choose presence over fusion, breath over bracing, truth over appeasement, we strengthen a new pathway. A path where love includes self, where connection honors sovereignty.

Joining is not a boundary drawn in resentment. It is a boundary drawn in reverence. It says, "I will not disappear to love you. I will stay and invite you to meet me, whole and intact." This is the sacred middle ground where profound intimacy lives. Where relationships thrive—not because one person becomes small, but because both are allowed to be fully human. In choosing to join rather than merge, we reclaim the nervous system as a site of both resilience and relationship. We learn that connection need not come at the cost of ourselves. And in that knowing, we become the kind of presence the world needs: grounded, generous, and whole.

Case Study
Amina Learns to Hold Her Own Heart

At twenty-four, Amina carried herself like someone older—fierce, efficient, always the one with tissues in her purse and a charger in her bag. Her friends called her the "mom" of the group, a badge of honor she wore with a smile. But privately, she was exhausted. Not just from work or graduate school, but also from the unspoken job she had held since she was eight years old: holding her family together.

The eldest daughter of Nigerian immigrants, Amina was fluent in sacrifice. As a child, she translated phone calls, filled out government forms, managed grocery lists. When her mother worked night shifts and her father worked doubles, she fed her siblings, bathed them, soothed their tears. She learned early that her own tears were less welcome. Her mother would scold, "Why are you crying like that? Toughen up." Her father, quick to anger, dismissed her sobs as "too much." So she learned to bury them. But buried things don't vanish; they decompose and leak into their surroundings, contaminating the healthy earth around them.

By the time she entered adulthood, Amina's emotions spilled out like water through a cracked jug. She cried at commercials. She snapped at small slights. She needed reassurance constantly. In relationships, she felt like a storm—always too much, too fast, and too fragile. Partners often told her, kindly or not, that they felt overwhelmed by her intensity. "It's like I'm trying to prove I'm worthy of staying," she admitted once in therapy. "Like I have to earn love every single day, or I'll lose it. This has me constantly on edge and hypervigilant in all my relationships."

Her therapist gently introduced the concept of merging. At first, Amina resisted, feeling confronted and defensive. "I'm just passionate, and when I love, I love hard," she said. But as they traced her patterns, a painful clarity emerged. When a friend was upset, Amina's day unraveled. When her boyfriend got quiet, she panicked. She didn't just feel with people; she also felt *as* them and *for* them. Their moods became her moods. Their silence became her self-doubt. Sometimes she felt the feelings her loved ones were actively avoiding or repressing, as though she was doing their feeling for them as a labor of love. "I don't know where they end and I begin," she whispered one day, eyes wide with realization.

Her nervous system had been trained for this. According to polyvagal theory (Porges, 2011), her body constantly scanned for threat; and when others were upset, her system interpreted it as danger. The sympathetic branch activated: she'd talk faster, overapologize, promise to do better. Her body didn't feel safe unless everyone around her was calm. This was the inheritance of parentification, the nervous system wired for hyperresponsibility and hypervigilance.

"I was the emotional janitor," she said. "I cleaned up everyone's messes, but no one taught me what to do with my own." In her family, loyalty meant silence, and big emotions were tolerated only if they weren't hers. But her body could no longer carry the unspoken grief. She started somatic therapy—not to understand her pain, but to survive it.

They began with interoception, noticing her own body in moments of overwhelm. Amina learned to feel the rapid beat of her heart, the tremble in her hands, the clenching in her stomach when her sister vented for an hour without asking how *she* was doing. "This is where I leave myself," she began to say. "Right here, in this moment."

Together, she and her therapist practiced joining instead of merging. This meant anchoring in her own sensations during difficult conversations. When her mother called to unload her day, Amina placed her bare feet on the hardwood floor, tracking the coolness under her toes. When her boyfriend went quiet after an argument, she resisted the urge to chase. She placed a hand on her chest and asked herself, "What am I feeling that belongs to me?"

It wasn't easy. The guilt came in waves. "I feel selfish," she said often. "They need me." But each time she stayed with herself, her nervous system learned a new truth: Boundaries do not betray love. They protect it. When she told her brother, "I can't help with your paper tonight," she defensively braced for the backlash—an anger she projected he would have with her. But it didn't come; he didn't have it. He shrugged and said, "Okay." The world didn't end.

Amina began to journal after hard interactions, tracing what was hers and what wasn't. She used visualizations, picturing her energy like warm light, learning when it dimmed or spilled. Slowly, she started asking questions no one had let her ask before: *What do I want? What do I need?*

The transformation wasn't dramatic. It was slow, cellular. One day, she cried in therapy—not from despair, but from recognition. "I'm starting to feel like I'm in my own body more than I'm not," she said, hand resting gently on her chest.

Amina didn't stop loving deeply. She didn't become stoic or detached. She still offered help, still cried during sad movies, still sent long voice memos to friends. But now she also said, "Not today." She ended phone calls when she felt herself unraveling. She let silence be part of the conversation. In time, the bigness of her love for the people in her life began to feel less messy and conflicted and more easeful.

Most profoundly, she began to love herself with the same intensity she once reserved for everyone else.

"Joining," she told her therapist one day, "feels like holding my own heart in one hand while I hold space for yours in the other." Her nervous system, once tuned only to the needs of others, began to hear the sound of her own breath, steady and sovereign.

Amina's story reminds us that love is not measured by how much of ourselves we give away, but by how fully we are able to remain present within our own being as we show up for others. The nervous system thrives in clarity—not in the chaos of emotional enmeshment, but in the grounded awareness of self. Merging may have once been necessary, a form of emotional camouflage to survive environments that offered conditional care. But as adults committed to healing, we are invited to something different: presence without self-erasure, empathy without absorption, love without leaking.

To join is to stay whole. It is a brave and sacred reclamation of self in a world that often confuses overextension with care. The more we practice anchoring into our own sensations, tending to our own needs, and discerning what is ours to carry, the more we restore dignity—not just to ourselves but also to our relationships. In joining, we say to the world, "I will not abandon you, but I will not abandon myself either." This is the heart of mature love, nervous system healing, and emotional freedom.

Case Study
Learning to Land: Nadia's Story

Nadia, a thirty-two-year-old painter, had spent her life chasing inspiration and approval. Her creative fire was undeniable, her brushwork evocative and raw. Galleries loved her.

Students admired her. But beneath her acclaim lived a private chaos: She couldn't bear the stillness that followed each exhibition. The praise was a drug, and the silence afterward felt like withdrawal.

She moved from one relationship to the next, never really single. Never truly alone. Each partnership began before the last had ended. "I needed someone else's presence like gesso on a canvas," she said. "Without it, I didn't know where to begin."

As a child, Nadia had learned that attunement meant abandoning herself. Her mother's moods were tidal and consuming—joyful one hour, rageful the next. Her father had checked out emotionally by the time she was six, often disappearing behind a newspaper or retreating into long silences. Nadia became an emotional barometer, absorbing her mother's distress in the hope of soothing the chaos. Her body learned early that love meant fusion. Her body memorized the rhythms of merging early: feel what others feel, need what they need, become the brilliant star they need you to be. It was the only way to stay safe.

By thirty, Nadia's nervous system was chronically attuned to everyone but herself. Her romantic partners shaped her schedule, her moods, even her art. She sought constant advice from friends, needing external direction to quell her inner fog. "I felt like I was borrowing other people's clarity," she said. "I didn't trust my own voice to last longer than a day."

It was a creative block that finally drove her to therapy. For months, she'd been unable to paint. She sat in her studio, paralyzed. The colors blurred. The ideas slipped away. "I didn't know what *I* wanted to say on the canvas anymore," she said. "I'd painted for galleries, for professors, for partners who wanted portraits. But not for me."

Through somatic and inner child healing, Nadia began to trace her patterns back to their source. She practiced orienting to her own body, scanning for what was hers versus what she had absorbed. She began to track sensation: the way her chest constricted when deferring to others, the flutter in her stomach when she made a choice without consulting anyone. Her therapist taught her to find her "home frequency"—a subtle, but steady sense of self that lived beneath the noise.

A breakthrough came after a gallery show. As the applause and congratulations rang out, Nadia did something she'd never done before: She placed a hand on her heart and took three slow breaths. Instead of reaching for someone to validate her, she stood still and allowed herself to *feel* the moment. "That was my art," she whispered inwardly. "That was my voice."

From then on, she began painting differently, slowly, deliberately, and from the body up. She painted not for praise, but for process. Her nervous system, once flooded by others' needs, began to soften into her own rhythm. Her solitude became sacred.

The more she anchored into her own experience, the more alive and engaging her art became. Viewers said her new work had "depth," "presence," even "healing energy." And she believed them because, for the first time, it was true. She wasn't merging into the gaze of others. She was meeting herself—fully.

"I used to think I needed someone else's gaze to feel real," she reflected. "Now I trust my own eyes, my own hands, my own breath. I've become the keeper of my own canvas."

Nadia's story reminds us that the journey from merging to joining is not just relational; it is also creative. When we stop painting ourselves out of the frame and begin to reclaim our own outlines, we discover a richer palette. A deeper pulse. And the quiet beauty of finally fully belonging to ourselves.

Journal and Reflection Prompts

1. **Where do I tend to lose myself in the emotional experience of others?**

   Reflect on moments when you felt drained, foggy, or overwhelmed after an interaction. What somatic cues signaled that you may have merged rather than joined?

2. **What beliefs or messages from my upbringing taught me that love inherently means sacrifice or self-erasure?**

   Gently explore the inherited narratives that shaped your ideas of closeness, duty, and responsibility. Do they leave enough space for your existence?

3. **How does my body feel when I am truly rooted in myself, even in the presence of someone else's pain?**

   Recall a moment when you stayed present with yourself and another. What sensations arose? How did your body respond?

4. **What boundaries, spoken or unspoken, would support me in practicing joining more often?**

   Consider physical, emotional, or time-based boundaries that protect your energy without shutting down connection.

5. **What would it feel like to say, "This is not mine," and let that be enough?**

   Practice releasing with love what does not belong to you. Imagine how your nervous system might respond to that permission.

Somatic Ritual: Returning to Your Own Field

This ritual is an invitation to re-anchor in your own body's rhythm when you have merged with another's emotions and to practice *joining*—providing your presence without self-erasure. Choose a quiet space where you can stand or sit comfortably. If possible, have a small bowl of water nearby to symbolize fluidity and a stone or object that feels grounding in your hand or lap.

1. **Arrival: Orient to the Room**

   Let your eyes slowly scan the space you are in.

   Notice color, light, shadow, and shape.

   Let your body register that *you are here*—in this room, in this moment, not inside anyone else's weather.

   Gently turn your head from side to side, softening your neck. Feel the air move across your skin.

   Whisper inwardly, *I am here. This is me. I am home.*

2. **The Breath That Belongs to You**

   Place one hand over your heart and one on your lower belly.

Inhale through your nose for four counts. Exhale through your mouth for six.

Let the exhale lengthen just slightly more than the inhale. This is signaling your vagus nerve that it is safe to soften.

As you breathe, imagine tracing the outline of your own body with air.

Redraw your edges with each exhale.

Feel the subtle warmth of your own boundary returning.

3. **The Boundary Gesture**

Bring your palms together at your heart. Then slowly open your arms outward in a wide arc, as if creating a sphere of space around you.

This is not a wall—it's a *field*.

This field surrounds the home of your body.

Breathe into that invisible circle, about an arm's length in all directions, and softly say the following:

This is my field.

Within it, I am safe to feel.

Outside it, I can witness with love.

Repeat until the words feel true in your body.

4. **The Water and the Stone**

Dip your fingertips into the bowl of water. Let them drip back into the bowl.

Feel how water moves. It touches, flows, receives but can return to itself with intention.

Then hold the stone in your hand. Feel its weight and steadiness. Its determined and constant separateness.

Say the following quietly:

Like water, I can feel with you and then return to myself.
Like stone, I can stay with myself at all times.

Allow this duality—fluidity and firmness—to settle somewhere inside you.

5. **Discernment Breath**

Bring to mind someone whose extra emotional energy you may have been carrying. It could be from a loved one, client, partner, or friend.

Notice what arises in your body as you think of them: warmth, pressure, tightness, fluttering.

Without judgment, place a gentle hand over that place.

Inhale and silently say, *This belongs to them.*

Exhale and say, *I release what is not mine.*

Repeat three times, letting the breath untangle what has fused.

Shake out and off anything that doesn't belong to you.

Feel your own aliveness—your pulse, your breath, your frequency reemerging.

Then inhale again and whisper, *This belongs to me.*

6. **Integration: Joining, Not Merging**

Stand or sit tall.

Sense your spine, the sacred column connecting the earth beneath your feet and the sky above you.

Imagine roots unfurling down through your feet or seat and a soft light expanding from your heart outward.

Steady, radiant, and intact.

Say aloud (or write afterward in your journal) the following:

I can be with you without becoming you.

I can love you without leaving myself.

I can join you without merging into you.

Let these words vibrate through your cells like a tuning fork resetting your nervous system.

7. **Closing**

Take one final breath in gratitude for your body's wisdom and its capacity to both connect and contain.

Touch your heart and say, *Here in myself, I am home, in my field.*

If you wish, anoint your wrists or forehead with a drop of water, thereby sealing the ritual with a reminder that clarity is sacred.

Daily Life Integration Prompt:

Throughout your day, notice when you begin to merge and when you absorb another's mood or tension.

Pause, breathe, and recall *the stone and the water.*

Ask, *What is mine? What is yours?*

Let your body answer before your mind does.

5

Building Safety in the Body
and Returning Home

Your pain is the breaking of the shell that encloses
your understanding.

—Kahlil Gibran, *The Prophet*

There are entire days when the body forgets it's allowed to rest. When the shoulders rise without reason until the blades are touching, the breath flattens into the chest, its rise and release unfelt; and the heart listens for danger even in silence.

These are not signs of failure. They are signs of the brilliance of a body that has learned, again and again, to protect what is precious. To build safety in the body is not to erase these signals. It is to honor their wisdom and offer new possibilities. Safety is not the absence of pain; it is the presence of something deeper: a felt sense of trust, containment, and belonging. A knowing, beneath words, that we are allowed to be. To breathe. To soften. To stay.

This chapter is about returning to that knowing.

Dr. Bruce Perry and Maia Szalavitz (2006) remind us that regulation is the first and most essential ingredient in healing. A nervous system on high alert cannot reflect or connect, cannot

93

learn or repair. This is why healing begins not with insight, but with nervous system regulation through coregulation with others when available and through self-regulatory practices when alone. It is why we begin with the body.

This is particularly tender work for those who never felt truly safe in childhood. When caregivers were unpredictable, withdrawn, or overwhelmed themselves, we often adapted by shrinking, performing, caretaking, or disappearing (Ogden et al., 2006; Heller, 2019). These strategies were brilliant. They kept us tethered to love or at least in proximity to it. But over time, they narrowed our sense of what was possible inside our own skin. They taught the body to prepare for danger, even in peace.

Dr. Gabor Maté and his son Daniel (2022) offer us this reframe: Trauma is not the event itself, but the wound of disconnection it leaves in its wake. The rupture is internal in the severing of trust, of presence, and of embodied belonging. And so the repair must also be internal. Healing is not about erasing the past, but about creating new living experiences that tell the body a different story.

This chapter is an invitation to gently return to your own body—not with demand, but with devotion. Together, we will explore how to recognize the subtle signs of dysregulation as they arise. You'll begin to understand the cues your body uses to say, "I'm overwhelmed" or "I'm bracing."

We'll explore how the language of sensation can become your compass. Through breath, rhythm, movement, and stillness, you will begin to offer your body what it has longed for: signals of safety, presence, and care. As these signals accumulate, something begins to shift. The shoulders lower. The breath deepens. The edges of experience soften. You are not suppressing anything. You are expanding your capacity to stay present with it. This is what building safety in the body looks like: not perfection, but permission. Not control, but connection. A moment-by-moment practice of choosing, again and again, to be with yourself.

And this too is an act of love.

When we talk about safety in somatic healing, we are not merely referring to the absence of physical threat. We are also speaking of *neuroceptive safety*, a concept introduced by Dr. Stephen Porges (2011), which describes the body's automatic subconscious detection of safety or danger. Long before we form a conscious thought, our nervous system asks, "Am I safe enough to soften? To breathe deeply? Or must I brace again?"

In the aftermath of trauma, this system becomes sensitized. The body, so wise in its instinct to protect, may begin to interpret neutral or even loving cues as dangerous. A raised voice, the stillness of intimacy, the unpredictability of joy—any of these can awaken survival responses. The nervous system, shaped by years of unpredictability or pain, learns to expect harm. It becomes exquisitely attuned to danger, real or perceived, and often misses the cues that signal safety. This is not a flaw. It is adaptation. It is the nervous system's history, written in sensation.

To build safety in the body is not to silence these protective signals, but to accompany them. We do not coerce the nervous system into calm. We court it, with tenderness and patience, until it learns that rest is now an option. In the language of polyvagal theory, we call this process "ventral vagal regulation," which refers to a physiological state that supports connection, openness, and presence (Porges, 2011). We do not drop into this state through logic alone. We arrive there by way of *felt experiences* that whisper, "You are safe now. You belong here. You can let go." Healing does not demand that we unlearn vigilance all at once. It begins with noticing moments of *glimmer*.

The concept of glimmers comes from the work of Deb Dana (2021), a clinician and pioneer in applying polyvagal theory to trauma healing. If trauma tunes us to warning signs, glimmers cue us to regulation: They are the body's way of noticing small signs of safety, connection, or pleasure. They are fleeting, delicate moments when the nervous system shifts, however briefly, into a ventral vagal state. In that state, we may feel just a bit more grounded, connected, or open.

A glimmer might be the warmth of the morning sun on your skin. A slow exhale as you lie down to bed. A steady humming. A loving gaze. The sound of birdsong at dawn. The rustling of leaves outside your window. The lilt of a familiar laugh. The way your breath slows when you hear your child's voice. These are not distractions. They are titrated medicine. They speak the language of the body and offer it a new map. These are not dramatic or life-altering experiences. They are micromoments, often overlooked because we are not taught to notice them. But to the nervous system, they are powerful. They are evidence. They say, "This moment is different. This moment is safe."

The more we learn to recognize glimmers, the more we begin to shape the way our nervous system responds to the world. Our brains are plastic, capable of change through repetition and relationship (Perry & Szalavitz, 2006). When we notice a glimmer and linger with it and savor it, even for a few seconds, we strengthen neural pathways associated with safety and connection. In this way, glimmers become more than moments; they become portals to regulation, hope, and healing.

Using glimmers as a somatic tool means turning your attention toward what soothes and settles you—not as an escape, but as a way to resource yourself. For those with trauma histories, this can feel unfamiliar or even wrong. The nervous system may resist. You might dismiss the comfort of sunlight or laughter as unimportant. But with time and practice, the body begins to trust again.

To begin working with glimmers, you might do the following:

- **Notice what feels settling, even for a second.** This could be a texture, a sound, a temperature, or a rhythm.
- **Linger there.** Let yourself feel it—not to analyze, but to allow. Five seconds is enough. The body notices.
- **Track the sensation.** What shifts? Does your jaw slacken? Do your shoulders drop? Does your chest open? Does your breath deepen? Is there a softening inside?
- **Repeat.** Glimmers are like tiny candles in the dark. The more you find, the easier they are to see.

More importantly, glimmers are not meant to bypass pain. They are not a distraction. They are a counterbalance, part of your body's full emotional range. And for those who have known mostly suffering, cultivating glimmers is not a luxury. It is a radical act of nervous system reclamation.

So if you find that a certain song makes you feel a little more alive, let it. If a warm beverage steadies your breath, hold it longer. If the way your cat curls beside you helps you exhale, receive that comfort without apology. These moments are not trivial. They are threads. And over time, they weave a new fabric of felt safety. This is the heart of somatic healing: not the elimination of pain, but the expansion of capacity through resourcing. We do not become regulated by force. We become regulated by allowing, by noticing, and by returning, again and again, to what helps us stay with ourselves.

And glimmers are the beginning.

In a culture increasingly driven by disconnection, by speed, by digital mediation, by the outsourcing of human experience to machines and intellectual frameworks, turning toward the body is an act of quiet rebellion. Each time you pause to feel the warmth of your own breath, each time you honor the softening of your shoulders, each time you choose to stay with your experience rather than flee from it, you are participating in a countercurrent of healing.

To build safety in the body is not merely personal work. It is also cultural repair. It is a way of saying, "I refuse to abandon my humanity, even when the world around me fragments and distracts." By restoring trust and connection within your own skin, you become more equipped to extend that same trust and presence to others. This is how somatic healing ripples outward, empowering us not only to heal ourselves but also to soften the spaces between us and to build communities rooted in empathy, care, and embodied aliveness.

Your breath is a revolution. Your presence is a form of resistance. And your willingness to stay with yourself, here and now, is a powerful antidote to an overculture that would just let you disappear. Your body is always in conversation with you. It speaks in breath and pulse, in sensation and tension, in the subtle shifts you feel before your mind can catch up. When we learn to listen, to really listen, we begin to recognize the rhythms of our own nervous system. We begin to notice when we are drifting out of our window of presence and when we are coming home again.

In the language of the nervous system, this is called "autonomic state awareness." Dr. Stephen Porges's (2011) polyvagal theory outlines the three primary states for noticing and naming, introduced in the earlier chapters:

- **Ventral vagal regulation**, which supports safety, connection, and presence
- **Sympathetic activation**, which prepares us to mobilize by fighting or fleeing
- **Dorsal vagal shutdown**, which causes collapse, freeze, or disconnection

Each of these states brings a unique felt sense to the body. None are "bad." Each is adaptive, designed for survival. But when trauma has been a frequent visitor, the body may become rigidly stuck in protection. The cues of danger stay loud. The cues of safety grow faint.

Signs of sympathetic dysregulation—when the body is flooded with activation and moves into fight, flight, or fawn—may include the following:

- A racing heart or shallow breath
- Tightness in the jaw, fists, or chest
- Heat in the face, chest, hands, or feet
- Feeling "amped up," irritable, or unable to sit still
- Looping thoughts or catastrophizing

- A sense of hypervigilance, urgency, panic, or the need to escape
- A fragile rigidity around routines, schedules, and transitions
- Overapologizing or agreeing to things you don't want to do to avoid conflict
- Feeling frantically responsible for other people's emotions or comfort

In this state, the body is primed for action. It is trying to protect you from harm. But without a real immediate threat, this energy can feel chaotic and overwhelming. It becomes hard to access reason, empathy, or grounded presence.

Signs of dorsal vagal dysregulation, when the body moves into freeze or collapse, may include the following:

- Numbness or a sense of hollow emptiness
- Heavy limbs, fatigue, or dissociation
- Cold extremities
- Feeling far away, underwater, or "checked / zoned / spaced out"
- Difficulty speaking, initiating action, or connecting with others
- Hopelessness or a sense that nothing matters
- A loss of hours in the day that cannot be accounted for
- "Bed rotting" for hours or days—awake, but not present

In this state, the body has gone into conservation mode. It believes there is no way out, so it shuts down to survive. This can be a particularly painful place for those with trauma histories as it often presents with depression, shame, and/or profound disconnection from self.

Signs of regulation, when the nervous system is in a ventral vagal state, may look and feel like the following:

- A sense of safety or ease in the body
- A steady, smooth breath
- Spontaneous tears or laughter
- A tingling warmth in the face, chest, or hands
- Curiosity, compassion, or creativity
- A willingness to connect, speak, rest, or play
- Feeling like you have *enough* time, space, support, or capacity
- Comfortable silence

You may not live here all the time. Few of us do. But just *touching into* this state, even briefly, helps to repattern your nervous system. It says, "You can return here. This place exists within you."

Janina Fisher (2021) encourages us to understand these shifts not as personal failures, but as *state changes*. Your body is not betraying you; it is navigating a complex inner world shaped by experience. Becoming aware of your state is the first step in building the capacity to shift it. And the more you recognize these states in real time, the more you can meet yourself with gentleness rather than judgment.

Start here:

Notice what happens in your body when you feel safe.

Notice what happens when you feel threatened.

Notice the in-between states too when you are beginning to tense and to fade.

Each signal is a conversation. Each sensation is a guide.

And remember, your nervous system is not a problem to be fixed. It is a relationship to be tended.

The ventral vagal state is our inner home. It is the place from which we feel most like ourselves: connected, creative, calm, and capable. But for many of us, this home may feel unfamiliar or, at best, a place we visit only briefly before being swept back into patterns of vigilance or collapse. The work then is not to live here perfectly, but to return more easily. To spend a little more time in safety. To build a life that nourishes this state of being—not by accident, but on purpose.

Ventral regulation is not an intellectual achievement. It is a felt sense. It arrives not when we think we are safe, but when the body *believes* we are safe. And because the body learns through experience, not logic, we must speak its language: rhythm, warmth, breath, sensation, attunement, and repetition.

Here are some ways we can offer the nervous system the experience of regulation:

1. **Breath as Anchor**

   The breath is one of the few functions that is both automatic and voluntary. This means we can work with it gently, without force, to invite the body into safety. Slow rhythmic breathing tells the nervous system, "There is time. There is space. We are not in danger."

   Try inhaling for a count of four and exhaling for six. Let the exhale be longer than the inhale. This activates the parasympathetic branch of the nervous system, encouraging ventral vagal tone (Porges, 2011). No need to perfect it. Just notice. The breath is always waiting for your return.

2. **Orienting to the Environment**

    Look around the space you're in. Let your gaze soften. Notice the colors, shapes, light, and shadow. Orienting is a primal animal gesture, and it says to the body, "I'm here, and I am not under threat." Let your head and neck move slowly as you scan. This practice signals the brain stem that you are safe enough to rest. As Peter Levine (2010) notes, orienting can be a deeply settling experience for those with trauma histories who are often unconsciously bracing against unseen danger.

3. **Rhythmic Movement**

    The nervous system responds beautifully to rhythm. Rocking, swaying, walking at a steady pace, or even gentle shaking can help discharge sympathetic energy and return us to a grounded state. Trauma often disrupts rhythm, creating chaos or rigidity. Restoring rhythm through movement invites the body back into flow. You might sway from side to side, bounce gently on your knees, or rock in a chair. Let your body choose. Let it remember.

4. **Safe Touch and Self-Contact**

    Touch is one of the most ancient and intuitive forms of regulation. If available, a warm trusted hand on your back, two hands clasping your shoulders, or cupping your cheeks can cue the nervous system toward coregulation. Self-touch can be powerful and profoundly shifting. Press your hand gently into your chest and hold your own heart. Wrap your arms around yourself and soften into your own embrace. Hold your face and melt into your palms. Try drifting off to sleep in a self-holding. These gestures, when done with intention, say, "You are here. You are witnessed. You are held."

5. Vocalization and Sound

The vagus nerve runs through the muscles of the face, throat, and middle ear. This is why humming, singing, chanting, or even speaking softly can regulate the nervous system (Porges, 2011). The voice, your voice, can be a medicine. It is vibration. It is vibration inside the body. If it feels right, hum a lullaby. Sing to your younger self. Let your sound be a tether back to now.

6. Connection with Others

Coregulation is a biological necessity, not a weakness. Being with someone who is regulated and attuned can help our nervous system return to safety more easily than we could alone (Fisher, 2021). This might mean calling a trusted friend, being near someone whose presence feels calm, letting a purring cat rest on your chest, or simply allowing yourself to be seen. Social connection is not a luxury. It is a physiological need.

7. Engaging Glimmers with Intention

Return to what we've already begun: noticing glimmers. Seek them out gently. Stay with them longer. Let them saturate your awareness like sunlight through a window. A few seconds of true safety can reorient the nervous system's expectations. Over time, this practice reshapes the map of what the body believes is possible.

When practiced regularly, these moments of regulation begin to accumulate. They build what Dr. Dan Siegel (2010) calls "neural integration," the ability for different parts of the brain and body to communicate, self-soothe, and adapt. This is not a onetime fix. It is a relational process. A practice of reintroducing the body to something it may have forgotten: ease, belonging, breath, enoughness. And every time you offer your nervous system even a brief pause, a breath, a gentle rhythm, you are building safety. You are offering the body a different ending to an old story.

There will be days when safety feels far away, when your breath is tight, your thoughts are loud, and your body feels like a battlefield. On those days, the invitation is not to force regulation, but to *resource yourself.* To draw upon something inside you or around you that can help you feel just safe enough to stay with the moment.

Resourcing is the practice of identifying and anchoring into experiences that bring a sense of steadiness, warmth, or capacity. It is a foundational somatic tool, one that helps us expand our ability to be with discomfort without being overwhelmed by it. When we're resourced, we are more able to respond rather than react, to remain present without collapsing or fleeing.

A resource can be anything that supports regulation and connection in your nervous system. It can be the following:

- A sensory experience (the weight of a blanket, the smell of lavender, the feel of warm water, the feeling of a brush against your scalp, ASMR)
- A memory (a time you felt safe, loved, or proud)
- An image (a favorite landscape, an ancestor's smile, a symbol of resilience)
- A person, pet, or presence that helps you feel grounded
- A part of yourself—your creativity, humor, faith, or an inner protector

Resources are deeply personal. What calms one person may agitate another. This is why resourcing begins with curiosity, not prescription. It is a process of gentle discovery: *What brings me a little ease? What helps me feel more like myself?*

One especially powerful type of resource is in the imaginal realm. Sometimes the body learns through what the mind cannot recall because it hasn't experienced it firsthand but can imagine for it. When you picture yourself being held by a loving ancestor, standing in a shaft of golden light, or walking again beneath trees you once knew, your nervous system leans into the image as if it were real. Muscles soften. Breath widens. The heart steadies. These are imagined experiences that evoke safety, warmth, or empowerment. While the thinking brain may recognize these moments as imagined, the nervous system often does not. The body responds to imaginal experiences much like real ones: The breath deepens, tension softens, and an internal sense of safety is restored (Farb et al., 2013). This is not a trick. It is a doorway. Neuroscience shows that mental imagery activates many of the same brain regions as lived experience, including the sensory cortices, limbic system, and prefrontal areas involved in emotion regulation (Kosslyn et al., 2001). In other words, when we vividly imagine, we are rehearsing new pathways of safety and capacity in the nervous system. Over time, this rehearsal strengthens adaptive neural networks through neuroplasticity, much like practicing a skill or instrument (Schwartz & Begley, 2003).

For trauma survivors, this can be especially profound. If the body has rarely or never known what safety feels like, imaginal resourcing offers a first imprint. It provides a sensory blueprint that the nervous system can return to again and again. This imagined felt sense of support, containment, or protection can gradually become embodied memory, teaching the system that another way of being is possible (Ogden et al., 2006). You are not "making it up." You are making it real in the only place it matters for regulation purposes: your felt sense. Every time you call upon imaginal resourcing, you are cultivating neural and emotional soil that is fertile for repair. In this way, imagination becomes both medicine and rehearsal, nourishing the soul and reorganizing the nervous system toward greater resilience.

By working in the imaginal realm, you are teaching your body how to return to itself. You are giving it practice in the language of safety, of feeling and knowing that you are safe. You are helping your nervous system encode a new pattern—one that recognizes safety not as an idea, but as a lived bodily truth, ready to be carried out into the world and your relationships.

To begin, you might ask the following:

- When was a time I felt even a little bit safe?
- Who or what helped me feel seen or soothed?

- What sensations in my body let me know something was okay?

As you explore, let your body speak. Don't analyze. Feel and engage your senses. A good resource should create a subtle sense of expansion, softening, or grounding. You might notice your jaw unclench. Your breath deepen. Your mind quiet just a little. These are signs the resource is resonating with your nervous system. Once you've identified a resource, you can return to it again and again, especially when you feel the early signs of dysregulation. Like a lighthouse in a storm, your resource does not need to stop the waves. It simply gives you something to steer toward.

Here is one way to practice resourcing:

1. **Settle** – Find a quiet place or let your body settle as best it can where you are.
2. **Recall** – Bring your chosen resource to mind. Imagine it in vivid detail. What do you see, hear, smell, or feel?
3. **Notice** – Observe how your body responds. Is there any shift? Any sensation of warmth, calm, or presence?
4. **Stay** – Linger with the resource for thirty seconds to a minute. Let it wash over you. Let it imprint.
5. **Return** – As you come back to the present moment, notice if anything feels different, even slightly.

Dr. Peter Levine (2010) writes that trauma healing involves *restoring the capacity for regulation and resilience*. Resourcing is not about denying what is painful; it is about building the inner scaffolding that allows you to *stay* with what is painful without becoming consumed by it.

In later chapters, we'll explore how resourcing interacts with more advanced practices, like *pendulation* (moving gently between distress and comfort) and *titration* (breaking overwhelming material into manageable pieces). But resourcing comes first. It is your ground. Your gathering place. Your nervous system's first yes.

Over time, as you strengthen your connection to your resources, you will build a more stable bridge between safety and discomfort, between activation and restoration. And when the waves come, as they always do, you will not be without oars.

You will have a compass.

You will have a tether.

You will have something within you that says, "I can be with this. I am not alone inside my own skin."

To build safety in the body is to choose, again and again, to stay. Not because it is easy, but because it is the most intimate act of self-devotion. It is to say to the muscles that have tensed for decades, "You may soften now." To say to the breath that has learned to hide, "You may take up space." It is to say to the younger parts of you, those who braced against storms too big for them, "I'm here now. You are not alone inside this body."

This work is not linear. You will forget. You will brace again. Your shoulders will climb. Your jaw will clench. Your breath will vanish without warning. But the point is not to prevent these returns to protection. The point is to know how to come home. To know what helps you soften, what helps you stay present, what helps you remember that this body—the body you are in today—is no longer a battlefield. It is a living altar of return.

When you begin to listen to your nervous system without shame, when you name its signals without blame, when you offer it small consistent experiences of safety, you are not just tending to yourself; you are also rewiring centuries. You are caring for the inheritance of pain you carry, softening the places where abandonment and rupture once left their mark. Each pause for breath, each glimmer welcomed into awareness, each choice to stay with yourself is an act of quiet repair. With every gesture of care, you are breaking old cycles and returning to something older than trauma in your system: trust.

And slowly, almost without notice at first, you begin to belong to your body again. Not as an idea, but in sensation. In rhythm. In warmth. In presence. This is the work of building safety in the body and returning home. It is not freedom from pain, but the discovery that even pain can be held. Even sorrow can breathe. And even here, in the immediacy of your own skin, you are worthy of rest, of belonging, of coming home to yourself.

Case Study
Micah Stitches Together A Blanket of Safety

Micah is a thirty-two-year-old queer and nonbinary artist who works with textiles and experimental performance. Their art often explores themes of gender, fragmentation, and spiritual reclamation—all artistic threads woven directly from the fabric of their life. Born into a conservative, religious household in rural Tennessee, Micah learned early that the body was a battleground. Their queerness was unwelcome. Their gender fluidity was ignored and unnamed. Silence became a survival strategy.

Micah experienced emotional and physical abuse from their father, a man who interpreted discipline as godly righteousness and difference as hellfire rebellion. Their family's faith community reinforced these messages, treating deviation from cisheteronormativity as a moral failing. Micah was told to repent. To be less visible. To disappear. When they couldn't comply, they were cast out. First emotionally and then physically.

By the time Micah left home at eighteen, their nervous system had become fluent in freeze and fawn. They learned to disappear inside themselves. They learned to make others comfortable with charisma. They often said yes when they meant no, nodded when they wanted to scream, smiled while bracing for harm. For years, their art was the only space where they could tell the truth.

Therapy began slowly. At first, Micah struggled to describe sensations in their body. They lived primarily in their intellect, orbiting the body like a distant moon. When asked what safety felt like, they hesitated. But in time, small openings appeared. Micah began to notice *glimmers*. The feel of velvet beneath their fingers. The sound of a singer's voice on the el train. The way their chest softened when their friend Kit touched their arm during dinner. The ritual of Sunday night "framily" potlucks, a gathering of chosen family of friends who brought one another food, stories, and shelter from the unpredictable storms of judgment and hatred found in the outside world.

One day in session, Micah named their first felt sense of ventral regulation: sitting on the floor, watching their friend handsew a patch on a jacket, surrounded by quiet laughter and cups of tea. "I think my body felt like it was in the right place," they said. That moment became a resource.

Their therapist invited them to return to that moment in future sessions by closing their eyes and feeling the weight of the cup in their hands, the rhythm of the needle, the laughter of their chosen family, the warmth and safety of the room. Over time, Micah learned to use this memory to anchor themselves during moments of overwhelm. They weren't escaping discomfort; they were expanding capacity. Resourcing.

Micah also began to experiment with self-touch. Placing one hand on their heart and another on their belly before bed. Swaddling themselves in a weighted quilt made by loving hands. They tried humming softly during panic, letting vibration echo through their chest like a prayer.

Still, dysregulation didn't disappear. There were moments when Micah froze in the face of perceived rejection. When their breath vanished in public bathrooms. When their voice shrank at the DMV. But instead of collapsing into shame, Micah began to ask, "What do I need right now?" Sometimes the answer was a long walk listening to queer revolutionaries' podcasts that encouraged hope and resilience and promised liberation one day. Sometimes it was crying into Kit's sweatshirt. Sometimes it was painting their nails.

The work was not about erasing dysregulation. It was about returning. And each return, however small, rewrote the old narrative: *You are not wrong. You are not alone. This body belongs to you.*

Micah still lives with a nervous system shaped by years of harm, but it no longer dictates their every move. They have learned to listen. To pause. To touch their own face with care. They have gathered a constellation of glimmers and wrapped them like a shawl around their shoulders.

Safety, for Micah, is no longer a place they are waiting to reach. It is something they are learning to create within themselves. Not perfectly. Not always. But more often than before.

And that is healing.

Journal and Reflection Prompts

1. **What does safety feel like in your body, if only for a moment?**

   Describe a time when you felt even slightly grounded, soothed, or at ease. What sensations accompanied that experience? Where did you feel it?

2. **What glimmers have you already encountered in your life without realizing it?**

   Think of small moments that brought warmth, softness, or aliveness. What might it feel like to return to those memories or to seek them out more intentionally?

3. **When do you notice your body shift into dysregulation?**

   What are the earliest signs that you're entering fight, flight, freeze, or fawn? How does your body try to protect you in those moments?

4. **What or who helps you feel more like yourself?**

   This could be a place, a person, a texture, a practice, a scent, or a memory. What resources can you turn toward, internally or externally, when you need support?

5. **How would your life begin to change if you trusted that your body was worthy of safety?**

   What might soften? What might open? What would you be free to feel, express, or receive?

Somatic Ritual: A Place to Land

This ritual is an invitation to return to your body—not to fix or change it, but to *be with it*. You will need about 10–15 minutes, a quiet space if possible, and something comforting: a blanket, a warm drink, a soft object, or anything that helps you feel resourced.

1. **Prepare the space.**

   Let this moment be intentional. Dim the lights. Sit or lie down in a way that feels supportive. Wrap yourself in something soft. Let the atmosphere mirror your intention: *to tend to your nervous system with care.*

2. **Orient to the here and now.**

   Look slowly around your space. Name five things you can see. Three sounds you can hear. One thing you can touch. Let your body know, "I am here. I am safe enough in this moment."

3. **Meet the breath.**

   Place one hand on your heart and one on your belly. Let your breath rise and fall without effort. You are not changing it; you are simply meeting it. With every exhale, invite a quiet message: *You may soften. You are allowed to rest.*

4. **Call in a glimmer.**

   Bring to mind a recent moment of safety, sweetness, or connection—a glimmer. Let it bloom slowly in your awareness.

Where were you? Who or what was with you? What did it feel like in your body? Linger here. Let this memory imprint. Let it remind you what safety can feel like.

5. **Name a resource.**

Now bring to mind a resource, something or someone that helps you feel more whole. A friend, a song, a painting, a tree, a place, a memory. Let yourself feel their presence with you now. If it helps, speak a few words aloud: *Thank you for helping me stay. I remember you.*

6. **Come back with a gesture.**

As you close, offer your body a small gesture to mark the return: a hand over your heart, a stretch, a sway, a hum. Let your body choose. Let the ritual end not with abruptness, but with a quiet honoring.

You have just practiced building safety in the body. You did not need to be perfect. You needed only to show up, and you did.

6

Breath as an Anchor in Rough Seas

The breath of life is in the sunlight and the hand of life
is in the wind.

—Kahlil Gibran, *The Prophet*

There is a quiet power in the breath, a rhythm as ancient as
life itself. Before we spoke our first word, before we could name
joy or sorrow, the breath was there: rising and falling, keeping
time with the pulse of our becoming. And though the world may
pull us outward, into noise, urgency, and endless distraction, the
breath remains faithful. Steady. Patient. Always ready to bring us
back to ourselves.

Across cultures and centuries, breath has been revered not
only as a biological function but also as a sacred thread—a bridge
between body and spirit, self and world. In the language of the
Māori, *hā* refers to the shared breath of life, an expression of connection and mana (Wikeepa, 2023). In the Yoruba tradition, *emi*
is both breath and soul, animating the body with divine essence
(Gbadegesin, 1991). In yogic practice, prāṇa is life force carried on
the breath, cultivated through prāṇāyāma to harmonize body and
mind (Saraswati, 2009). Among the Navajo, breath is woven into

117

songs, healing ceremonies, and prayers that attune the body to the land and spirit (Lewton & Bydone, 2000).

These traditions remind us that breath is not separate from life; it *is* life. In traditional Chinese medicine, the concept of qi (also spelled "chi") is central to understanding vitality and health. Qi is often described as the vital energy or life force that flows through the body's meridians, and it is believed to be carried on the breath. Practices such as qigong and *taiji* (tai chi) are designed to cultivate, balance, and circulate qi through intentional breath, movement, and focus. Breath, in this view, is not just a physiological process; it is also a spiritual practice, an energetic tuning, a way of harmonizing the body with the cosmos. To breathe consciously is to align oneself with the natural rhythms of life and to restore harmony where disharmony once lived (Kaptchuk, 2000).

In moments of chaos, transformation, and healing, the breath is often our most accessible medicine. Think of the birthing body riding the waves of contraction through long exhales. Or the sigh that escapes the chest in grief. The steady inhale, exhale of a child calming in a caregiver's arms. In the everyday sacred—a candle blown out, a wish whispered, the steam of tea meeting lips—the breath is there, anchoring our presence.

Modern science affirms what ancient wisdom has long known: The breath is intimately connected to the autonomic nervous system, which governs your body's survival responses. This system includes the sympathetic nervous system (mobilization: fight or flight) and the parasympathetic nervous system (regulation: rest and digest). What makes breath extraordinary is this: It is the only function of the autonomic nervous system that you can consciously control. It is the doorway through which you can influence your state of being (Porges, 2011).

Fast shallow breathing can signal danger to your brain, activating tension and anxiety. Slow deep breathing tells your nervous system, "You are safe. You can soften." Diaphragmatic breathing, or belly breathing, involves drawing air deep into your abdomen rather than breathing shallowly into your chest. When you engage your diaphragm fully, the vagus nerve is stimulated, activating the parasympathetic nervous system and fostering a sense of calm (Levine, 2010). Practicing diaphragmatic breathing for just a few minutes can lower the heart rate, reduce muscle tension, and ground your nervous system. With just a few rounds of intentional breath, you can shift your body from chaos to calm (Levine, 2010).

The breath is your breathprint, a living signature, shaped by everything you've survived, longed for, avoided, and embraced. Like a fingerprint made of air and memory, your breathprint holds the subtle imprints of your personal and ancestral experiences. No two are alike. Some breaths come from a lineage that had to hide, hold tight, or disappear to stay safe. Others carry songs passed down through the lungs of elders, lullabies that softened night terrors or welcomed dawn with sacred repetition.

Trauma tends to make the breath shallow, fractured, or even frozen. The breath is held tight in the throat, locked beneath the ribs, scattered at the edges of awareness. These held breaths are survival strategies, not failures. The body remembers what it once had to do to endure. In contrast, joy reopens the rib cage. It stretches the breath wide, like sunlight entering a once-closed room. Grief too leaves its signature—sometimes as sighs, sometimes as hollowness, sometimes as trembling inhales that never quite make it to the bottom of the lungs.

Your breathprint shifts with seasons, with age, with emotion. It responds to the presence of safety or threat, to silence or song, to solitude or touch. When you become curious about the shape of your breath in any given moment, checking in to find it tight, shallow, expansive, heaving, or broken, you are not just noticing a pattern; you are also listening to a story your body is still telling. You are entering into relationship with the part of you that never stopped breathing, even when the rest of you had to go numb. To listen to your breathprint is to say, "I care about what shaped me. I care enough to stay. I care enough to listen, not just to the words of my mind but also to the movements of my lungs." This is a cornerstone of nervous system repair.

The breath is the bridge between mind and body. When your thoughts spiral or dissociation sets in, the breath can tether you to sensation and the present. You do not need to stop the thoughts. You simply need to feel the breath as it enters, moves, and exits. By focusing on your breath, you pull awareness back into your body, reconnecting with sensation rather than story. This shift allows space between stimulus and response, a pause, or a sacred gap, in which healing can happen.

This gap is not just metaphorical; it is also neurobiological. Every conscious breath lays the foundation for new neural connections. Through the science of neuroplasticity, we now understand that the brain is capable of rewiring itself across the lifespan (Doidge, 2007; Siegel, 2010). Each time you return to your breath instead of reacting automatically, you are building a new pathway.

A pathway that favors awareness over reactivity, compassion over collapse. Regular breath-focused practices increase the density of gray matter in areas of the brain associated with emotional regulation, such as the prefrontal cortex and insula (Hölzel et al., 2011). Breath invites the brain to shift out of survival reflexes and into creative choice. In this way, breath is not just calming; it is also transformative. It becomes a tool of conscious evolution, helping us carve new trails of safety, presence, and connection within our nervous system. It is in this gap that choice, clarity, and healing begin. Consciously returning to the breath is not just a wellness practice; it is also a quiet act of resistance. In an era of relentless distraction, of bodies bypassed in favor of screens and algorithms, choosing to feel your breath is a reclamation. It says, "I am here. I am alive. I am worth my own attention."

Dr. Stephen Porges (2011), the founder of polyvagal theory, explains that slow, extended exhalations activate the ventral vagal branch of the parasympathetic nervous system—promoting feelings of safety, connectedness, and regulation. Long exhales increase heart rate variability (HRV), a biomarker of resilience and adaptability. When you extend your exhale, you are telling your nervous system, "I am not in danger. You may rest now." Try inhaling for a count of four and exhaling for a count of six or eight. As you breathe out, imagine tension draining from your body. With each breath, you are practicing self-contact. You are rewiring your body for peace.

Breath is also a source of vitality. Breath and movement practices, like yoga and tai chi, and even simple gestures like raising arms on an inhale and lowering on an exhale help entrain the nervous system into balance. When you are sluggish, fatigued, or frozen, upregulating breathwork can reignite energy. Breath of Fire, for example, uses quick rhythmic breaths to activate alertness and focus. Upregulating practices should always be approached gently, especially if you have a history of trauma or panic. Always let your body lead.

The sigh is another underused breath tool. It is nature's reset button. Often spontaneous, sighing releases trapped tension, efficiently releasing what words cannot express. A spontaneous sigh is the body's silent exhale of surrender. It arrives often unbidden—often after tears, during longing, in moments of transition or overwhelm, as if the nervous system is giving itself a moment to soften without asking for permission. Biologically, a sigh reinflates the alveoli in the lungs, improving oxygen exchange. Emotionally, it is a threshold: the place where the body acknowledges it can no longer hold everything in. There is grief in a sigh, but also relief. When used intentionally, the sigh becomes a ritual of release, the nervous system's exclamation point. Inhale deeply, slowly. Exhale with sound through the mouth or nose. Let it be loud. Let it be soft. Let it be real. The sigh does not require explanation. It only asks to be honored.

Breathwork is not about control. It is about relationship. Listen before you guide. Be curious before you change. Let your breath be a partner, not a project. The breath is your quiet companion, ever present, asking only to be noticed. In its rhythm, we find resilience. In its depth, we find a way home. You don't need a yoga mat or an altar to practice breath awareness. You need only a moment: three breaths before opening your inbox. A deep exhale while standing in line. One hand on the chest during a hard conversation. A sigh before dinner. These microrituals are medicine. They return you to your breathprint. They remind your body that even in stress, you are still home.

Micropractices for Everyday Breath Rituals

These breath rituals are small accessible ways to return to presence in the midst of daily life. Let them be gentle companions woven into the texture of your day:

- **While Walking:** Match your inhale and exhale to your footsteps—perhaps four steps in, four steps out. Let your breath fall into rhythm with the earth beneath you.

- **While Cooking:** As you stir, chop, or season, inhale the scent of your ingredients. Let your breath slow and deepen as you nourish yourself and others.

- **While Bathing or Showering:** As warm water touches your skin, exhale fully. Feel the breath release tension from your body like water down the drain.

- **While Brushing Your Teeth:** Take three intentional breaths as you begin. Let this be a moment of self-contact, not just a task.

- **While Driving:** At each red light, inhale slowly and exhale longer than you inhale. Let the pause be a portal back to calm.

- **While Waking:** Before you rise, notice the first breath of the day. Let it remind you that you are alive.

- **While Listening:** With a friend, partner, or child, soften your breath. Let it be slow and steady. Let your breathing become an anchor for deep presence.

These practices don't require extra time, only extra noticing. With each breath, you return to the sacred rhythm of being here.

Practice Instructions
Diaphragmatic Breathing
- Sit or lie in a comfortable position.
- Place one hand on your chest and the other on your belly.
- Inhale slowly through your nose, allowing your belly to rise while your chest stays still.
- Exhale gently through your mouth, letting your belly fall.
- Continue for 5–10 breaths, focusing on the slow rise and fall of your belly.

4-7-8 Breathing
- Sit comfortably and close your eyes if it feels safe.
- Inhale quietly through your nose for a count of 4.
- Hold your breath for a count of 7.
- Exhale completely through your mouth for a count of 8, making a soft whooshing sound.
- Repeat for 4 rounds or as needed.

Breath of Fire (use with caution)
- Sit upright with your spine straight.
- Take a deep breath in. Then begin rapid rhythmic exhalations through your nose, allowing passive inhales between each exhale.
- Focus on pumping your lower belly with each exhale, keeping your chest relatively still.

- Continue for 30 seconds to 1 minute. Then inhale deeply and exhale slowly to finish. Repeat up to 3 rounds if comfortable.

Case Study
Rosa's Return to Breath

Rosa, a thirty-eight-year-old teacher and mother of two, arrived in therapy saying she felt like she was "holding her breath all the time." Her anxiety was constant with symptoms of a tight chest, racing thoughts, and frequent overwhelm. Traditional meditation hadn't worked; it made her feel more agitated. She wondered if she was simply bad at calming down.

Rather than asking her to still her thoughts, Rosa's therapist invited her into the body through breath. They began with diaphragmatic breathing. At first, it felt unnatural. Rosa realized she had been chest breathing for years. But gradually, she noticed that even one deep breath made a difference. She could feel her body start to soften.

She began using 4-7-8 breathing before parent-teacher meetings and at bedtime when her children were restless. Later, she incorporated Breath of Fire in the mornings to shake off exhaustion. These practices became anchors.

Eventually, Rosa brought breathwork into her classroom, guiding her students through three slow breaths before lessons and using sighs as resets during conflict. What began as a personal regulation practice rippled outward. Rosa reclaimed her breath, her body, and her rhythm. And she taught others to do the same.

Case Study
Kelly's Grief and Chronic Illness

Kelly, a fifty-four-year-old musician recently diagnosed with an autoimmune condition, came to therapy engulfed in a grief that had no single origin. He had lost his father months earlier, his career had been paused by debilitating fatigue, and his once-reliable body now felt foreign. "I feel like I'm disappearing," he said in one session, eyes dim with exhaustion.

Rather than rushing to cope or fix, his therapist invited him into the slow, steady companionship of breath. They began each session with a breath scan: five minutes of noticing the breath's shape, texture, and rhythm. At first, Kelly could barely feel it. His breath was shallow, almost imperceptible. But over weeks, something shifted. He began to describe moments when the breath "filled in the hollow places."

Diaphragmatic breathing became a ritual before infusions and doctor visits. Inhalations became his cue to name a single word for what he was feeling—be it grief, anger, or relief. Exhalations became his release. On days when breathwork felt like too much, they honored that too, placing a hand on his chest as a gesture of presence.

Over time, breathwork helped Kelly relate differently to his pain. It didn't erase the illness or the sorrow, but it gave him a way to stay in contact with himself. He began composing again, short songs inspired by breath rhythms. In reclaiming his breath, Kelly reclaimed his voice. Not in spite of his illness, but alongside it.

Journal and Reflection Prompts

1. When I pause and notice my breath, what sensations or emotions arise?
2. What is my breathprint today? Shallow? Deep? Held? Flowing?
3. What breathing practice soothes me? Which one energizes me?
4. How can I use the breath as a tool of connection in my relationships?
5. What part of Rosa's story did I relate to, and why?

Somatic Ritual: Breath as Sanctuary

Set aside 10–15 minutes in a quiet space. Sit or lie down with a blanket or shawl.

Place one hand on your heart, the other on your belly. Close your eyes.

Begin with three deep belly breaths with longer exhalations than inhalations. Feel the rise and fall. Feel the contact between your palms and your body.

Next, let your breath find its natural rhythm. Whisper an affirmation on each exhale: *I am safe. I am here. I belong.*

Let the breath carry the words into your cells.

To close, place both hands over your heart. Inhale slowly, exhale with a sigh. Thank your breath.

Sit for a few moments in silence.

Open your eyes.

Return.

7

Surfing the Waves with Titration and Pendulation

After great pain, a formal feeling comes—
The Nerves sit ceremonious, like Tombs—
The stiff Heart questions "was it He, that bore,"
And "Yesterday, or Centuries before?"

—Emily Dickinson, "After great pain, a formal feeling comes"

There are moments when emotions rise like floodwaters, threatening to sweep us away. The body tenses, the breath catches, and the familiar ground of calm vanishes beneath our feet. This is the lived experience of overwhelm, an ancient survival response encoded in our nervous system. But within this intensity lies the possibility of something extraordinary: transformation.

This chapter is an invitation to meet those rising tides with the quiet courage of titration and pendulation and to cultivate the art of tracking sensation like a skilled navigator at sea. We move beyond technique into an inner ecology where curiosity becomes our compass and where the nervous system is not an enemy, but a wise ancient storyteller. Each tremor of sensation, each flicker of emotion, each subtle image is a breadcrumb on the path of healing.

Healing unfolds in rhythms. The tides pulse against the shore and return. The moon waxes and wanes. The sun rises, softens, then sinks. Our bodies echo these patterns: the rise of heartbeat, the lull of breath, the cycles of sleep and wake, contraction and release. These elemental cadences teach us that intensity and stillness are not opposites; they are partners in a dance as old as the stars. To titrate is to honor this pulse. To pendulate is to follow its arc.

Titration: Healing, One Drop at a Time

Titration is the art of healing in doses. Rather than plunging headlong into overwhelm, we touch experience lightly, like dipping a toe into water. A flicker of heat in the belly. A dull ache in the heart. A flutter in the chest. When we allow ourselves to feel just a fragment and then return to ground, we teach our nervous system that we can move toward pain without becoming submerged (Levine, 2010). This approach requires both bravery and restraint. It teaches us to stay connected without drowning, to feel without fragmenting. Like the ancient practice of adding strong medicine drop by drop, titration honors the body's pacing. Over time, this becomes a rhythm of restoration: touch, rest, touch again.

Clinically, titration allows clients to work at the edge of their window of tolerance, engaging with activation while maintaining coherence (Ogden et al., 2006). This slow exposure helps build affect tolerance and enhances emotional regulation, particularly in clients with developmental trauma whose nervous systems were wired for survival rather than connection (Schore, 2012).

One client, Lena, a thirty-six-year-old mother with a history of sexual abuse, entered therapy with the belief that healing required emotional purging. She would dive into traumatic memories, only to leave sessions feeling shattered and destabilized. Her therapist introduced titration. Rather than retelling full trauma narratives, Lena was guided to track a single somatic cue, a heaviness in her chest. She stayed with it for three full breaths, then shifted to a warm memory of holding her newborn. In doing so, she began to experience her body's wisdom in real time. She said, "It's like I finally have a dial instead of a floodgate."

Titration is the invitation to befriend the edges. It is the nervous system's native pacing, a language that says, "We can go slow." This slowness is not weakness. It is the pace of integration. In somatic healing, slow is fast. The body does not heal through force, but through consent and curiosity.

Pendulation: The Rhythm of Resilience

Pendulation is the natural swinging between activation and rest, a back-and-forth movement that restores rhythm (Levine, 2010; Dana, 2021). Just as waves return to the shore or breath expands and contracts, our nervous system thrives in cycles. Pendulation allows for exploration of once-overwhelming material with safety and structure. As we learn to move in and out of difficult emotional terrain, we find that our internal world becomes less terrifying. In somatic therapy, pendulation acts as a neurobiological reset, an opportunity to move from sympathetic arousal into parasympathetic states and back again without collapse (Porges, 2011). This swinging rhythm not only regulates emotional intensity but also restores interoceptive awareness, helping clients reorient to the present moment and widen their window of tolerance (Fisher, 2021).

Pendulation is not about avoidance; it is about rhythm. Like the contraction and release of the heart or the waxing and waning of the moon, pendulation reflects life's essential pulse. The body, given the right support, knows how to find its way back from distress. What was once dysregulating becomes bearable, then familiar, then transformed.

One client, Jules, twenty-eight, came into therapy with severe somatic symptoms following years of emotional neglect and covert abuse. Their body oscillated between hypervigilance and shutdown. By learning pendulation, Jules practiced moving between a sense of internal threat and small moments of safety through feeling their feet on the floor, the warmth of a blanket or hearing the sound of their own breath. Over time, these small swings rewired their sense of what was survivable. Jules later described it this way: "It's like I've grown an internal hammock. I swing, but I don't fall."

Override: When the System Protects

Within somatic work lies the essential concept of override, the moment when the nervous system pushes past its window of tolerance and into a survival response too overwhelming to integrate in real time. Override happens when the sensation caused by activation breaches the capacity of the nervous system to remain integrated. It often shows up as habituated patterns of bracing, fawning, or dissociating that feel automatic and over time can result in numbness, panic, or collapse when these survival states are chronically relied upon (Fisher, 2021; Porges, 2011). Everyday examples might include wanting to cry but blinking back tears, wanting to scream but locking your jaw, or needing to rest but forcing yourself to push through. These protective surges are not signs of failure. They are signs that the body is doing what it knows to do: protect.

Every person has a different sensation threshold, where stimulus becomes unbearable and a distress management strategy, like override, needs to be deployed. For some, it's interpersonal conflict. For others, it's loud noise. Trauma thresholds are personal and shaped by our past experiences, our nervous system, and how we were cared for early in life (Perry & Winfrey, 2021). Our brains build patterns through repetition, forming networks that hold both protective responses and body memories. When trauma pushes us past our limit, those protective patterns get stronger, making it easier to slip into override again (Siegel, 2020).

These override patterns are shaped by relationships, early disconnection, and stress in childhood that disrupt healthy brain development (Schore, 2012). If we grow up under constant stress, our bodies may learn to stay on high alert or shut down as a way to survive. But there is good news: Our brains can change. With steady support, safety, and practice, the nervous system can create new patterns. This is called "neuroplasticity," the brain's ability to rewire itself. Even long-held survival responses can soften and become less automatic over time with the right care (Doidge, 2007).

Tracking Sensation: Finding Our Edges

At the center of titration and pendulation lies the sacred art of tracking: the subtle practice of noticing what moves within.

Tracking sensation means bringing gentle sustained awareness to the inner terrain like an ache behind the eyes, a coolness along the spine, a flutter beneath the ribs. This is not analysis, but intimacy. It is how we reestablish contact with the body's language. Tracking is the nervous system's version of being witnessed. When you offer attention to sensation without needing to change it or make it go away, you validate your body's experience. This kind of attuned witnessing activates neural networks associated with safety and connection, particularly within the right hemisphere and limbic system (Schore, 2012; Cozolino, 2017). For trauma survivors, whose bodies may have been denied attunement or treated as sites of danger, this quiet attention is radical repair.

One essential skill in tracking is learning how to locate and return to a *neutral sensation* in the body, a place of relative ease or stillness. This might be the gentle pressure of your feet on the ground, the rhythm of breath in the belly, or the soft weight of your hands in your lap. Neutral does not mean emotionless or blank; it means steady, tolerable, undramatic. By identifying a neutral anchor, you create a tether—a place to pendulate back to when activation begins to rise. This is foundational to nervous system regulation. Just as a child looks for a familiar face in a crowded room, the nervous system looks for cues of safety to orient and settle. Using a neutral sensation as your pendulation base allows you to explore difficult edges with greater safety and return capacity.

Within somatic sessions, clients are often guided to explore the felt sense of an activating memory or image and then return to a neutral or even pleasant sensation, working back and forth, breath by breath. This rhythmic practice teaches the nervous system that activation is not a trap, but a wave that can be met and released.

What does this look like in practice? One client, Amir, who had survived a car crash, noticed that even the sound of keys could make his shoulders brace. Rather than dismissing the reaction, his therapist helped him stay with the sensation of his shoulder tightening for just a moment, then pendulate to the feeling of his spine supported by the back of the couch. Together, they identified that the gentle contact with the soft fabric against his back offered a neutral resourcing sensation—a place his body associated with stillness and support. This became his anchor. Over time, Amir learned to return to that sensation anytime he noticed the beginning of a startle or brace. This simple act of noticing, without rushing, began to change his relationship to the bracing. "I'm not frozen in it anymore," he said. "Now I notice it, and I know where else I can go."

Tracking, practiced over time, becomes a kind of emotional levee—holding space for rising tides before they breach the nervous system's edge. Like a seasoned sailor reading the winds, the practiced tracker scans the horizon of sensation, discerning the early signs of turbulence and signaling when to pause, breathe, and return before the storm of overwhelm arrives.

SIBAM: A Compass for Somatic Perception

SIBAM stands for *sensation, imagery, behavior, affect,* and *meaning.* It is a model developed by Peter Levine (2010) to help map the components of experience during traumatic events and in the process of healing. Each element represents a channel through which experience is received, processed, and expressed by the bodymind.

Sensation refers to physical feelings and bodily states: pressure, warmth, pain, movement. *Imagery* involves internal visual experiences or symbolic impressions: a flickering candle, a flash of memory. *Behavior* includes motor impulses, urges, or physical responses: an urge to run, freeze, or collapse. *Affect* encompasses emotional tone: grief, rage, joy, or numbness. *Meaning* involves the personal narrative or interpretation attached to the experience: "I am unsafe" or "I survived."

The brilliance of the SIBAM model is in its ability to disentangle the overwhelm. Trauma fuses all channels into one flood. By identifying each element distinctly, we unbraid the knotted rope of trauma. This unbraiding supports repatterning at the level of the nervous system, activating prefrontal engagement and increasing coherence between the cortex and limbic brain (van der Kolk, 2014; Ogden et al., 2006). Clients become less identified with any single experience and more able to hold multiplicity without being swallowed by it.

Consider Sam, a thirty-four-year-old veteran who experienced flashbacks, muscle pain, and emotional numbing. Using SIBAM, he learned to sequence an event: the image of a burning truck (imagery), a jolt in his sternum (sensation), the urge to hide (behavior), a wave of dread (affect), and the thought "It will never end" (meaning). With his therapist, Sam practiced naming and separating these components. This gave him room to respond instead of react, slowly rewiring the panic loop.

SIBAM is not only a model; it is also a map back to wholeness. A way to turn confusion into clarity. To help the body remember that what was too much then can be metabolized now. To allow the story to unravel—not in words alone, but through breath, image, gesture, and feeling.

Discovering Your Dominant Channel

Clinically, SIBAM allows practitioners to meet clients in their dominant channel and use it as an entry point to integration. A client who is highly visual may find safety in imagined landscapes. A kinesthetic client might respond more fully when naming bodily sensations. Over time, cultivating awareness across all five channels builds somatic fluency—an internal literacy of experience that transforms dissociation into choice.

Within the SIBAM framework, each individual tends to lean naturally toward one or two primary perceptual channels. These dominant channels are not a fixed identity, but a doorway—an initial entry point into the complex mosaic of one's embodied experience. Discovering this channel allows us to listen more deeply and respond more precisely to our body's language. For some, sensation leads: They feel first. A tightening in the chest, a lightness in the belly, a wave of heat across the shoulders. For others, imagery arises first via flashes of color, symbolic dreams, or visual memories. Still, others process initially through movement or behavior: a compulsion to fidget, a sudden stillness, a tilt of the head. Emotional affect might be the first spark, felt as grief swelling without story, joy trembling without cause. And some will enter through meaning: a belief, a phrase, an intuitive truth.

Identifying your dominant channel(s) helps you regulate more effectively. If you are a visual processor, you might ground through visualization: picturing a soft forest path or a steady flame. If sensation is primary, placing a weighted object on your lap or a hand to the heart may reorient your nervous system. If affect leads, naming the emotion and offering it breath create space. Knowing your channel empowers you to reach for what works with less effort. Clinically, awareness of the dominant channel helps therapists tailor interventions. A client who dissociates visually might benefit more from kinesthetic grounding than guided imagery. A body-first processor might prefer to sway, press, or stretch rather than speak. This attunement builds trust between client and practitioner and between the client and their own body (Ogden et al., 2006).

Over time, working across channels expands one's perceptual range. Just as cross-training strengthens the body, cross-channel awareness builds neuroplastic flexibility. This integration promotes deeper self-regulation and greater inner coherence (Cozolino, 2017). The bodymind becomes fluent in its own language, becoming an oracle to itself. The answers you seek are (literally) within you, and your dominant channels reveal them to you.

As with all somatic work, there is no rush. Begin where your system opens easily. Track what rises first. Let that be the door. And trust that with time, other doors will open too.

Cultural Rhythms of Titration and Pendulation

Processing life's intensity through undulating rhythm, breath, and ritual is an ancient inheritance, not a modern innovation.

Around the world, Indigenous and ancestral cultures have long understood the body's need for pacing, cycling, and returning. Their practices echo what somatic therapy has named: that healing moves in waves.

In the Andes, Quechua and Aymara cosmologies revere wind, or *wayra*, as both messenger and medicine. It is understood as a carrier of spirit, breath, and transformation. Healing ceremonies often involve rhythmic breath, prayer, and exposure to the natural elements—helping individuals titrate emotional intensity through contact with land and air (Apffel-Marglin, 2011). A related ritual known as Saminchay, meaning "to bless," invites the invocation of life force (*sami*) to connect with the land and one's own spirit. In these practices, breath becomes a ritual of attunement—not only to the self, but also to the earth.

In traditional Chinese medicine and qigong, pendulation is mirrored in the natural flow of qi, or life force energy. This energy moves along the body's meridians in cyclical rhythms, reflecting the yin-yang oscillation of activation and rest. Qigong breath practices emphasize gentle wavelike motion, using inhale to gather and exhale to release, thereby mimicking the body's innate pendular wisdom. Practitioners learn to "ride the qi," allowing sensations to crest and fall, thus regulating emotional intensity and restoring internal harmony (Kaptchuk, 2000).

A third thread can be found in the Adowa dance of Ghana's Akan (particularly Ashanti) people. Performed at funerals, festivals, and rites of passage, Adowa allows dancers to express a full spectrum of emotions, from sorrow to celebration, through symbolic hand movements, footwork, drumming, and call-and-response singing (Ampomah, 2014). This communal dance forms a rhythmic container for emotional expression, supporting both individual grief and collective reconnection. While not framed in therapeutic terms within its cultural context, Adowa exemplifies pendulation by balancing individual emotion with communal presence within a shared ritual space.

Consider Amma, a forty-five-year-old social worker and Ghanaian immigrant living in the United States. Amma sought therapy for chronic fatigue, emotional numbness, and professional burnout following her father's death. Verbal processing felt distant and ineffective. When her therapist introduced somatic rhythm practices, Amma recalled the Adowa dances of her childhood. They began integrating simplified Adowa-inspired movements into sessions, combined with breath and a recorded drum loop. Slowly, Amma found herself weeping—not as collapse, but as return. The familiar rhythm, rooted in her lineage, gave her grief rhythm and direction. She described it as "coming home to a part of myself I thought I'd lost."

These practices show us that pendulation is not merely personal; it is also communal, cultural, and ancestral. The rhythm of returning has always been with us. And in reclaiming it, we do not simply regulate; we also remember.

Case Study
Mariana's Return to Rhythm

Mariana, a forty-two-42-year-old elementary school teacher, entered therapy after a prolonged period of burnout. She described feeling like her body was a taut wire, one small tug away from snapping. Years of caregiving, both in the classroom and at home for her aging parents, had left her numb, fatigued, and emotionally brittle. "I'm either completely checked out or on the verge of tears," she told her therapist during their first session.

In their early work together, Mariana struggled to identify any bodily sensations at all. Her default was to intellectualize, to narrate her feelings from the neck up. Her therapist gently introduced titration and pendulation, inviting Mariana to notice, for just one moment, the temperature of her hands. She blinked, surprised. "They feel cold, like I'm not in them." That moment of contact—fleeting, but real—became the first drop.

Over the following months, Mariana practiced tracking sensations in small doses. One week, she brought in a memory of standing barefoot in her garden. Her therapist encouraged her to pause, feel the imagined soil beneath her feet, and notice any change in her breath. Mariana exhaled slowly. "I think . . . my shoulders just dropped," she whispered. Together, they named that as "pendulation," a movement from activation to regulation.

Later sessions included exploring moments of override. Mariana began to recognize how often she pushed through exhaustion, saying yes when her body begged for no. "I feel the clench in my stomach, but I keep going," she admitted. Her therapist helped her practice pausing at that edge. Sometimes they would spend an entire session naming each layer of tension—jaw, belly, chest—and then returning to a neutral place, like the soft weight of a pillow in her lap.

One turning point came when Mariana had a conflict with a coworker. Instead of ruminating or shutting down, she noticed her heartbeat speeding, placed her hand on her sternum, and recalled the feeling of grass under her feet. "It's not that the anxiety vanished," she explained. "But I didn't override. I didn't abandon myself."

By the end of their work together, Mariana's nervous system no longer felt like a live wire. It felt like a tide—sometimes high, sometimes low, but always returning. She had grown the internal rhythm to meet herself where she was. "I know how to find my way back now," she said with a quiet smile. "I'm not afraid of the waves."

Journal and Reflection Prompts

Use these reflections as an invitation, not a prescription. Choose one or two prompts to sit with or journal about and notice how your body responds as you do.

1. **Tracking Your Natural Rhythms**

   What daily rhythms already support your nervous system? Think about your breath, your energy shifts, or even the way you wind down at night. What's one small way you could honor your body's pendulation today?

2. **Healing, One Drop at a Time**

   Choose a memory or emotion that feels slightly uncomfortable, but not overwhelming. What would it look like to approach it in a small dose? Try imagining, sketching, or writing a single sentence. How does that feel compared to diving in all at once?

3. **Sensation as a Guide**

   Next time you feel anxious or shut down, ask yourself the following: What is one sensation I can feel right now? Name it without judgment. Then see if you can find a neutral or calming sensation, like the feel of your back against the chair or the air on your skin. What happens when you shift attention between them?

4. **Listening for Override**

   When do you notice yourself pushing past your limits: ignoring hunger, staying silent when you want to speak, or forcing productivity? Write about one moment of override. What might your body be asking for instead?

5. **Ancestral and Communal Rhythms**

   Are there any cultural or family practices that involve rhythm, movement, or ritual (song, dance, prayer, shared meals)? How might these be part of your healing? If none come to mind, is there a rhythmic activity—like drumming, swaying, or walking—you'd like to try?

Let each reflection be a step toward tuning in to your inner rhythm. And if something feels like too much, pause. Take a breath. Come back later. Healing flows best when given the space to arrive in waves.

Somatic Ritual: Riding the Wave

This is to be practiced after reading this chapter or whenever overwhelm threatens to pull you under.

1. **Find your shore.**

   Begin by settling into a quiet, undisturbed space. Standing, let your body land with your feet planted, seat supported, and spine gently tall. Take a moment to look around and orient. Choose three objects in the room to visually connect with. Say each one softly to yourself: "I see the lamp. I see the window. I see the book." This anchors you in the here and now.

2. **Let the breath begin.**

Bring your awareness to your breath—not to change it, but to follow it. Inhale like a wave rising. Exhale like a wave returning to sea. Let your breath show you that all things crest and settle. Say silently, "This too will pass."

3. **Track and touch.**

Gently scan your body for sensation. Find a place that feels slightly activated. Maybe it's tight, tense, or fluttering. Notice its edges of sensation. Place a hand there if it feels safe to do so. Now find a place in your body that feels neutral or pleasant—perhaps the weight of your legs, the contact of your back with the chair, or the softness of your hands. It can be a place as tiny as your pinkie nail or earlobe. Rest your attention there.

4. **Pendulate with presence.**

Shift your awareness gently between the two: the edge and the ease. Back and forth. Not to fix, but to witness. Let your nervous system learn that both can be held. This is pendulation: the practice of coming and going without abandoning yourself.

5. **Close with ground and gaze.**

Return to the room by once again finding and naming those same three objects. Feel your feet and seat supported by gravity. Offer your body one simple gesture of gratitude, like a stretch, a hum, a hand on your heart. Whisper to yourself, "I return. I remain here with myself."

8

What Didn't Get to Happen: Discharging Stored Energy

Every motion of the soul has its natural appearance,
voice, and gesture.

—Cicero

The body is a living archive. Every startle, every grief, every unresolved survival impulse has a place it lodges in our tissues, waiting for the safety and conditions to complete itself. When we experience overwhelming or traumatic events and don't have the time, space, or support to fully process them, that energy often becomes trapped and stored as muscular tension, chronic pain, dissociation, or a sense of being frozen. This isn't simply a poetic metaphor; it is a biological reality rooted in how the nervous system responds to threat (Levine, 2010; van der Kolk, 2014). Trauma, in its essence, is not just what happened to us but also what didn't get to happen. It is the scream stifled, the sprint halted, and the arms that didn't get to push or protect. Our survival responses were thwarted, and the energy they mobilized had nowhere to go.

This chapter invites us into the liberatory practice of discharging this stored energy. Not through force or dramatic catharsis, but through slow, titrated, and body-led movements. The nervous system, when offered safety and attunement, knows how to complete what was once interrupted. Healing becomes less about narrative and more about nervous system completion: letting the body finish what it started (Levine, 2010).

Somatic therapy teaches us that trauma is not the event itself, but the body's response to that event, especially when it's left incomplete. For example, a child frightened into stillness may have wanted to run or scream but was told to sit still or be quiet. That override becomes habitual; and over time, it maps tension into muscles, breath patterns, posture, and immune function (Ogden et al., 2006). These become frozen adaptations, and though they were once protective, they become burdens.

Yet the body, when supported, seeks restoration. Stored energy wants to move. That is where somatic discharge practices come in. One of the most primal and effective is shaking, shivering, or tremoring. After threat, animals shake instinctively—a reset mechanism. Humans have a need for this too but have learned to suppress it. Standing with soft knees, arms loose, and feet planted, you can invite tremors through subtle bouncing or swaying. Follow what arises. Let the body lead. Let the shaking come if it wants to. This is where the phrase "shake it off" comes from—not as metaphor, but as a biological directive: a literal invitation to let the body finish what threat interrupted.

Another powerful practice is the silent scream. Our voices are often silenced in trauma; and that unexpressed energy nests in the throat, jaw, and diaphragm. To release it, find a safe private space. Open your mouth wide. While it may be actually heard only as a whisper or a breath, let the action of a scream move through your viscera. Let your face contort. Let your diaphragm contract and release. Stay in the experience until the urge subsides. This isn't for performance; it's for completion.

Crucially, all of this must be done with care. Discharge is not about intensity or drama. We are not aiming to "let it all out" but to allow what was frozen to thaw in small doses. This is titration: engaging with energy incrementally. After each release, pause. Breathe. Feel your feet and your seat. Notice sensation. Are you present? Grounded? Calm? If not, return to a resource like a comforting object, a scent, a breath, or a soft sound. Use pendulation, moving between activation and calm, to restore rhythm (Levine, 2010).

This distinction is particularly important when we consider the legacy of catharsis-oriented therapies, which gained popularity in the 1970s and 1980s. These approaches—often involving intense emotional expression, like primal screaming, aggressive physical exertion, or dramatic reenactments—were believed to release repressed feelings and lead to healing. While these methods sometimes brought momentary relief or emotional intensity, research and clinical experience have shown that unchecked catharsis can overwhelm the nervous system, reinforce traumatic patterns, and lead to retraumatization (Scaer, 2005). Without careful containment, support, and integration, big emotional releases can leave clients flooded, disoriented, or even more disconnected from their bodies.

That is not to say catharsis is wrong or shameful. In many Indigenous and ancestral traditions, catharsis finds its safest and most powerful expression in communal spaces, where rhythm, ritual, and shared presence form a sacred container for release and reintegration. There are moments when tears, rage, laughter, or sobbing rise up organically and offer a profound sense of release. These moments are not to be feared. But they are not the goal. They are a by-product of safety, not a path to it. In somatic work, we are not chasing catharsis. We are cultivating completion. The goal is not to get bigger, louder, or more dramatic, but to get closer to the body's truth; and the body whispers more than it shouts.

Among the Yoruba people of West Africa, drumming and ecstatic dance are not mere performance, but spiritual technology with ritualized embodied practices that allow grief, rage, and joy to be expressed and metabolized communally (Thompson, 2005). In traditional Hawaiian hula, storytelling through dance becomes a vehicle for ancestral remembrance and emotional release, with chants (*oli*) and movement acting as vessels for deep feeling. In many Indigenous Amazonian ceremonies, including those involving plant medicines, cathartic purging through crying, trembling, sweating, shaking, and even vomiting is seen as sacred processing and the body's way of clearing emotional and spiritual weight (Winkelman, 2010). In pre-Christian Irish keening (*caoineadh*) rituals, banshee women (*mná caointe*) wailed collectively over the dead, giving public voice and body to grief, allowing it to move through the body and be shared by the community (Ó Madagáin, 1985).

These traditions understood something essential: Catharsis, when held in sacred context and collective rhythm, can be healing. It is about not losing control, but surrendering to a current that carries us home to ourselves, together. When catharsis is held in communal ritual, the messiness of our humanity is reflected back with tenderness; and we come to know, in our bones, that our need to process and alchemize our big emotions is not a burden, but a shared reality.

Catharsis also plays a vital role in collective protest, in rallies, marches, chants, cries, and actions that allow groups of people to give voice and body to their pain, their rage, and their hope. Protest, in this way, becomes a ritual of release—an expression of refusal and reclamation. Through the body and voice, people say, "This hurts. This matters. I will not carry this alone and silently anymore." In movement, sound, and shared emotion, protest becomes both a demand for change and a somatic expression of truth (hooks, 2000). When bodies gather in defiance and devotion with feet pounding pavement, arms raised skyward, voices braided in chant, something ancient awakens. The nervous system, so often isolated in trauma, begins to regulate through rhythm and resonance. Drums echo heartbeats. Shouts become patterns of shared breath. Grief is no longer private, but witnessed, validated, and amplified. A protest becomes a communal nervous system: holding, discharging, alchemizing, and providing an antidote to feelings of isolation, abandonment, and aloneness.

These gatherings function not only as political interventions but also as embodied ceremonies of remembering: remembering dignity, remembering rage as sacred fuel, remembering that justice is not only a policy but also a pulse. In these moments, catharsis is not individual chaos without a container. It is collective coherence. It is the body's wisdom leading toward systemic regulation, ancestral memory, and the insistence that liberation must be felt, not just theorized. Cathartic as protests and rallies are, they offer an opportunity for discharge to be completed because they provide both the container of community and the safety of ritualized process.

What is possibly most important to remember is that within these experiences of protest and ancestral traditions, the emphasis is not on drama for its own sake. Any catharsis is collectively held. It is witnessed. It is integrated. It is purposeful. The body is not left raw or alone. There is always rhythm and ritual underpinnings. There is always a return. And the return is not an abrupt ending, but a soft closing: As the chants quiet, as bodies embrace, as people say their goodbyes and begin the journey homeward, the spirit of the protest or the ritual is intended to travel with them. As they leave, they carry it back with them into their kitchens, into their workplaces, and into the daily fabric of their lives.

The body learns to trust the process of discharging emotion and find safety in it through repetition and containment. The nervous system must relearn the following: *I can go there, and I can come back. I can shake, scream, move, and still return to center.* In processing and discharging stuck or overwhelming emotion, the bridge between large-scale safe catharsis and gentle processing is the concept of the container. While big expressive release may grab our attention, it is often the subtle consistent practices like breath, swaying, and pressing into a surface that form the true foundation of somatic reintegration and emotional processing.

A container is not a cage. It is a vessel, a holding space, a boundary that keeps intensity from becoming fragmentation and dissociation. In somatic work, a container can be the body's own boundaries, a therapist's grounded presence, or the predictable structure of a ritual or protest. These forms provide the nervous system with something to lean on when touching into charged material. They transform chaos into coherence. Just as trauma fragments experience, healing restores continuity of lived experience. Without a container, catharsis risks becoming a flooding river with no levee, creating more chaos. With one, it becomes a wave that moves through, cresting and then carrying us home to our shoreline, restoring calm and coherence.

Slow micromovements support the process of gentle discharge of emotion. Trauma often constricts our range of motion. Gentle, slow movement—like rolling the shoulders, rotating the hips, opening the chest, or pressing into the wall—begins to restore agency and expand capacity. With movement, we reclaim territory. We witness ourselves. We drop in and feel every muscle, tendon, and fascial stretch in our viscera during the movements of discharge. We remind the body that it is not trapped. That there is space.

Sometimes symbolic reenactments help complete an unfinished impulse through the actions we wanted to take in a moment of harm or trauma but couldn't. When we ask ourselves "What didn't get to happen?" the body cues up and remembers these urges. They linger like open parentheses in our nervous system, waiting to be closed. If you once needed to push someone away but froze instead, you might press your palms firmly against a wall or the floor to feel your own strength and reclaim the boundary that was once breached. If you needed to run but couldn't move, walking in place with strong, deliberate steps can help your legs remember their power. If you needed to hide, curling into a ball beneath a blanket and breathing deeply might restore the safety that was denied. These are not regressions; they are remembrances. They are the body's way of saying, "Let me finish what I started."

These movements, while simple, can unlock profound shifts. They bypass the verbal brain and speak directly to the midbrain and limbic system, where survival memory lives. Even when a movement cannot be performed in physical space due to limitation, fear, or circumstance, it can still be imagined. In somatic work, the nervous system responds to vividly imagined actions almost as if they were real. While the thinking front brain knows the difference between literal and symbolic, the body often does not. Imagining yourself pushing someone away, running through an open field, or curling into safety can evoke similar nervous system responses to actually doing it. This is the quiet power of the imaginal realm. It allows us to rehearse, reclaim, and repattern experiences in ways that are neurologically real, even if metaphorical. For the nervous system, what is felt is often more important than what is fact (Farb et al., 2013). In somatic psychology, this is called "completing the defensive response"—an opportunity for the body to complete what was once interrupted (Levine, 2010). This completion signals to the nervous system that the danger has passed. That we are no longer trapped. That we have agency now.

In this way, symbolic action becomes ritual. Not performative, but reparative. A quiet ceremony of reclamation. A way of telling the body, "You did not fail. You adapted. And now we return to what was once unfinished—not to relive it, but to finish and release it."

When working to complete defensive responses, safety is foundational. Before engaging in any kind of release or discharge work, your environment must whisper to your nervous system, "You are allowed to soften here." Choose your setting with care. Dim the lights or let sunlight filter gently through a curtain. Wrap yourself in a warm blanket. Place nearby objects that help you feel rooted, like a familiar smooth stone, a cup of your favorite tea, or a herbal scent that brings comfort. Let your skin touch grounding textures: the nubby weave of a rug, the grain of wood beneath your palms, the steady floor beneath your feet.

This is more than ambiance. It is neurobiological scaffolding. The body cannot heal in a state of vigilance. It needs cues of safety, what Stephen Porges calls "neuroception," to shift out of survival and into repair. When we intentionally create a space that signals calm and choice, we activate the social engagement system of the ventral vagus nerve, inviting connection and integration (Porges, 2011). Let the ritual of healing feel sacred. Light a candle. Play music that soothes or inspires. Set an intention. These acts tell the limbic system, "You are not in danger." They transform the space into a container—not for performance, but for presence.

Allowing discharge is not about forcing catharsis. The goal is not to scream, weep, or tremble on cue. The goal is reconnection with the parts of self that got left behind. We are wanting coherence in our system. We are offering a gentle return to self. True release comes not through intensity, but through rhythm. Through curiosity and choice. The nervous system does not respond to pressure. It responds to permission. When the body knows it can stop at any time, it begins to trust the process. It learns the following: *I can go there, and I can come back. I am not alone. I am not trapped. I am safe.*

After any discharge, whether subtle or strong, take time for integration. This is the moment when healing settles into the body. Lie still if that feels safe. Let yourself be held by the ground. Feel the ground's steady presence beneath you—a quiet reminder that you do not have to hold everything alone. Breathe slowly, without agenda. Inhale gently. Exhale even more gently. Place a hand over your heart, your belly, or wherever you feel sensation most clearly. This is a gesture of return. Of reassurance. Of anchoring.

Let the nervous system settle in its own time. Think of this as the exhale after a storm. The body may need stillness; or it may want to rock, hum, sway. Follow the impulse without forcing. Allow a pause, not just of movement but also of meaning-making. Let the experience speak before you translate it into words. Then when you're ready, reflect: *What did I feel? What shifted? What remains? Was there a moment of release, like a tear welling up, a spontaneous yawn, a groan, a sob, a sigh that surprised you, or even a small laugh rising unbidden?* These are all signs of completion. The body lets go in mysterious ways. A single breath out breath may hold the fullness of release.

Sometimes the shift is enormous, like a wave of heat moving through the spine or trembling that finally quiets. Sometimes it is almost imperceptible, a quiet sense of softening in the jaw or the faintest widening of the breath. Trust whatever arises. Welcome it as a messenger. There is no right way to release. There is only the honest way, the present way, the way your body chooses. Integration is not an afterthought; it is the healing. It is where sensation becomes meaning and movement becomes memory. It is how your system learns the following: *I did something different, and I survived. I am allowed to feel. I am allowed to rest.*

As you begin to work somatically and embark on the lifelong journey of traversing your inner terrain, you might ask yourself some guiding questions: *Where do I brace? Is it in the jaw, the belly, the shoulders? Where does my body clench against the world or against memory? What does my body do when it feels safe?* Maybe it softens. Maybe the breath deepens. Maybe the eyes become less guarded. *What does letting go feel like?* Not just as an idea but also as a texture, a temperature, or a rhythm. *Can I stay with the sensation a little longer?* Not to analyze, but to witness. These are not questions the mind can answer. They are invitations the body responds to—with tremors, with sighs, with shivers, and with stillness. With tears that come out of nowhere. With laughter that erupts like a spring.

As we discharge the old through movement, sound, breath, or image, we make room for the new. Space opens. The breath expands, the posture uncoils, the muscles unhook from old shapes. Emotion flows more freely. Vision brightens, not only literally but also existentially. You may find yourself suddenly knowing what matters or feeling a long-lost desire return like a forgotten friend. Energy doesn't just return; it also reorganizes. We become less driven by avoidance and more available for presence. We stop bracing against life and begin to participate in it. We stop fearing the next wave and begin to trust our capacity to ride it.

This is not about fixing yourself. There is nothing broken. This is about freeing yourself, from what you no longer need to carry, from reflexive defenses that once protected you but now confine you. From inherited burdens and muscle-held memories. This is about returning to your own rhythm. Your own breath. Your own truth. A truth the body never forgot and the mind is relearning.

Case Study
Helen's Release

Helen, a seventy-three-year-old retired professor and grandmother, arrived to somatic therapy with a familiar story etched not in words, but in joints and silence. Her knees ached constantly. Her hips creaked with every step. Her jaw was perpetually clenched. She had not cried in decades—not at the loss of her beloved sister to cancer, not through her divorce after thirty years of marriage, not even when her grandson was hospitalized with a rare autoimmune illness. "I just get on with it," she would say. Her voice was kind, clipped, and carried the cadence of someone who had long relied on intellect over emotion: sharp, measured, and meticulously controlled. But her body told another story.

In early sessions, Helen struggled to locate sensation beyond pain. Numbness clouded her awareness. When asked how she felt, she would often pause, scan for the "right" answer, and then reply with something vague and intellectual—"It's interesting" or "It's complicated"—as if emotions were a puzzle to be solved rather than sensations to be felt. But slowly, with guidance, she began to track subtle internal cues. She noticed that her throat felt tight when she spoke about her children. That her breath would pause when she mentioned her ex-husband. That her hands would clench in her lap, even as she said, "It's fine, I know I'm blessed in life."

Together, she and her therapist explored gentle movements. Slowly pressing her palms against the wall, swaying slowly to classical piano music, and curling into a blanket on the therapy couch. These symbolic reenactments touched something old and unfinished in Helen's system. In one session, she described an image of herself as a girl, hiding under the table while her parents fought. Her breath caught. Her jaw tensed. Her eyes welled, but still, no tears.

The therapist invited her to press her back gently into the couch cushions, to feel supported. Then without words, Helen brought her hands to her face. Her body shook, first imperceptibly, then with fuller tremors. A sound emerged, almost like a sob, but quieter, as if testing the air. "I didn't think I was allowed to feel all of this," she whispered.

In subsequent sessions, Helen practiced "micromourning," spending a few minutes each morning with a photograph, a song, or a memory and letting her body respond. Sometimes there were tears. Sometimes only sighs. But something shifted. Her knees felt looser. Her jaw softened. Her dreams became more vivid. She began to say things like "I feel more real" and "I think I'm finally catching up to everything that's happened in my life."

Somatic work had not made her pain vanish, but it had begun to give it language. Movement. Meaning. Helen's story is not one of dramatic catharsis, but of quiet revolution. Of a body long silenced now learning to speak.

She began to walk with a new kind of awareness—no longer bracing for life, but moving with it. Her laughter returned, soft and surprising. And once, during a session, she wept without fear, holding her own hand the entire time. "This," she said, "feels like coming home to myself."

Journal and Reflection Prompts

1. **Where does my body hold on?**

   When you are stressed or triggered, where in your body do you tighten, clench, or brace? Scan from head to toe. Which part speaks first, and which part stays quiet?

2. **What didn't get to happen?**

   Reflect on a painful or unresolved moment in your past. What did your body want to do that it couldn't at the time? Did you want to run, cry, yell, or hide? What impulse remains incomplete? What movement or expression has my body been craving?

3. **What helps me feel safe enough to let go?**

   Think about environments, textures, sounds, or rituals that help your nervous system soften. What makes your body feel safe, not just in theory but also in sensation?

4. **What does release look or feel like for me?**

   Have you ever felt a spontaneous yawn, shiver, sigh, or tear arise without warning? Describe what that felt like. What preceded it? How did your body respond afterward?

5. **What small ritual could I create for integration?**

   Imagine a simple daily practice like a breath, a movement, or a gesture that could help you integrate emotional experiences. What might it look like? How could you honor both the activation and the return?

Somatic Ritual: Completing the Cycle

Find a quiet private space where you can move freely. Let the space feel sacred, a threshold between the ordinary and the healing. Dim the lights, light a candle, or wrap yourself in a soft shawl. Allow this act of preparation to tell your nervous system, "We are entering a space of care."

Bring to mind a mildly upsetting recent event, something that registers as a 1–3 on a scale of 10. This might be a moment of irritation, a small hurt, or a minor disappointment. You are not diving into deep overwhelm; you are inviting a manageable wave to practice riding.

Begin with grounding. Stand or sit. Press your feet gently into the floor. Feel the contact. Place one hand on your heart and one on your belly. Breathe slowly, without force. Notice where tension lives. Name it gently, like a friend arriving at your door.

Invite gentle movement.

Sway from side to side.

Bounce softly on your knees.

Roll your shoulders.

Stretch your arms like wings.

Let your body tremble if it wants to.

Let breath move naturally.

If you feel the urge to vocalize, do so softly.

Practice the silent scream.

Open your mouth and let your diaphragm engage, even if no sound escapes.

Press your palms firmly against a wall or floor.

Rock. Curl. Extend.

Let your body complete what it needs.

As movement rises and falls, track your sensations. What shifts? What releases? What calls your attention? This is not performance; it is deep presence.

After several minutes, begin to slow. Return to stillness. Lie down or sit with support. Place both hands on your belly. Inhale slowly through your nose. Exhale fully through your mouth. Feel the exhale ripple through your body. Let yourself land.

If it feels right, gently close your eyes. Let yourself feel held, by the floor, the breath, the moment. Sense what is still moving inside you and what has quieted.

When ready, journal your experience. What did your body show you? What sensations or images arose? What shifted? What remains?

Whisper to yourself the following: *I am allowed to release. I am allowed to return home to myself.*

Let that be your closing prayer and your nervous system's lullaby.

Remember, this ritual is a practice in building discharge capacity. By working gently with small waves of sensation and activation, we strengthen our ability to stay present through the discharge process. Over time, the body learns that it can go there and come back. That release is not danger. It is ritual return.

9

Dancing Down the Pain, Playing with Pleasure

Dance, when you're broken open.
Dance, if you've torn the bandage off.
Dance in the middle of the fighting.
Dance in your blood.
Dance when you're perfectly free.

—Rūmī

The body is the original storyteller. Long before we had language to explain our experiences, our muscles, gestures, and movements carried the imprint of our joys and sorrows as evidence of our essential embodiment. We danced before we spoke. We reached, curled, trembled, and leapt to express the inexpressible as very young humans. The language of embodied movement is older than words and still lives within us, waiting to be remembered. In embodied movement and creative expression, the body finds an extremely direct and easily accessible path to restoring vitality. Emotions, after all, are not just felt in the mind; they are also physical events—waves of sensation and energy that surge through muscles, fascia, and breath. When we suppress their expression, we ask the body to hold what should move, becoming bog-like, stagnant, heavy, and overgrown with the detritus of unspoken pain. Even today, beneath the layers of social conditioning and technological distraction, our bodies retain this ancient language. They know how to grieve and celebrate, to release and restore through movement and expression. Embodied movement practices and creative expression support emotional healing and nervous system regulation by helping us bypass the limitations of intellect and reconnect with the deeper rhythms of sensation, presence, and authenticity.

Modern somatic therapies, as well as ancient traditions, recognize that the combination of embodied movement and creative expression is powerful medicine being ingested in real time. Indigenous cultures have long known that dance, drumming, painting, and song are not luxuries, but necessities—rituals that restore coherence to the psyche and nervous system. In the ceremonial dances of the Diné or the powwows of the Plains peoples, in the spirited storytelling of the Yoruba, or the rhythm of Irish céilís, we see creative movement used to process grief, restore joy, honor transitions, and connect with the unseen. These practices teach us that healing happens not only in stillness but also in motion. Embodied movement allows the body to metabolize what talking alone cannot. It stirs up what is stagnant. It clears out what is stuck. Even gentle gestures—like a swaying torso, circling hips, or opening and closing hands—can unlock old, frozen parts of ourselves when done with intention and emotional attunement. These small shifts matter. A shoulder that loosens. A breath that deepens. A laugh that escapes midmovement. In these moments, the body begins to trust itself again.

Despite what society's messaging may suggest, embodied movement is not the same as exercise or performance. Somatic psychology recognizes that trauma often severs our connection to the body as the nervous system braces against perceived threats (van der Kolk, 2014). Moving with expression and intention—allowing somatic urges to mingle with creative impulses—animates stuck energy, awakens dormant vitality, and reconnects psyche with soma. Emotions are inherently energetic; they rise, crest, and fall. When suppressed or unacknowledged, however, they stagnate—showing up as disembodied tension, numbness, or agitation. Embodied movement restores this natural flow—bringing brain, body, and spirit into coherence. Whether through a slow sway, a spontaneous stretch, or an exuberant dance, the body relearns that it is safe to feel, to move, to exist in its fullness. In this process, what was once braced begins to soften; and joy, creativity, and freedom reawaken.

Similarly, flow states accessed through creative expression offer us a clear path to embodied healing—one that brings expansion where trauma once brought stagnation. When we dance, draw, sing, sculpt, or write from the body rather than just the mind, we invite a different kind of intelligence and communication forward. The written word gives story to what was once erased. Two-dimensional visual art gives visage to what was once unseen. Three-dimensional art gives form to what was once formless. Sound gives voice to what was once silenced. Dance restores the motion that was once restricted or shamed. These acts bypass the analytical brain and access the felt sense, allowing long-held emotions to move through the body, surfacing in safe and symbolic ways for gentle witnessing and processing.

Clinically, the expressive arts therapies have shown strong efficacy in supporting emotional release and nervous system regulation (Malchiodi, 2007). Through the expressive arts, we meet ourselves beyond the realm of logic and reason in a place where sensation, representation, and metaphor become the language of our deepest truths. These acts of creation become acts of liberation, allowing us to process emotions without needing to explain, justify, or even fully understand them. In this way, creativity becomes a path into embodiment, offering a somatic bridge that allows us to safely metabolize and notice feelings through rhythm, image, gesture, word, and sound.

We don't need to invest tremendous amounts of time or money into classes or workshops to access personal material ripe for creative exploration. We can start with our everyday speech, where the body whispers its truths in metaphors, shaping phrases before we even notice them rising to our lips. Sometimes the poems inside us take shape on their own, carried by the body's whisper through the words we choose. Our everyday language carries traces of sensation, urgency, and unmet needs. Listen closely to the phrases that arise in passing: "I'm carrying the weight of the world," "I'm about to snap," "I feel boxed in," "My heart's not in it." A person who feels "stuck in molasses" may have an urge to move or change that hasn't yet reached conscious awareness. Someone who "can't open up" might have a blocked impulse to express anger, grief, or longing. These turns of phrase are nervous system breadcrumbs, evidence of inner truths trying to surface. By becoming curious about the language we use, especially in moments of discomfort, we can begin to uncover what the body is holding. These aren't just figures of speech; they're also clues. Somatic metaphors often point to unrealized urges, repressed instincts, or unmet needs ripe for exploration and creative expression. Expressive practices, like free verse poetry writing, can give those clues a safe passageway toward integration and relief.

Performance-based creative practices beyond dance, like improvisational acting, also reveal how embodied expression can become a portal to healing. When we allow ourselves to respond in real time, without scripting or controlling the outcome, we learn to follow the body's truth as it emerges. Actors and improvisers have long understood this principle. Sanford Meisner taught his students to "use it, use it, don't lose it"—encouraging them to work with whatever emotion or impulse was genuinely present in the moment rather than resisting or suppressing it (Meisner & Longwell, 1987). Similarly, the foundational rule of improvisational theater ("Yes, and . . .") models the power of acknowledgment and expansion: You accept what arises and build upon it, without judgment or control (Johnstone, 1981).

These theater principles mirror the core of somatic healing: We meet what is here, we include it, and we let it move. In both healing and in improv, you must be willing to put your ego on the line. To not know what will come next. To be surprised by your own impulses. This kind of presence requires vulnerability. But it also makes space for joy, creativity, playfulness, and truth to emerge in real time. It is in these unscripted moments that the nervous system learns the following: *I can trust myself here. I can be with what arises. I can use it for good. I can even enjoy it.*

Playful movement holds a special place in somatic healing. Often, trauma creates rigidity—physically, emotionally, and psychologically. Play dissolves that rigidity. It invites spontaneity, curiosity, and delight back into the body. Try jumping, spinning, or wiggling without a plan. Let yourself be silly. Laugh out loud. Make faces. Move like a child. This kind of play reconnects us with our inner child—the part of us that still knows how to dance without inhibition, to sing without fear of judgment, to express freely and fully. Through play, we create new neural pathways that say, "Joy is safe, expression is allowed, and presence is pleasurable" (Siegel, 2010).

Working with our inner child during creative expression is deeply healing. When we dance or draw with that younger part of ourselves in mind, we are actively reparenting ourselves. We are giving that tender part of us the freedom, attention, and validation it may never have received. Consider a practice where you put on a song from your childhood or one that makes you feel lighthearted. Then imagine dancing with your inner child. Invite them in. Ask, "What would you like to do? How would you like to move? What feels good in your body?" Then follow their lead. This is not regression; it is integration. It is honoring the parts of ourselves that still seek movement, connection, and joy.

Incorporating play and pleasure into these practices is not indulgent; it is essential. Inspired by the work on *pleasure activism* of adrienne maree brown (2019), we begin to understand that pleasure is a form of resistance for our adult selves. In a world that often tells us to numb, to perform, or to push through pain, choosing creative expression and joy is revolutionary. Moving toward what feels good—what lights you up, what softens you, what excites you—reclaims your body from the grip of survival. Let movement be an act of playful pleasure. Let drawing be a love letter to your senses. Let singing be a prayer of aliveness. When we center our pleasure, we create sustainable healing that is rooted not in deprivation, but in nourishment.

Creative expression also restores our sense of agency. When we shape our inner experience into something tangible, we begin to take authorship of our story. We move from being solely the ones who endured suffering to also being the ones who shape beauty from its depths. This shift can be especially transformative for those who have experienced powerlessness, erasure, or voicelessness. In the process of creating, we reinhabit the body not just as a site of pain but also as a place of artistry and authorship.

Through art, we communicate and connect. Through embodied movement, we take up space and reclaim our right to be seen, heard, and felt. Through creative expression, we retrieve the parts of ourselves that trauma, silence, and separation once fractured. We give texture to grief, temperature to rage, and color to longing. We let what was once buried rise up into the light—not as pathology, but as poetry. And in that rising, something ancient stirs: a remembering that we are not only survivors but also the vibrant cocreators of our reality.

Indigenous and ancestral cultures have long understood the power of embodied movement and creative expression in healing and resourcing. From ceremonial dances to sacred songs, these traditions honor the body as an alchemic vessel for emotion, memory, and spirit. In many tribal rituals, creative movement is not separated from spirituality; it is a way of communing with ancestors, with the earth, with the unseen. Among the Māori people of Aotearoa (New Zealand), haka dances serve not only as war chants but also as communal expressions of grief, celebration, and solidarity in ancestral pride. In Thai traditions, drumming and dance are woven into rites of passage and healing ceremonies. The Wai Khru ritual, performed in schools of dance and martial arts, honors teachers and ancestors through embodied reverence (Pidokrajit, 2011; Guffey & Kaewkaen, 2017). Meanwhile, the Poy Sang Long ordination festival among the Tai Yai (Shan) people marks the entry of young boys into novice monkhood through vibrant processions of ritual dress, music, and communal movement (Phromrekha, 2019). These dance-based practices, like many others across cultures, remind us that creative expression through rhythm, gesture, and ritual are foundational to honoring threshold crossing, transformation, and belonging. These communal movement practices create safety and containment in experiences where there may have otherwise been fear and disintegration.

One powerful example of a culturally rooted dance and embodied movement tradition that blends mourning, celebration, and nervous system regulation through pendulation is the New Orleans jazz funeral with a second line parade. Originating from a blend of West African, French, and African American traditions, these funerals begin with a somber march to the cemetery, led by a brass band playing dirges and hymns. After the burial, the music shifts, the tempo quickens, and the second line forms. As the music changes and the collective bodies reassemble, the experience of the mourners shifts from somber expressions of grief and heartache over the loss of a loved one to ecstatic expressions of joy and gratitude for their existence. In this shift, the mourners are supported in pendulating their grief with their gratitude for the person lost. In the second line, mourners and community members dance colorfully through the streets, waving handkerchiefs and parasols, tears and laughter buckjumping through time together.

This ritualized expression of grief and joy creates a communal container for emotional release, transforming heavy sorrow into creative movement and music. It allows the community to process loss not in isolation, but in rhythm, remembrance, and celebration (Sakakeeny, 2013). This pendulated blending of solemnity and joy—through dance and music, rooted in cultural continuity—offers a vivid example of how creative movement and expression can alchemize pain into connection and resilience.

To integrate these practices into daily life, create space each day, even for a few minutes, to move or express freely and creatively. Begin your morning with a stretch and a hum. Sing and sway in the shower. Take a break from work to doodle. Dance in your kitchen on Sunday morning as you drink your coffee. Write a haiku about your day on your calendar. Ask your inner child if they need five minutes of play. Shake out the residue of the day before bed. These small rituals anchor you in your body and help prevent the buildup of stress and stagnation. Over time, they become sacred moments of reconnection. You don't need a studio, a stage, or an audience. All you need is willingness and a tender commitment to meet yourself where you are through movement and sound.

As you practice, take time to reflect. Ask yourself, "What did I feel while moving? What surprised me in my drawing? What did I release in my sound?" Keep a journal or voice memo log to track your insights and patterns. These reflections help you deepen your relationship with your body and recognize the progress you're making. Healing is not always dramatic; sometimes it's the quiet shifts, the small doodles and releases, the unexpected laughter and dance that mark the deepest transformation.

Movement and creative expression are not supplemental; they are central to healing.

They speak the language of the body and invite us into a fuller, freer existence.

When we move, we remember.

When we express, we reclaim.

When we dance down the pain and play in pleasure, we soften what once seemed immovable and make space for joy to rise.

Deeper Explorations for Embodied Movement and Creative Expression:

Dance

- One of the most accessible forms of this practice is free-form dance. In this space, there are no right or wrong steps, only honest movement. To explore free-form dance, find a moment alone and create a felt sense of safety in your space by locking the door, closing the blinds, or simply orienting to the room. Choose a song that resonates with you as something playful, inspiring, or deeply emotive and allow your body to respond. Let your arms rise or your feet stomp. Let your hips sway or your spine curl. If tears come, let them. If laughter bubbles up, follow it. Free-form dance is not about looking a certain way; it's about feeling fully. It invites us to be seen by ourselves in our raw embodied truth. Afterward, take time to reflect. How does your body feel? What shifted inside you? This simple practice can become a sacred ritual of renewal within yourself—the dance of return.

Drawing

- Drawing and visual art offer a different, yet equally profound path. When we engage in expressive drawing, we bypass the analytical mind and let the hand speak for the heart. Begin with a blank page and a few simple tools; you don't need more than crayons, pencils, or markers. Close your eyes, take a deep breath, and tune in to your body. What emotions or sensations are present? Let them guide your hand. You might scribble furiously or draw a spiral. You might use bold colors or soft strokes. There is no need to judge or interpret the outcome. The act itself is the medicine. Over time, your drawings can reveal patterns, release emotions, and become a visual journal of your healing journey.

Vocalizations

- Sound too holds transformative power. Many of us have learned to silence our voices, to hold back screams, sobs, or even songs. But the body remembers. Vocal expression—whether through humming, chanting, sighing, or screaming—activates the vagus nerve and helps regulate the nervous system (Porges,

2011). One powerful practice is *embodied sound*. In a safe private space, inhale deeply and let a sound emerge on your exhale. It might be a low moan, a sharp cry, or a melodic tone. Let it move through your chest, throat, and jaw. Notice what shifts. Often, this simple act can release long-held tension and bring a sense of aliveness and relief. Don't worry about being on pitch or sounding "nice." This is not a public performance; it's a conversation between your breath and your being, shaped by the basket of your diaphragm and the vessel of your throat.

Breath

- When we combine movement with breath, the effect becomes even more potent. Simple exercises like raising your arms overhead as you inhale and lowering them as you exhale can help integrate the body and mind. These gentle rhythms mimic the ebb and flow of the nervous system's natural pendulation between activation and rest. As you practice, notice how your breath deepens, your heart rate slows, and your body begins to trust the safety of the moment. Notice how your breathprint shifts. In these moments, healing becomes tangible—not as an abstract goal, but as a felt sense of coherence and ease.

Boundaries

- Boundaries also find expression through embodied movement. When we move with awareness, we begin to discern what is ours and what is not. We feel the edge of our own skin. We notice when we are leaking energy or merging with others. Grounding movements, like pressing your feet into the floor or making strong intentional gestures, help anchor you in your own energy. Try standing tall, placing one hand on your chest and the other on your belly, and swaying gently from side to side. Feel the perimeter of your being. Ask, "Where do I end and others begin? How can I hold myself while staying open to connection?" Movement, used in this way, becomes a map for self-containment and self-trust. Through grounding movements, you can allow yourself to *be where your feet are*. Let the ground remind you that you can find safety here, in this very moment. You don't have to leap forward or retreat into the past to be safe. You can root yourself in the now.

Case Study
Héctor's Dance of Becoming

Héctor was forty-two when he walked into his first Latin dance class, though he told himself he was there only "for the exercise." A tall quiet man with an easy smile and shoulders that rarely dropped from their habitual hunch, Héctor had spent most of his life in silence. Not because he lacked language, but because somewhere along the way, he learned that his voice did not matter.

Raised in a working-class Puerto Rican family in Chicago's Humboldt Park, Héctor grew up with the unspoken rule that men should be strong, steady, and selfless. Visible only through action, not emotional expression. His father rarely spoke of feelings and expected Héctor to perform, provide, and protect without complaint. When Héctor, as a boy, tried to explain why he cried at the sound of violins or why he sometimes wanted to be held more than be left alone, he was met with silence or, worse, mockery. So he shut it down. He became the quiet one. The strong one. The invisible one.

He married young and became a dedicated provider, raising two children and working long shifts at a transit job that left him physically exhausted and emotionally numb. The years passed. His body stiffened. His words dried up. His wife said he was "a good man," but never "present." When she eventually left, her parting words echoed: "You're a ghost in your own life." He didn't know what to do with that.

A friend dragged him to a Saturday night merengue class at a local community center. The music was already pulsing when they walked in, the guitars rippling like river water, the beat like a heartbeat you'd forgotten was yours. Something inside Héctor stirred awake.

That first class was awkward. He stepped on toes. He blushed every time he had to make eye contact. But the teacher, an older woman named Reina with brightly painted lips and a laugh loud and clear like a church bell, kept saying, "Your body already knows this. Trust your hips. Let the rhythm find you." And somehow it did.

Week after week, he returned. At first, it was just the music that called him back. Then it was the warmth, the brief moment of holding someone's hand without needing to explain who he was. The simple sacred way his body could speak without words. He began to loosen. To feel. To move.

As the months went by, something remarkable happened. Héctor's gait changed. His chest began to open. He started making eye contact, not just in dance but also in life. He joked more.

Smiled more. Laughed even. He began to notice sensations in his body again through the thrill of a spin, the heat of a hand resting at his back, the safety of following the beat. In a world where he had once felt invisible, the dance floor made him feel *seen*.

In dance, Héctor discovered that needs weren't shameful. They were human. The need to connect, to lead and follow, to be held and known. His movements told the stories he had locked away— of grief, of longing, of hope. The studio became his sanctuary. The social dances his temple.

One evening, during a particularly fluid bachata, Héctor felt a surge of emotion rise in his chest like a wave. He didn't suppress it. He let it move through him as he danced. Tears came. Not from sadness, but from the relief of being alive in his body, of being allowed to feel and be felt. It was the first time in decades he had cried without shame.

Later, when he began working with a somatic therapist, he brought what he learned on the dance floor into the room. He could now describe sensations—"tightness in my chest," "tingling in my hands"—and track emotional waves as they moved. He started to speak. Not just about his past but also about his *present*. He told his therapist, "I don't want to disappear anymore. I want to be seen and heard."

Today, Héctor teaches beginner salsa classes at that same community center. He tells his students, "You don't have to know the steps. Just start with the rhythm and your breath. Let your body speak."

Héctor is no longer a ghost, disappearing into the margins of his own life. He moves with presence now. A man who found his voice not through talking it out, but through dancing it out—each step a liberatory act of return to himself.

Journal and Reflection Prompts

1. **Embodied Emotion**

    Recall a recent moment when you felt a strong emotion. How did your body respond? What movements or sensations accompanied that feeling?

2. **Movement as Expression**

    Choose a piece of music that resonates with you. As you listen, allow your body to move freely. Afterward, reflect: What emotions surfaced? How did movement help in expressing or releasing them?

3. **Creative Exploration**

    Engage in a creative activity (drawing, singing, writing) without any specific goal. Let your body guide the process. What did you discover about yourself through this uninhibited expression?

4. **Inner Child Connection**

    Think back to a joyful movement or activity from your childhood. Recreate it now. How does this reconnection feel in your body and spirit?

5. **Pleasure and Play**

    Identify a movement or activity that brings you pure joy. Incorporate it into your routine.

    How does prioritizing pleasure impact your overall well-being?

Somatic Ritual: Expressing Your Embodiment

This ritual is designed to facilitate emotional release and self-discovery through spontaneous movement and creative expression.

1. **Setting the Space**

   Find a quiet, comfortable area where you can move freely. Gather materials like paper, crayons, or markers.

2. **Grounding**

   Begin with deep intentional breaths. Feel your connection to the ground, anchoring yourself in the present moment.

3. **Spontaneous Movement**

   Play music that evokes emotion. Allow your body to move without judgment or structure. Let the music guide your movements, expressing whatever arises.

4. **Creative Expression**

   After moving, sit down and use your art materials to create something that represents your experience. This could be abstract or literal. Focus on expression, not perfection.

5. **Reflection**

   Observe your creation. What emotions or insights emerge? Journal about the experience, noting any shifts in your physical or emotional state.

6. **Closure**

   Conclude with a few deep breaths, acknowledging the courage it takes to explore and express oneself. Consider integrating this practice regularly to deepen your connection with your body and emotions.

10

Working with Triggers
and Repairing the Ruptures Within

The cure for pain is in the pain.

—Rūmī

A trigger is not merely an inconvenience or a fleeting mood swing. It is also a soul echo, a sharp reminder that something within us is still seeking resolution, still calling out to be seen, heard, and held. In this chapter, we step into the delicate terrain of working with triggers: those moments when the nervous system flares in alarm, when the past overtakes the present, and when we respond not just to what's in front of us but also to everything that came before. Here, we do not turn away from the discomfort. Instead, we become fluent in its language. We learn to meet it with curiosity, grace, and grounded skill. We endeavor to repair the ruptures within.

When a trigger arises, it is not a failure. It is the body's attempt to make sense of the present using the language of the past. Triggers are messengers. They point us toward what once overwhelmed us and what still longs to be witnessed. Often, they activate fear, not just the sharp kind but also the subtle bracing kind: tightening in the chest, shrinking in the voice, scanning for danger in benign moments.

Your fear is valid. And also, your fear is courage asking to be known.

Beneath the trembling is the impulse to protect. Beneath the withdrawal is the longing to belong without threat. When we stop judging fear as weakness, we begin to recognize its sacred role: to signal that something matters. That something once hurt. That an old rupture still needs tending. Beneath the fear is a courageous desire for repair and healing. For safety.

A trigger is any stimulus, external or internal, that activates a strong emotional or physiological response. This might be the tone of someone's voice, a particular smell, a crowded space, or even a fleeting thought. In these moments, the body responds as if the original wound were happening again. We may feel fear, rage, or shame wash over us without warning. Our breath quickens, our muscles tense, and our vision narrows. The past bleeds into the present, hijacking our capacity to respond rather than react (van der Kolk, 2014).

These reactions are not signs of weakness; they are signs of a nervous system doing its job to protect us, albeit based on outdated information. Understanding our triggers begins with recognizing the core beliefs beneath them. These beliefs often crystallize in early life and are formed through repeated experiences that reinforce them. Beliefs such as "I am not safe," "I am not enough," and "I am alone" are not facts; they are survival strategies encoded into the body and mind. When a current event pokes at one of these beliefs, the whole neural network associated with that belief lights up, bringing with it a cascade of emotional memories (Levine, 2010). The neural network acts like a grove of trees sharing one root system. Burn one branch, and the whole root network responds as if it's on fire, adjusting its chemistry in response to the perceived threat.

While triggers can feel overwhelming, they are also directional. Each activation is not only a flashback; it is also a flare. It marks the coordinates of an old wound that is finally ready to be met. In this way, triggers are not interruptions to our healing; they are invitations. They point directly to the places where our nervous system is still holding on, still guarding, still hoping for resolution. When approached with care, these moments of heightened emotion become portals and opportunities to move closer to what was once unbearable and to offer it what it never received: attention, compassion, and choice. As somatic therapist Pat Ogden teaches, the body doesn't just remember trauma; it also remembers the impulse to heal (Ogden et al., 2006).

To navigate this with compassion, we must become detectives of our inner landscape. When triggered, pause. Ask yourself the following: *What core belief is alive right now? What is this reaction trying to protect me from?* As we name the belief, we loosen its grip. And as we reframe it, we begin to write a new story.

Some of the most common core beliefs include the following:

"I am not enough."
"I am too much."
"I am abandoned."
"I don't belong."
"I am unworthy of love."

"I am unlovable."
"I have to earn my worth."
"It's not safe to rest."
"I am responsible for everything."
"I must be in control to survive."

These beliefs often take root in early childhood, shaped by repeated attachment ruptures that the child self experiences as fear, disconnection, or unmet needs. At the time, they served as adaptive strategies—ways the young nervous system scanned for threat and prepared itself for pain or disappointment. In many ways, these negative beliefs were like familiar maps: They may have limited us, but they also helped us recognize and endure dangers we already knew how to face. It is often easier and preferable to survive the devil we know than the devil we don't.

Over time, however, we come to see that our reliance on these beliefs begins to constrain us more than protect us—sometimes even sabotaging our ability to move toward connection, joy, or fulfillment. While these strategies once helped us survive, they are not ultimate truths. They are old stories waiting to be rewritten—not by force, but by gently offering the body and mind new evidence of safety, belonging, and worth. Neurolinguistic programming (NLP) offers a powerful tool for this. By taking a limiting belief and rephrasing it with the word "regardless," we plant the seeds of resilience and hope. For example, "I am unlovable" becomes "I am learning to love and be loved, regardless of past wounds." The word "regardless" acts like a bridge; it connects us to a possibility beyond the pain (Dilts, 1990) without denying the reality of our lived experience. In this way, belief reframes can help us repair the ruptures within, restoring trust in ourselves and widening the paths available for healing.

Using "Regardless" to Reframe Common Core Beliefs

- *I am not enough.* → I am worthy of care and belonging, *regardless* of how others have treated me.

- *I am too much.* → I am allowed to take up space and feel deeply, *regardless* of who was overwhelmed by me.

- *I don't belong.* → I am learning to find my people and my place, *regardless* of where I started.

- *I am unlovable.* → I am learning to love and be loved, *regardless* of past wounds.

- *I have to earn my worth.* → My existence has value, *regardless* of my productivity or performance.

- *It's not safe to rest.* → I am allowed to rest and receive, *regardless* of what I was taught about survival.

- *I will always be abandoned.* → I am building relationships rooted in trust, *regardless* of the losses I've known.

- *I must be in control to survive.* → I can soften into life's flow, *regardless* of the chaos I've endured.

Once we've identified the underlying negative belief, we can invite in a new positive one. NLP teaches us to install empowering beliefs by recalling moments when the opposite of our negative underlying belief was true. Even if brief or subtle, these memories hold powerful medicine. If you frequently feel "I am unsafe," picture a time when you felt safe, even for a moment. Let that memory expand. What do you see, hear, smell, taste, feel? Embody it. Breathe it in. Let it wash over you until your nervous system softens. As you sit with the sensations of safety, repeat out loud to yourself, "I can create safety in my life, regardless of past experiences." In this way, we resource the body with new truths. Truths that can guide us through future storms (Dispenza, 2017).

At times, we need more than reframing; we need protection. In somatic and imaginal practices, the concept of a competent protector offers a profoundly stabilizing tool. A competent protector is an internal or imagined figure—real, symbolic, or ancestral—who embodies strength, calm, and reliability. When you feel overwhelmed by a trigger, you can pause and call upon this protector. Close your eyes, breathe deeply, and ask yourself, "Who could support or protect me right now?" Then visualize this being, character, or energy standing beside you or within you, keeping you safe from harm. They might be a wise grandparent, a fierce animal, a spiritual figure, or a future version of yourself. Let them speak to you. Let them steady you. With their presence, return to your body and to your window of tolerance (Ogden et al., 2006).

Many Indigenous cultures and faith traditions have long incorporated competent protectors into their spiritual and healing practices. In Yoruba cosmology, the orisha gods and goddesses, such as Ogun (protector of warriors) and Yemoja (the nurturing mother of waters), are invoked for protection and inner strength during times of distress (Awolalu & Dopamu, 1979). In Native Hawaiian tradition, ancestral spirits (aumākua) are believed to guide and shield descendants, offering wisdom and comfort through dreams, rituals, and everyday signs (Handy & Pukui, 1999). In Catholic traditions, figures such as St. Michael the Archangel (defender against evil), Mother Mary (compassionate intercessor and source of refuge), and Brigid (patroness of healing, poetry, and protection) are revered as guardians who embody both strength and tenderness. These spiritual figures are not abstract ideals; they are culturally living presences with specific energies that can be called upon for grounding, guidance, and regulation. Through prayer, dance, chant, or visualization, individuals can summon these protectors to support emotional resilience and somatic containment.

Touch too can become a ritual of reclamation. When emotions surge, wrapping your arms around yourself or placing your hands on your heart and belly can offer containment. This self-holding sends a signal to your nervous system: "I am here. I am safe. I am holding myself." You can also imagine placing overwhelming emotions into a locked container of your unique design that only you can lock and unlock, knowing you can return to them when you feel more resourced. These visualizations do not deny emotion; they offer structure to help us metabolize it gently over time (Fisher, 2021).

Another gentle, yet potent tool is bilateral stimulation. Borrowed from eye movement desensitization and reprocessing (EMDR) therapy and adapted for everyday use, this practice involves alternating stimulation on the left and right sides of the body through eye movements, tapping, or sound. When done slowly and with intention, bilateral stimulation can help discharge the emotional charge of a trigger while reinforcing new beliefs and inner safety (Shapiro, 2017). It is as though the brain is walking itself back into balance—left foot, then right; left, then right——until the whole system begins to calm.

Bilateral stimulation works by gently engaging both hemispheres of the brain, creating a rhythmic back and forth that can help soothe distress and rewire limiting and rigid beliefs. Neuroscientists believe this left-right movement fosters communication between the brain's emotional and rational centers, allowing charged memories and maladaptive beliefs to be processed with greater ease (Shapiro, 2017). It's like rowing across a river: one oar, then the other—alternating strokes that carry you forward across the waters of your experience. Without both sides working in coordination, you might spin in circles. But when each side takes its turn, you begin to move with intention, guided and whole. This pendulum-like rhythm does not erase pain. But it helps metabolize it, giving the nervous system a structured pathway toward coherence and allowing new adaptive beliefs to take root—beliefs that resource us and support greater vitality.

Slow bilateral tapping can be paired with NLP reframes, creating a powerful practice rooted in EMDR resourcing techniques. For example, as you repeat an empowering belief ("I can seek and cocreate love, regardless of my past"), tap gently on your shoulders or knees, left, then right—letting the rhythm support the installation of this new truth. As you continue, invite memories of times when this belief felt true and imagine future moments when you hope to embody it. In doing so, you engage both memory and imagination, weaving resilience into your nervous system. Over time, this practice becomes a soothing ritual, one that helps anchor new beliefs into lived experience (Dispenza, 2017).

Pendulation, the somatic rhythm of moving between activation and calm, also finds resonance here. As you begin to explore a trigger or emotion, do so with lightness and care. Dip into the discomfort, then shift into a resourced state by utilizing a calming breath, a safe memory, or a grounding practice. With each pendulation, the nervous system learns that it can feel intensity and return to safety. You are teaching your body that overwhelm is not forever. You are proving to your heart that it can feel deeply without descending into chaos while being tenderly held (Levine, 2010).

Indigenous cultures have long understood the power of ritual and storytelling in working with triggers. In many traditions, emotional pain is not pathologized, but honored. Ceremonies, songlines, and healing circles provide containers for emotional release and communal witnessing. Among the Diné people, the Beauty Way ceremony restores harmony after hardship (Kahn-John (Diné) & Koithan, 2015). In the Irish *seanchaí* tradition, myths and stories were shared aloud to make meaning of grief and trauma (Ó Madagáin, 1985). Through these rituals, the nervous system is not left alone to process pain; it is held within the arms of culture, rhythm, and meaning.

To work with your own triggers, begin with awareness. Reflect on a recent moment of reactivity. What sparked it? Where did you feel it in your body? What story did it awaken? Use these reflections not to judge yourself, but to get closer to the wound with compassion. Then begin to apply the practices in this chapter. Name the belief. Reframe it. Call on your protector. Use your hands. Use your breath. Slowly tap. Move. Speak aloud a new truth. Let these tools become a bridge from the old to the new.

You may not be able to stop triggers from arising, but you can change your relationship with them. You can soften the edges. You can shorten the recovery time. You can move from reaction to response. And over time, the things that once undid you will become portals to your strength. Triggers, once seen only as danger, become invitations, opportunities to revisit what was once unbearable and to rewrite the ending.

In the quiet after a trigger, in the breath that follows a remembered pain, you can say to yourself, "I survived that. I am here now. I am safe." And little by little, your nervous system will believe you.

Case Study
Jordan and the Lizard Brain

Jordan was thirty-six when they finally received a diagnosis: complex post-traumatic stress disorder (C-PTSD). It came after years of being misdiagnosed with anxiety, depression, and even bipolar disorder—none of which fully captured the tangled, aching reality of their inner world. Raised in a chronically chaotic home by a parent with untreated mental illness and another who was emotionally absent, Jordan learned early that the safest way to exist was to not exist fully at all.

They moved through life in a constant state of alert. Relationships exhausted them. Conflict shut them down. Even praise made them squirm. At the heart of it all was a ruthless internal narrator—what Jordan, half jokingly and half terrified, called "my lizard brain."

"It's like there's this angry little creature in the back of my skull," they said during one session. "And it's constantly whispering the worst possible things about me. About everything. Like 'You're too much. You're not enough. No one will stay. Everything good will crumble. Everyone will leave, especially if you need them.' It never shuts up. It just forecasts doom like the weather."

Their lizard brain didn't just speak in words; it also shouted through hard-to-ignore sensations. A tightening in the chest when someone didn't reply to a text. Nausea when asked to speak up at work. Numbness when someone complimented them. Underneath it all was the body memory of having once been too vulnerable, too visible, and not protected.

In therapy, Jordan began by identifying the pattern: the moment of activation, the belief it woke up, and the bodily reaction that followed. Jordan became a quiet observer of their own nervous system. After a conflict with a friend, they'd journal, "The lizard brain says I ruined it. That I'm unlovable. But is that true, or is that just an old fear showing up to a new party?"

Slowly, Jordan's therapist introduced new tools: bilateral tapping paired with new affirmations. "Regardless of what my lizard brain says, I am here. I am learning. I am loved." Jordan found comfort in the rhythm. "It's like I'm rocking myself through the panic," they said.

Next came the introduction of a competent protector. At first, Jordan scoffed. "You mean like a superhero?" But when invited to explore further, an image arose: a great blue heron, standing calm in stormy waters. Tall. Still. Watchful. "That's who I want with me when my brain starts spinning out." They began visualizing the heron standing beside them during moments of overwhelm, seeing the heron on the subway, during hard conversations, and in the grocery store when the crowd felt too thick.

In therapy, Jordan also used pendulation with their therapist's guidance. Jordan practiced touching into the discomfort just long enough to name it, then shifting into a resourcing practice, calling forward a favorite song, a warm blanket, a memory of being held. Their nervous system began to learn the following: *I can feel and survive. I can return.*

Over months, the voice of the lizard brain softened. It didn't disappear. C-PTSD healing is not linear, and Jordan still had days where everything felt raw. But there was a difference now. They could say, "That's my lizard brain talking," and choose not to obey. They could feel the fear without becoming the fear. They could ask their competent protector to walk them home to themselves.

One day, after a vulnerable conversation with a friend that ended in reassurance instead of rejection, Jordan smiled through tears. "The lizard brain predicted the worst again. But this time, it was wrong, and I didn't let it crash the bus."

This is the heart of trigger work—not eliminating our protective instincts, but retraining them. Honoring the lizard brain for trying to keep us safe while also letting our deeper self, the one committed to healing, take the lead.

Journal and Reflection Prompts
1. What Does My Lizard Brain Say?

When you feel triggered, what is the internal narrative that arises? Write down the exact words or tone your "lizard brain" uses. Whose voice does it sound like? What does it try to protect you from?

2. **Mapping a Trigger in the Body**

   Recall a recent triggering moment. Where did you feel it in your body? What was the shape, color, or sensation? What happened next—emotionally, physically, relationally?

3. **Rewriting the Script**

   Take one of the negative beliefs your lizard brain repeats and apply the "regardless" reframe. For example, "I am a burden" becomes "I am worthy of support, regardless of what I was taught to believe." How does that shift feel in your body?

4. **Calling in Protection**

   Visualize or describe your competent protector. What qualities do they hold? What do they say or do to help you feel safe and anchored? How can you remember to call on them in moments of overwhelm?

5. **Reclaiming Response over Reaction**

   Think of a time when you were able to pause and respond instead of react. What helped you do that? What can you carry forward from that experience into future trigger moments?

Somatic Ritual: From Fire to Ground

A ritual designed to help regulate the nervous system after a trigger, reclaim a sense of agency and install a new compassionate belief through breath, movement, and visualization. To begin, find a quiet space. You may wish to bring a journal, a blanket, or an object that feels grounding or protective to you.

1. **Grounding Through Touch (2–3 minutes)**

   Place one hand on your heart and the other on your belly. Feel your breath rise and fall. Say the following to yourself slowly:

"I am here."

"I am with myself."

"In order to be here now, I have successfully survived every moment of my life."

2. **Naming the Narrative (3–5 minutes)**

   Gently name the trigger and belief that arose. You can say aloud the following:

   "I was triggered by . . ."

   "My lizard brain says . . . [insert negative belief]*"*

   Take a moment to thank this voice for trying to protect you. You might say the following:

   "Thank you for trying to keep me safe. I see you. But I choose something new."

3. **Bilateral Tapping with Reframe (3–5 minutes)**

   Cross your arms and tap *slowly* left-right-left on your upper arms or knees while repeating a reframe such as the following:

   "I am safe now, regardless of what I once believed."

   "Regardless of past experiences, I am learning to stay with myself, even when it's hard."

   "Regardless of what I have lived through, I am worthy of care, even in moments of overwhelm."

4. **Calling in the Protector (2–3 minutes)**

   Close your eyes and visualize your competent protector. Feel their presence beside you. Imagine them placing a hand on your shoulder, whispering a message of safety and strength. Stay with this image until you feel your breath begin to slow.

5. **Anchoring in the Present (2 minutes)**

Open your eyes and name three objects around you. Wiggle your fingers and toes. Press your feet into the floor. Say aloud the following:

"This is now. I am safe in this moment. My body belongs to me, here and now."

6. **Sealing the Ritual (1–2 minutes)**

Place your hands over your heart. Offer gratitude to your body for showing up, to your protector for guiding you, and to yourself for returning. You might say the following:

"I choose healing. I choose presence. I choose me."

11

Opening the Window of Tolerance
to Let the Light In

Although the world is full of suffering,
it is also full of the overcoming of it.

—Helen Keller, *Optimism*

There is a threshold within each of us, a subtle line between what we can hold and what overwhelms us. Some days, that threshold is wide and generous. We meet frustration with grace, grief with presence. Other days, the smallest touch of stress sends us spiraling into panic, numbness, or dissociation. This range of emotional capacity is known as the "window of tolerance," a term coined by Dr. Dan Siegel to describe the optimal zone where our nervous system can process life without collapse or chaos. Trauma narrows this window. Healing, through daily practices of nervous system hygiene, invites it to widen.

Healing is not a destination; it is a rhythm. An unending dance of rupture and repair. Expanding the window is not about holding ourselves in perfect regulation, but about learning to stay with ourselves through the glorious mess of being alive. It is about threading somatic awareness into the blanket of everyday life, so safety is not a place we visit, but where we live. And slowly, we begin to understand that we must spill out some tears to make room for joy. We must let the ache have its say so that delight can find its echo. The body cannot receive what it has not made space for. Pleasure needs space to land; and the body, emptied of what it no longer needs to carry, becomes a vessel ready to receive.

We begin by listening to our activation. Each body speaks its own dialect. The flutter in your chest, the fog in your mind, the heat behind your eyes—these are not nuisances to ignore. They are guides. Hyperarousal may feel like a clenched jaw, racing thoughts, or a pounding heart. Hypoarousal might show up as a heavy fog, a numbing stillness, or the urge to disappear. Both are natural nervous system responses. Neither is a failure. They are your body trying to protect you the only way it knows how.

Instead of fearing these states, we learn to meet them with gentle inquiry. Curiosity becomes a balm, a doorway, a method of reentry. What if we didn't recoil from activation but moved toward it with kindness? What if we could hold it—not as a danger, but as a signal, seeing it as a flare from the inner world saying, "This needs your attention"? When we stop pathologizing our symptoms and start listening to them, we begin to unlock the body's encoded messages. These responses are not random. They are patterned. And every pattern has a story.

Start by recalling a time when you felt at ease, perhaps sipping tea on your porch or watching the morning light dance across your bed. What did your body feel like in that moment? Was your breath slow? Your gaze soft? That is the center of your window of tolerance. Now remember a moment of overwhelm. Where did you go? What shut down or spun out? This is one of your edges. To expand your window is to stretch gently toward those edges and return, supported by the brain's neuroplasticity, which allows us to rewire patterns of threat detection and build new associations with safety. It is not about forcing yourself to feel more; it is about teaching your body that feeling is survivable. That returning is possible. That presence, even in discomfort, can be practiced.

This is where glimmers come in. Coined by Deb Dana, glimmers are the micromoments of safety and joy that often go unnoticed: sunlight on your face, the laugh of a child, the exact right line in a poem. Glimmers are not the opposite of triggers; they are the antidotes. Orienting toward them each day—not as a luxury, but as a necessity—reminds the nervous system that safety is not a fluke. It is a state we can find, nourish, and return to. This is daily work. Not a one-and-done workshop or weekend retreat, but a way of being.

This work of tending to the nervous system also includes rest, not just collapse but also true restoration. Tricia Hersey, founder of the Nap Ministry, teaches that rest is not laziness, but resistance against systems of oppression. In a society that demands constant output, productivity, and urgency—often at the expense of Black, Brown, disabled, and marginalized bodies—choosing to rest becomes a radical act of reclamation. Hersey invites us to see rest as a portal to healing and repair, as well as a refusal to conform to White supremacist and capitalist systems that profit from our exhaustion (Hersey, 2022). This is not the dorsal vagal collapse of dissociation, but intentional nourishing rest that brings the body back into regulation. A slow breath under a blanket. A still moment with your eyes closed, letting gravity hold you. These are acts of defiance and devotion. They say, "I am not a machine. I am a being. My worth is not in what I produce, but in who I am." Rest then becomes both a somatic medicine and a political statement against the dehumanizing forces of capitalism, one that restores dignity to our nervous systems and honors our ancestral right to rest.

Indigenous cultures have long practiced daily forms of nervous system hygiene through ritual, song, movement, and storytelling (Dumont, 2014; Haskie, 2023). In Andean traditions, the *despacho*, an offering to Pachamama (Mother Earth), serves as both spiritual reverence and grounding ritual. In West African Yoruba culture, daily drumming and invocation of the orisha help attune the body to rhythm, regulate emotion, and restore communal harmony. These rituals are designed not to transcend the body, but to consciously inhabit it with grounded reverence and presence (Mead, 2003).

Similarly, in many contemporary religious traditions, daily embodied practices serve as powerful regulators of the nervous system. In Islam, the five daily prayers (salat) invite grounding through rhythmic movement, breath awareness, and connection to the divine (Gebirrebbi, 2025). Catholicism offers the rosary and contemplative prayer—engaging breath, repetition, and the regulation of emotion through structured ritual (McGuire, 2003). In Zen Buddhism, walking meditation and breath-focused mindfulness cultivate present-moment awareness and internal spaciousness (Dudeja, 2022; Kabat-Zinn, 2005, Maezumi & Glassman, 2002). Hinduism incorporates daily puja (ritual worship), chanting, and yoga as integrated body-spirit practices that align and soothe the system (Frawley, 1997). In Judaism, practices such as morning blessings (*birkot hashachar*) and the wrapping of tefillin create structured, somatically informed moments of connection, containment, and meaning (Levine, 2010). These traditions, in their own ways, affirm what somatic psychology now teaches: that daily embodied ritual helps us regulate, remember, and return to ourselves.

Pleasure is not indulgence. It is medicine. It is a balm for a body that has braced too long, a light in the neural dark. As adrienne maree brown reminds us in her work on pleasure activism, pleasure can be a revolutionary act. A daily embodied declaration that we deserve wholeness and joy, even in a world shaped by oppression and trauma. She teaches that choosing pleasure is not selfish, but strategic. It reclaims the body as a site of liberation, reminding us that aliveness is our birthright and that joy is not a distraction from justice; it is a fuel for it (brown, 2019).

One breath taken in full awareness. One note of music felt resonating in your chest like a tuning fork. One bite of food savored slowly, as if it were sacred. These are not small things. They are microrevolutions. Each act of sensual presence says, "I deserve to feel good. My body is a site not only of pain but also of pleasure. I am allowed to inhabit this skin not only as survivor but also as celebrant. I can dance down the pain inside me, stomp it through my feet, and offer it to the earth for regeneration."

Pleasure reminds the nervous system that safety is possible. Each time we allow ourselves to feel pleasure, not just in theory but also in the texture of the moment, we expand what is possible inside our window. This is not wishful thinking; it is neurobiological reality. Mindfully savored pleasure stimulates the release of dopamine, oxytocin, and serotonin—the neurochemicals associated with reward, bonding, and well-being (Porges, 2011; Siegel, 2020). These chemicals, in turn, reinforce the brain's sense of safety and connection, supporting a shift from sympathetic arousal into parasympathetic restoration.

Our relationship with pleasure is also where we begin to reclaim the nonsexual erotic—the quiet sensuous field of aliveness that lives beneath productivity, beyond performance. This form of eroticism is not about sexuality, but about vitality. It is the warm press of sun on skin, the weight of a soft blanket across the thighs, the thrill of a color that stirs something unnamed in the chest. It is the hum of presence when chopping garlic or dancing alone in the kitchen, the pulse that rises when something feels sacred, even if no one else sees it. It is the enjoyment of coming home to ourselves and the celebration of shamelessly being in our body, however momentarily, as we build our capacity for even more self-intimacy. These experiences aren't solely reserved for moments of intimacy with others; they are profoundly important intimate moments with the self.

To engage the erotic in this way is to acknowledge the body as a site of perception, of wonder, of responsiveness. It is to relate to life not from numbness or distance, but from participation. This is a somatic practice. To notice when your breath catches in beauty. When your body leans toward a scent or a song. When your skin prickles with memory or awe. The nonsexual erotic invites you to root your awareness in your felt sense—not to be consumed, but to be *in communion* with the aliveness that moves through you. It is where the sacred meets the sensory. It is the body remembering that it is not only functional; it is also exquisite.

When we honor this dimension of ourselves, we allow more texture into our emotional palette. We begin to notice nuance. Subtlety. Desire that isn't transactional, but devotional. We soften the hardened edges left by trauma and return to the tender curiosity that signals safety. This is nervous system expansion through the portal of embodied pleasure—an awakening not to stimulus, but to *sensation*. A reminder that your aliveness does not need to be earned. It already lives here, pulsing beneath your skin.

Over time, these small doses of goodness begin to rewire the nervous system. We stop orienting solely toward what might go wrong and begin to recognize what is already right. We stop holding our breath and start living into it. We learn to linger in warmth, to dwell in beauty, to follow the trail of what feels good without apology. And in doing so, we don't turn away from the world's pain; we simply refuse to forget our joy within it.

This daily orientation to somatic presence means giving our emotions and urges the space they've long been denied. It is a conscious refusal to abandon ourselves the moment discomfort arises. Rather than overriding with logic, numbing with distraction, or shoving the feeling aside in the name of productivity, we pause. We listen. We allow. We make the radical choice to *stay*. To feel. To name.

The urge to lash out may not be aggression. It might be a flare of old pain, a reflex born of fear, a defense shaped by betrayal. The tightness in the chest, the heat behind the eyes, the tear you blink back may carry a message, a whisper from the body saying, "This matters." Emotions are not interruptions to be silenced; they are information to be honored. They are signals from the interior, alerts that something within us wants tending. They are not mistakes. They are messengers.

Over time, we want to come to a place where we can trust our activation. We may rightfully never *enjoy* being triggered, but we can begin to see it as a form of internal communication, not a personal failure. Activation is the body's way of saying, "Something needs your attention." It may be pointing to a current threat or reactivating an old wound still waiting to be acknowledged. Either way, the signal is sacred. It is not proof of brokenness; it is proof that something in us is alive and trying to speak. The answers we seek aren't always found outside of us. Often, they live inside the activation itself, waiting for us to enter into conversation with it— to meet it, support it, process it, and let it resolve.

And like waves, emotions rise and crest. If we let them come, if we allow ourselves to be moved rather than braced against, those waves will pass. They may leave us weeping, trembling, sighing, or utterly still. But more often than not, they leave us softened, not broken. Changed, not ruined. Cleansed, not undone. This is the nervous system completing its cycle, feeling what needs to be felt, then settling.

To live this way, to truly orient to somatic presence, is to live with reverence for every flicker of sensation, every stirring of feeling. It is to trust that what arises has wisdom. That discomfort is not the enemy. That we are vast enough to hold the full complexity of being alive. To be embodied, or *em-bodied*, is to be in your *emotional body*—in tune with the sensations attached to your emotions. And it is to remember, again and again, that feeling fully is not weakness; it is *freedom*. Freedom from numbness, from self-abandonment, from the invisible prisons built by unprocessed pain.

Play, humor, and laughter are not sidenotes to this work; they are central. Neuroscience shows that curiosity and fear cannot exist in the brain at the same time. The same is true of anxiety and laughter. When we laugh, even softly, we signal safety to the nervous system. When we play, we disrupt the rigidity of trauma and remind the body that not all surprise is danger. Try it: Make a ridiculous face in the mirror. Watch a toddler dance. Let yourself giggle. These are not childish things. They are radical nervous system hygiene practices. Neuroscientific studies reveal that laughter stimulates the prefrontal cortex, the part of the brain involved in emotional regulation, and activates the vagus nerve, enhancing parasympathetic activity and reducing stress hormones like cortisol (Porges, 2011; Sapolsky, 2004). Laughter and play say, "Joy is safe. Levity is allowed. They help to open the window."

Healing doesn't always have to hurt. Some days, healing is downright hilarious. It doesn't only come to shore through deep dives into grief; it can also sail in on a fit of laughter, loud and unexpected. Let yourself be taken up by it: the kind of laughter that foot-stomps and table-slaps, that folds you forward until you can't breathe. Then do just that—*breathe*. Inhale deeply, stretching the inner spaces of your mouth, your throat, your diaphragm. Let the tears run freely down your cheeks—not from sorrow, but from release. As your breath slows and your body opens back up and outward, feel your nervous system follow. Settling and softening, reset by the rising tide of your own joy.

Make it a habit. Let curiosity be your daily balm. Research in affective neuroscience suggests that curiosity and creativity are supported by neural pathways distinct from those activated during anxiety. Anxiety tends to narrow attentional focus and engage threat-monitoring circuits in the amygdala and anterior insula, while creativity and open exploration activate the brain's default mode network, associated with imagination and integrative thinking (Beaty et al., 2016). This means the brain struggles to be both creatively expansive and anxiously vigilant at the same time. By fostering curiosity, we invite the brain into a state that is neurologically incompatible with fear. Ask the following: What if this tension in my chest is trying to help me? What if I can move through this with wonder instead of dread? Laughter is not always the absence of seriousness; it is often the body's way of metabolizing the unbearable. It is both medicine and evidence of aliveness.

If we want to expand our window of tolerance, we must stop pretending we can do it alone. Self-regulation is vital, but coregulation is ancient. It is how we first learned to survive, and it is how we are meant to heal. Connection is not an accessory to healing. It is the architecture of it. Healing and repair are communal. Always have been. Always will be. Social connection, therefore, is not optional; it is foundational for widening our window of tolerance. It is the original regulator, the first language our nervous systems ever spoke. Before we had words, we had touch. We had the cadence of a caregiver's voice, the safety of being held.

Polyvagal theory reminds us that we are quite literally wired for coregulation. According to Porges (2011), the ventral vagal branch of the parasympathetic nervous system links the heart, lungs, and facial muscles—supporting our capacity for social engagement, softening the edges of our defenses, and allowing us to feel safe in the presence of others. In attuned connection, we are able to breathe more fully, speak more freely, and rest more deeply. In the eyes of another who sees us with compassion, our system exhales. This is why eye contact, shared rhythm, and attuned presence are not luxuries; they are lifelines. They pull us from the brink. They remind our bodies "you are not alone." Group singing, communal meals, call-and-response prayers, and storytelling circles are not merely traditions; they are also nervous system medicine. They have endured across time and culture not because they are quaint, but because they are effective. They remind us that healing was never meant to be solitary. We regulate with the most ease in the presence of others who are calm, present, and safe.

Make it a point to connect daily. Hug someone and stay long enough to feel the exhale. Send a silly video to a friend and let your laughter braid across distance. Let someone witness you, really see you, even for a moment. And if no one is physically near, let memory be your bridge. Recall a moment you felt loved or truly seen and let that warmth resurface in your body. The nervous system doesn't need proof, only a felt sense of safety, even if imagined. That is the brilliance of neuroplasticity: It allows us to build new pathways—moment by moment, breath by breath.

Remember, this is a lifelong daily practice. A thousand small returns and connections. Some days, you will feel like a storm.

Other days, like a quiet field. Neither is better. The point is not to stay calm. The point is to stay *with* yourself through it all. To become the one your nervous system learns to trust. Over time, your window will widen. Not just so you can endure more but also so you can *feel* more—more joy, more presence, more nuance. So you can dance in the tension between sorrow and celebration. So you can be fully, fiercely alive and beautifully human.

Case Study
Raquel's Window

Raquel, a forty-two-year-old former paramedic, used to describe herself as high-functioning, but perpetually on edge. She had spent years in the grip of emergencies, including car crashes, cardiac arrests, shootings, and suicides—training her body to override panic, to act swiftly and selflessly in the face of chaos. Long before that, she had been shaped by a childhood of inconsistent caregiving and emotional volatility. Her nervous system, forged in crisis, learned vigilance as safety. "Either I'm wound so tight I can't sleep," she told her therapist. "Or I crash for fourteen hours and sleep like the dead."

In therapy, Raquel began to gently trace the contours of her survival patterns. With compassionate guidance, she mapped her nervous system states, recognizing the telltale edges of her window of tolerance. Irritability, muscle clenching, and obsessive thinking marked her sympathetic overdrive. Numbness, social media scrolling, and disconnection signaled her drop into dorsal collapse. Both were familiar territories. What was new was the practice of noticing without judgment. She began to orient to these inner landscapes as weather patterns—temporary, responsive, and rooted in something intelligent.

Her therapist introduced her to the concept of *glimmers*, the subtle moments when the nervous system feels safe enough to soften. At first, Raquel struggled to identify any. Safety had long felt like a foreign language. But gradually, she began to notice flickers: the smell of coffee blooming in the morning, the golden arc of her cat stretching in a sunbeam, the aching beauty of a cello concerto. These weren't cures. They were footholds, tiny affirmations of aliveness.

Together, they practiced anchoring these glimmers through breath, touch, and bilateral tapping. One hand on the heart. One hand on the belly. Breathing into the now. These rituals became small acts of nervous system hygiene, like brushing her teeth or washing her face, but for her sense of safety.

Raquel also rediscovered something she hadn't known she'd lost: her laugh. Not the polite social chuckle, but the deep belly laugh that startled her with its sincerity. It reemerged in the most unexpected of places: an improv class. At first, it felt like a risk. But each week, she showed up, trembling, but willing. Improv invited her to be present without a script, to listen with her body, to say "yes, and . . ." to whatever arose. It was the first space where she didn't have to rescue or perform. She could just be. Fallible. Playful. Whole.

The freedom to follow her urges, to move toward what felt good without justification was revolutionary. In those rooms, she wasn't evaluated for competence or praised for sacrifice. She was celebrated for cocreation, for presence. Laughter became medicine. Vulnerability became an opening, not a danger.

"It's the only place I don't feel like I'm bracing for impact," she said. When a panic wave rose before class one evening, she placed a hand on her chest and one on her belly, breathing into the re-membered warmth of a scene that had once left her gasping with laughter. Instead of spiraling, she grounded.

Raquel also began to weave social connection into her daily life—not grand gestures, but gentle threads of belonging. She walked regularly with a neighbor, allowing silence to be companionable. She made a pact with herself: When she noticed the pull to isolate, she would send a simple text: "Thinking of you." It wasn't about fixing loneliness, but about interrupting the inertia of withdrawal.

Over the course of months, Raquel's window of tolerance slowly widened. Not because she stopped experiencing anxiety or shutdown, but because she no longer feared them. She knew how to listen, how to respond with care. She developed her own internal rituals: stepping outside for air when her chest tightened, humming when her voice felt stuck, letting her dog curl into her lap when tears came unannounced.

The rhythm of her healing became less about breakthroughs and more about maintenance in daily loving acts that said, "You matter. I'm with you." Her nervous system didn't need to be tamed. It needed to be heard, befriended, accompanied.

"For the first time," she told her therapist, "my nervous system doesn't feel like an enemy. It feels like a language I'm finally learn-ing to speak."

Journal and Reflection Prompts

1. What are some sensations or signs that let you know you are within your window of tolerance? What about when you are outside of it?

2. What does your body feel like when it experiences a glimmer? Can you identify three glimmers from today?

3. Think of a recent moment when your body truly needed rest—not the kind that comes from shutting down or crashing, but the kind that gently invites you to soften, slow down, and return to yourself. What signals did your body give you that rest was needed? How did you respond?

4. In what ways can you begin to tell the difference between restorative rest and nervous system collapse? What does necessary chosen rest feel like in your body? Is it warm? Spacious? Quiet? Connected?

5. What is one somatic practice that reliably brings you back into your body? Describe a recent moment when you used it.

6. How do you respond to urges or emotions that feel inconvenient? How might you create more space for them to be explored safely?

7. What roles do humor, play, and social connection currently have in your life? How might you invite more of them in?

Somatic Ritual: Return to the Center

This ritual is for moments when your inner landscape feels flooded or far away, when you've lost touch with your body's quiet center, or when joy feels just out of reach. Let this practice be a gentle tether, a way back to your aliveness.

1. **Begin in stillness.**

   Find a quiet, uninterrupted space. Sit upright with support or lie down in a shape that feels like a sigh. Allow your body to settle without effort. Let gravity hold you. Close your eyes if that feels safe or soften your gaze. Take three slow breaths, inhaling through your nose and exhaling out your mouth with sound. Let the exhale lengthen. Let your weight drop just a little more. You are not here to perform. You are here to be.

2. **Name your edges.**

   Gently bring to mind a recent moment when you felt overwhelmed, agitated, numb, or disconnected. Let the image or sensation arrive without trying to fix or change it. Now ask, "Where does this live in my body?" Scan gently. Maybe it's a tight jaw, a clenching in the belly, a hollowness in the chest. Wherever you find it, place one hand over that area. Name the sensation aloud: tightness, burning, buzzing, dullness, static, collapse. You are bearing witness. You are bringing curiosity and dialogue to the place that is activated within you.

3. **Call in a glimmer.**

   Now bring to mind a glimmer—a fleeting, but real moment from today or yesterday that brought ease. It could be sunlight on your skin, the sound of birdsong, the way someone smiled at you, the smell of tea, a line from a poem. Let it bloom slowly in your memory. Where do you feel this glimmer in your body? Does your breath shift? Do your shoulders lower? Place your other hand on this part of your body. Let the warmth of your palms hold both: the place of activation and the place of peace.

4. **Pendulate between the two.**

Begin to gently pendulate, moving your attention back and forth between the sensation of discomfort and the sensation of the glimmer. There is no rush. No need to force symmetry. You are building a bridge. Use your breath, sound, or bilateral tapping to support the movement: Tap gently on each knee or rock slightly from side to side. You might say to yourself, "This is discomfort, and this is safety. Both can exist. I can move between them." Repeat the pendulation three to five times. Rest between each round. This is how we build capacity, by not getting stuck in either extreme.

5. **Use laughter as medicine.**

Now invite in a moment of levity. Recall something that made you laugh, truly laugh, in recent memory. A misheard phrase. A child's unfiltered honesty. A moment when you surrendered to silliness. Let it rise. If you can't recall a moment, try making a silly face, humming a ridiculous tune, or letting your shoulders do a loose little dance. Feel what shifts in your body when you choose to make space for play. Let your face soften. Let a small smile, if it comes, be a form of resistance and repair.

6. **Return to the present.**

Begin your return. Slowly open your eyes or lift your gaze. Name three objects in your environment aloud. Let your voice be soft, but clear. Wiggle your fingers. Wiggle your toes. Roll your shoulders or stretch your spine like you're waking from a long rest.

Now say softly to yourself, "I am here. I am safe enough. I am allowed to return to myself, again and again."

Let your hands come to rest over your heart or one on your belly. Feel the rhythm. This is your center. This is your return.

12

Stories of Healing: Feeling Your Aliveness by Cultivating Meaning and Purpose

Out of suffering have emerged the strongest souls;
the most massive characters are seared with scars.

—Kahlil Gibran

Aliveness, meaning, and purpose are often spoken of as if they are one thing, braided so tightly we forget they are separate strands. Yet each arises from a distinct current inside the nervous system, and each returns through its own doorway. Healing invites us to learn the texture of each thread: their differences, their longings, and the way they find their way back to one another.

Aliveness is the first to stir. It is not a mindset nor an act of will; it is a physiological state. When the body senses even a whisper of safety, the ventral vagal pathways begin to glow again, restoring the rhythms of connection and curiosity (Porges, 2011). Breath deepens. Heart rate steadies. The window of tolerance widens, allowing life to feel less jagged, less overwhelming, more possible.

This is the return of interoception, the inner listening that lets us feel the subtle landscape within—the warmth behind the sternum, the soft pull toward color, the slight lift that comes when something in us says *yes*. Even after trauma, even in grief, even under the weight of oppression, this *yes* does not extinguish. It simply retreats until kindness, coregulation, stillness, or one small glimmer is enough to coax it forward again. Aliveness whispers, "I want to be here. I want to feel again."

Meaning enters differently. It does not rush; it settles. Meaning is the inner coherence that forms when our experiences, emotions, and memories begin to weave together into a narrative the body can trust. This coherence is the fruit of integration, as the brain links separated regions and restores a sense of wholeness after fragmentation (Siegel, 2010). Meaning is not an idea we invent; it is a harmony we feel.

We know we've touched it when something inside aligns with a soft inward click: a sigh that empties the lungs, a warmth gathering behind the eyes, a steadiness in the spine that feels earned. When trauma or chronic stress disrupts the nervous system's sense of continuity, meaning can dissolve into numbness or disconnection. But it returns in glimmers: a sudden laugh, a fleeting moment of beauty, a tenderness we didn't expect. These are not accidents. They are the nervous system reclaiming access to significance. Meaning is the depth beneath our days. It is the pulse that tells us, "This matters. I matter. My life belongs to something larger than my labor or my wounds."

Purpose moves differently still. If meaning roots us, purpose reaches outward. It is the forward-oriented energy of the nervous system, the somatic orientation toward what feels life-giving. Purpose awakens when the body begins responding to reward and motivation pathways, the neural circuitry that lights up when we move toward something aligned with our values, creativity, or contribution. These systems release dopamine, not in the service of hype or hustle but as the quiet fuel that gives us direction. And when purpose is relational or creative, oxytocin deepens the sense of safety, reminding us that our movement toward others is not dangerous but connecting.

Purpose does not require certainty. It asks only for resonance, a faint leaning toward what feels true. Even the smallest sense of direction can begin to gather the scattered parts of self, organizing inner chaos into coherence. This too is neuroscience: neuroplasticity shaping itself around what we move toward, not simply what we move away from. Purpose declares, "I have something to offer the world."

Aliveness opens the door.

Meaning deepens the ground.

Purpose gives direction.

Together, they form a living braid that stabilizes the nervous system and expands our capacity for sensation, complexity, and intimacy. Without safety, the body retreats into survival. Without meaning, life flattens. Without purpose, energy collapses inward. But with even one gentle cue of safety, the system begins its slow return. Neural pathways strengthen. Integration grows. The rhythms of curiosity and connection restore themselves.

For those who have lived inside trauma, grief, or dehumanizing systems, these capacities often go offline—not because of personal failure, but because the body has been asked to endure more than it has been allowed to inhabit. Survival narrows imagination.

Oppression constricts meaning-making. Grief smudges purpose until everything feels equally heavy. Yet the return always begins at the edges: the breath that softens the chest, the color that draws the eye, the task that leaves the body fuller instead of emptied, the single tear that feels like truth rather than threat.

These small openings are neurobiological thresholds, tiny but profound signs that the body is recalibrating toward life again. This chapter traces those thresholds: how aliveness rekindles through safety, how meaning pulses through integration, and how purpose gently reorients a life toward what feels coherent and true. These stories are reminders that the nervous system can mend, that the spirit can return to itself, and that a life once fractured can be rewoven—slowly, tenderly, inevitably—into something whole.

Eli: The Musician Who Found His Voice Again

Eli, a jazz pianist, lost his will to play after a devastating break-up and the death of his musician father. Grief silenced his hands. The piano became an artifact of a former life. He became disassociated from his sense of rhythm, joy, and expression. In therapy, Eli began using breath and gentle touch to reconnect with his chest and hands. He practiced orienting to glimmers: the smell of aged wood, the feel of keys under fingers. One day, he played a single note. It vibrated through the room and through his heart. That note became a doorway. He began to play again—not to perform, but to feel. In the safety of weekly community music circles, he explored his voice in new ways, including drumming and vocal improvisation. Over time, he began facilitating healing improvisation sessions for grieving men, integrating purpose with vulnerability.

"I don't just make music now," he said. "I let it move through me. It's how I remember who I am."

Maya: The Mother Who Reclaimed Her Joy

After postpartum depression and years of self-abandonment in parenting, Maya felt invisible. Her art supplies gathered dust. Her sense of self was faint. In her sessions, Maya and her therapists used body mapping and grounding to locate small sensations of color, pleasure, and longing. She began drawing again—not masterpieces, but doodles on envelopes, chalk drawings on the sidewalk with her daughter. Eventually, she created a daily altar, where she lit candles and painted abstract representations of her mood on index cards. Her nervous system softened. She reclaimed joy not just through art but also by witnessing herself as someone worthy of beauty. "This," she said, gesturing to the simple canvas filled with brushstrokes, "is what aliveness looks like for me."

Louis: The Activist Who Needed to Rest

Louis had dedicated his life to social justice. But burnout hollowed him out. His body pulsed with anxiety and rage. Rest felt selfish. Pleasure felt impossible. He worked with pendulation, by dipping into his grief, then orienting to the present moment. He began tending a small garden. Each morning, he placed his hands in soil, grounding through scent and sensation. His nervous system began to shift. "I thought I had to burn myself out to change the world," he said. "Now I see that resting is part of the resistance." He still marches. But he also naps, dreams, and teaches younger activists how to care for their bodies while holding the fight.

Aisha: The Perfectionist Turned Mentor

Aisha had lived her life by gold stars marking academic success, professional accolades, relentless achievement. And yet she felt empty. Her nervous system lived in a state of bracing. She often felt sick, anxious, and cold. Somatic tracking helped her notice moments of softness: hot tea, sunlight on her skin, a student's smile. She realized that her true calling wasn't to achieve, but to guide. She became a mentor to first-generation college students. "When I'm mentoring," she said, "my shoulders drop. My breath slows. I feel useful and peaceful." Purpose, for Aisha, wasn't a spotlight; it was a warm room with an open door.

These stories share a pattern: The return to meaning is always also a return to the body. But it's helpful to remember that meaning is not fixed; it evolves. What felt purposeful in one season may shift in another. Purpose is not a single destination, but a living practice. It ebbs and flows with our energy, our relationships, our grief, our joy.

The barriers to purpose are real. But so is the body's ability to remember, reconnect, and rise. Purpose is not a privilege for the healed. It is the path of healing itself. We are not waiting to be worthy of it. We are walking it, one trembling step at a time. We learn to follow what stirs us. Purpose is not always loud. It often arrives quietly, sensed more than declared. There are signs the body gives us when we are living in alignment with what matters. We feel grounded. We can feel our feet firmly planted in the present moment. We feel clear-eyed—that is to say, not free from doubt, but able to hold uncertainty without collapsing. The nervous system settles into a rhythm that makes space for reflection, for connection, for creativity.

When we are on purpose, we often experience an increased tolerance for discomfort. We don't need the path to be easy; we need it to be meaningful. Our bodies signal this through sensations of spaciousness, vitality, and integrity. There may be spontaneous laughter, unexpected tears, or a burst of energy after long fatigue. There may be a synchronicity and coherence that feel like confirmation or a feeling of being gently nudged forward. Curiosity often reappears when we are aligned. So does wonder. So does the desire to connect. These are not random experiences; they are nervous system cues that we are in touch with life. When you are on purpose, even your posture changes. Your breath deepens. You move toward, not away.

Pay attention to these signs. They are your body's way of saying, "Yes. This matters. Keep going."

Each of the stories in this chapter illustrates a truth: Purpose is not something we find all at once. It's something we return to in our own rhythm, again and again. Eli's reconnection with his voice shows how grief, when felt and honored, can become music. Maya's journey into joy reminds us that meaning lives in small daily expressions of beauty. Louis demonstrates that rest and resistance are not opposites, but partners. And Aisha's shift from perfection to mentorship reveals that purpose often begins in softness, not striving. Taken together, these stories teach us that purpose is not a formula; it is a felt sense, an inner orientation that grows more vivid with practice. It is deeply personal and often arises through service, through art, through connection, through stillness. When we learn to track the somatic signals of aliveness, we don't just understand our purpose; we also embody it.

This is your invitation to do the same. To move at the pace of trust. To let your nervous system guide you. To let meaning live not just in your mind but also in your breath, your bones, your daily gestures of care. Aliveness is not far away. It is already within you, waiting for your attention. To truly stay in relationship with that aliveness, we need more than insight—we need access. We need integration practices that help us cross the threshold from concept into connection, from thinking into being. This is where ritual comes in. There is a reason ritual holds such power. It is not performance. It is not routine. It is a forgotten language, a doorway into something deeper than cognition or behavior. Ritual builds a sacred chamber within the nervous system. When movement, breath, attention, and meaning converge, the psyche, soma, and heart align in a single direction: toward mending, toward coherence, toward wholeness. Ritual is the doorway through which the soul steps forward to meet us.

The soul, in this context, is not an abstract or ethereal concept. It is the animating essence of who we are. The soul is the part of us that holds longing and mystery, that remembers what we were born to do, and that aches when we abandon ourselves. It is less concerned with identity than with integrity. Less about role than about resonance and presence. It speaks to us not through logic, but through emotion, through the felt sense in the body. The soul lives in sensation. It knocks with longing. It cries out in despair. It stirs when we witness beauty or truth. The soul does not shout; it trembles, contracts, expands. And it asks us to pay attention.

This is where ritual becomes essential, regardless of one's orientation toward religion or lack thereof. Not optional. Not decorative. But necessary. Because ritual gathers the mind, the heart, and the body into one place. It slows us down enough to notice. It pulls our focus inward. It creates a container for presence, a threshold where something deeper can rise to meet us. In ritual, we engage movement, sound, breath, stillness. We name. We bless. We release. And through these embodied acts, we speak the language of the soul.

This is why grief rituals feel holy. Why dancing alone to a song that unlocks us can feel like resurrection. Why lighting a candle or kneeling on the earth can shift something no conversation could reach. Ritual communicates with the soul because it feels and the soul speaks in the syntax of sensation. For many, trauma has interrupted this channel, leaving us in what Latin American traditions call *susto*: the fright that dislodges the soul, the hollow that follows a shock too great to bear (Martínez-Radl et al., 2023; Glazer et al., 2004). In this state, we learn to override our emotions, to step outside the body simply to survive. We become fluent in the language of endurance, yet estranged from the language of soul. Ritual is what intertwines them back together—body and soul, survival and meaning—carrying us, breath by breath, back into wholeness.

Purpose is not just something we do. It is also someone we remember we are. And ritual is one of the most ancient reliable ways to access that memory and hear our soul's calling. As you reclaim your aliveness, consider that your soul may not ask you to *do* more, but it may ask you to *feel* more. To come home through your breath, your tears, your bare feet on the ground. To pause in a moment of ritual and ask, "What is my soul trying to say?"

The answer may not come in words. It may come as warmth in the chest. As a sigh. As tears. As a steadying.

But it will come.

Journal and Reflection Prompts

1. **When do you feel most alive in your body?** Describe the sensations, images, and movements that accompany this state. Where in your body do you feel a *yes*?

2. **What brings you a felt sense of meaning that is not tied to productivity or performance?** Explore how your body responds when you are connected to what matters rather than what is expected.

3. **How does your body say, "This matters"?** Reflect on the physical signals—possibly in your breath, posture, sensation, or emotion—that arise when you are in alignment with purpose.

4. **Who helps you feel seen—not for what you do, but for who you are?** How does your body respond in their presence? Can you trace the felt experience of being witnessed?

5. **What losses or griefs have clarified what truly matters to you?** In what ways has sorrow refined your sense of purpose or opened new doorways to meaning?

6. **What childhood instincts or imaginal games still live in your body?** Is there a sensory memory (a smell, texture, sound) that brings you back to a time when meaning was simple and embodied?

7. **What small daily ritual could serve as an anchor to your aliveness?** Explore gestures, rhythms, or sensory practices that return you to yourself.

8. **What kind of offering—be it creative, relational, or communal—helps you feel both grounded and expanded?** How

does your nervous system respond when you are in service from overflow rather than depletion?

Somatic Ritual: Anointing the Day with Meaning

This ritual is a simple act of devotion—a way to reclaim the sacred in the ordinary and honor the quiet moments that sustain you. It invites you to recognize meaning not as something to seek, but as something already present, waiting to be felt.

1. **Prepare your space.**

     Find a quiet place where you can be undisturbed for a few minutes. Dim the lights if you wish or light a candle. Let your body settle into the space.

2. **Come into presence.**

     Place one hand gently over your heart and the other over your belly. Feel the warmth of your own presence beneath your palms. Take five slow, nourishing breaths. With each exhale, allow yourself to arrive more fully in this moment.

3. **Remember what mattered.**

     Close your eyes and call to mind one moment from your day that felt quietly meaningful. It doesn't need to be grand. It could be the sound of birdsong, the smile of a stranger, a moment of rest, or an act of kindness you offered. Let your body linger with that memory. Notice any sensations that arise—softening, warmth, steadiness, or emotion.

4. **Name the sacred.**

Whisper softly to yourself, aloud or silently, the following:

This mattered. This was enough.

5. **Anoint with warmth.**

Rub your hands together until you feel heat and energy between them. When ready, gently place your warmed palms over your forehead, your heart, and your belly—pausing at each point to offer presence and gratitude.

6. **Seal the ritual.**

As you complete the ritual, say the following words: *I am walking in meaning. I am alive. I am enough.*

Let this act be a daily practice of devotion to what matters. Not a performance, but a reclamation. Not an effort, but an arrival.

13

Becoming the Medicine, Healing Ourselves, Changing the World

It is one of the most beautiful compensations of this life that no man can sincerely try to help another without helping himself.

—Ralph Waldo Emerson, "Compensation"

There is a moment in every healing journey when the focus shifts, when what began as a desperate search for personal relief transforms into something vaster. You begin to realize that the work you are doing in your own nervous system is not only for you. It radiates. It ripples. It touches the people you love, the spaces you inhabit, the children you raise or mentor, the systems you navigate. It becomes clear: Your regulation is not just healing. It is also medicine.

To regulate your own nervous system in a dysregulated world is a radical act. It is a refusal to pass on harm that was handed to you. It is a declaration that the violence will stop with you. That your body will not be a battlefield—not for your thoughts, your past, or anyone else's expectations. That you will learn to listen instead of override. Soften instead of harden. Choose to stay present, even when it hurts. This is not passive. This is power. And often, it initiates something quiet and unexpected—an invisible shift, a subtle magic, that begins to change not only you but also the room you're in.

We were not meant to live like this. The human nervous system was shaped over millennia in deep relationship with the earth, with seasons, sunlight, communal rhythms, and sacred rest. We are animals with ancient instincts, born to move and breathe and feel in tune with the pulse of life around us. But industrialization disrupted that rhythm. Capitalism exploited it. Technology rewired it. And now many of us live in a near-constant state of low-grade distress, dissociation, and sensory overload.

We wake to alarms. We scroll before we stretch. We answer emails before we speak to a loved one. We consume more information in a day than our ancestors encountered in a year. We sit indoors under artificial light. We eat quickly, often alone. We forget to look at the sky. Our bodies have not evolved for this speed, this fragmentation, this relentless input.

Chronic stress is no longer an exception; it is the norm. And the cost is profound. Neuroscience research has shown that excessive screen time and digital stimulation can reduce the brain's capacity for attention, memory, and emotional regulation (Christakis et al., 2018). The prefrontal cortex becomes overloaded while the amygdala, the brain's fear and reactivity center, remains in overdrive (McEwen & Sapolsky, 1995). This constant activation erodes our ability to track internal cues, regulate our breath, and respond with intention.

Even more concerning is what we lose in the absence of embodied rhythm. When we no longer move in sync with natural cycles of day and night, hunger and fullness, tension and release, we become untethered. The vagus nerve—essential to rest, digestion, and social connection—cannot operate efficiently in a system that never slows down (Porges, 2011). We lose our felt sense of boundaries. We forget what safety even feels like.

But this is not irreversible. The body remembers. Beneath the digital noise, the circadian rhythms still wait. The parasympathetic system still longs to hum. When we choose to reorient to the body and to step away from screens, to eat in silence, to walk without a destination, we begin to repair what industrialized life has fractured. We come back to our original technology: our breath, our blood, our senses.

This return to rhythm is more than personal; it is ancestral and relational. When we begin to repair our nervous systems, we not only restore our own sense of safety but also reenter a lineage of care that capitalism tried to sever. This is our responsibility. And it is also our privilege. Not everyone has access to healing, to safety, to time, to care. But if we do, even in small moments, then our healing becomes an offering. An ethical inheritance. A new story written into our cellular memory and passed down in our energy, our tone, our gaze, our choices.

What happens when we are no longer at war with ourselves? When our body becomes a sanctuary instead of a site of chaos? We become less reactive. More spacious. We listen better. We love with more integrity. We move through conflict without collapsing into it. We speak truth without needing to dominate. We begin to hold paradox and complexity instead of demanding control. This is what becomes possible when our inner world is no longer on fire.

And that matters. Because the world is on fire. And what the world needs now is not more burned-out activists or perfectionist healers or dissociated caretakers. The world needs nervous systems that can hold tension without adding to it. Hearts that can stay soft in the face of difference. Voices that can interrupt harm without causing more.

This is how healing becomes activism. This is how the micro becomes the macro. This is how our regulated breath becomes a ripple in the pond of humanity. We are not separate from the whole. Like a glistening strand in a spider's web, our presence is both distinct and connected—one vibrating thread that carries movement, meaning, and resonance across the entire structure of the living world. And just as one drop of water can tremble the entire web, so too can one moment of embodied feeling—one sacred tear, one reclaimed breath—send waves of healing far beyond its origin. This is the holy water of our becoming. This is how sacredness enters the system. And when we choose healing, the pattern shifts.

This is not just emotional intelligence; it is also somatic maturity. And sometimes when we least expect it, it becomes something even more surprising: a quiet magic that changes the room.

There is a moment in somatic healing that feels like wonder. You've been doing your practices: breathing, orienting, discharging, and softening. You've built capacity. You've rebuilt your neural networks and trained them to bend toward beliefs rooted in resilience. You've returned, again and again, to the present moment.

Then seemingly without effort, something shifts—not just in you but also around you. Your child's fists clench, their breath catches. But seeing your calm, they soften and climb into your lap, still trembling, but reachable. Your partner starts to pull away but pauses, exhales, and leans in just a little longer, resting their forehead against yours. Your parent, usually guarded, traces the rim of their coffee cup and says, "You always used to hum when you were coloring. I still think about that sometimes." Your coworker walks in tight-jawed and tense. But as you speak, their shoulders drop, and they let out a breath they didn't know they were holding.

You didn't offer them a strategy or teach them a tool. But something changed.

This is what I call "somatic magic"—the surprising, often inexplicable transformation that unfolds in the relational field when one person begins to regulate their nervous system in earnest. It is subtle, yet undeniable. A new tone enters the room. A softness. A coherence. A different rhythm. And that rhythm spreads as the presence of safety becomes known and contagious.

Neuroscience affirms that this is not an illusion. Human beings are biologically wired for coregulation. Our nervous systems constantly scan and respond to the cues of others. Through the mechanism of mirror neurons, we subconsciously reflect the facial expressions, vocal tones, and body postures of those around us, particularly those to whom we are emotionally attached (Rizzolatti & Craighero, 2004). Our vagus nerve, the primary conduit of the parasympathetic nervous system, attunes us to signals of safety or threat, including breath tempo, vocal resonance, and even the subtle shifts in eye contact or muscle tone (Porges, 2011). Social baseline theory further explains that our brains are metabolically more efficient and emotionally more stable when in proximity to trusted others (Coan et al., 2006). The implication is radical: Safety is not solely an internal state; it is relational, resonant, and shared.

But science doesn't fully account for the poetry of what happens here.

There are moments in healing that defy the linear.

They ripple.

They echo.

They leap across time, bloodlines, direct communication, and physical distance.

The British biologist Rupert Sheldrake (2009) proposed a theory of morphic resonance to describe this very phenomenon: the idea that once a pattern of form or behavior has occurred repeatedly in one place, it becomes easier for the same pattern to appear elsewhere—not through direct contact, but via a field of memory embedded in nature. This theory, while still debated, invites a new lens on healing. What if your regulation is not just helping your own body but also altering the field that others inhabit?

There are curious examples in biology that support this. In controlled experiments, rats trained to solve a maze in one laboratory were followed by rats in distant labs, who learned the same maze more quickly despite no genetic or environmental overlap (Sheldrake, 2009). Once a new compound has been crystallized for the first time, chemists have reported that the process becomes easier in other laboratories worldwide, suggesting that form itself becomes more "available" after its first emergence. Even in bird populations, such as the famous case of blue tits in twentieth-century Britain learning to peck milk bottle caps for cream, behavior spread with a velocity and distance that exceeded what traditional observations of social learning could explain. The field holds knowledge and spreads it.

In a similar way, the human body—your body—may become a transmitter of a new pattern. As you learn to breathe through conflict, settle through overwhelm, and stay in contact through discomfort, your nervous system becomes a tuning fork for others. Those closest to you—including partners, children, colleagues, and clients—can begin to orient to your signal. They soften. They mirror. They entrain. They receive an invitation to a new relational dance. The old dance steps no longer make sense, if they want to stay in step with you.

This isn't just poetic; it's also polyvagal (Porges, 2011). The ventral vagal system, when active, radiates signals of safety through tone of voice, facial expression, posture, and presence. These cues are received by others and interpreted by their own neuroception, the subconscious surveillance system that detects whether an environment or relationship is safe or dangerous. When our neurophysiology broadcasts calm, others begin to feel safe enough to regulate too.

The implications are profound.

We cannot control another person's reactions to us, and we definitely should not try. Healing is not something we can coerce or direct on someone else's behalf. Trying to fix, rescue, or manage their growth only entangles and merges us further. But we can offer a different presence. We can become a new resonance in the room. By letting go of control over the outcome and choosing presence over performance, softness over strategy, breath over reactivity, you begin to shape the field. We create new patterns, new relational possibilities, and quiet invitations that arc toward wholeness and health. We only need to tend to our own work and allow the unfolding of its magic in our life to ripple outward, unforced and unspoken.

This is the somatic magic that unfolds in family lines, in classrooms, in communities. It is the unspoken transmission of regulation, the biological basis of belonging, and the neurophysiological root of hope. When one person shifts their pattern, the collective pattern shifting toward regulation, repair, mutual care, and embodied truth becomes more possible. You are not just healing for yourself. Like a spider's web responding to movement, the web of life feels your shift and adjusts in kind.

You are remembering the truth your body always knew:

We heal in relationship.

We become whole together.

You have walked through these chapters—not as a passive reader, but as a courageous participant—allowing your body to speak, your tears to flow, and your sensations to guide you. The tears you've shed, the trembling you've honored, the breath you've reclaimed—these are not signs of weakness, but sacred rituals of return. In this work, we do not turn away from feeling; we make a sanctuary of it. We learn that tears are holy water, sacraments of the soul's thawing, ceremonies of release, baptisms into a more authentic aliveness.

The practices offered here are not prescriptions, but invitations. They are somatic rituals for feeling and aliveness, pathways back to yourself and the sacred intelligence of your body. Each ritual, each pause, each breath has helped you remember that regulation is not about perfection. It is about returning.

This is not the end of your journey. But it is a powerful beginning. You are not alone. You are not broken. You are your own sacred medicine. This medicine is not just for you; it ripples outward. You are a healing presence in your community, a living offering of what becomes possible when we choose to feel, to stay, and to heal.

In a fractured world, we often forget that healing doesn't always begin with intellect or explanation. It begins with presence, and deep presence is what ritual makes possible. Ritual is not simply a cultural artifact or spiritual ornament; it is also an ancient technology for wholeness. A remembering. It unites mind, heart, and body—holding them steady in the immediacy of now. Ritual is the portal to the soul. Not the soul as a theological abstraction, but the soul as your innermost knowing—your irreducible spark, your ache for beauty, your cry for justice, your capacity to feel and be moved. The soul is the part of you that remembers who you are beneath what happened. It is not separate from the body but expressed through it.

When we say "the soul speaks," we do not mean it uses words. The soul speaks through sensation. It trembles in grief. It warms in the presence of love. It pulses when we are near something true. Emotion is its language, and the body is its instrument. And that is why ritual is so powerful: It pulls our consciousness down and in—into the very places where the soul waits to be met. Ritual creates conditions for listening. It slows time while pulling focus. It gathers scattered parts. It engages the breath, the heartbeat, the gesture, the gaze. It honors the thresholds between birth and death, love and loss, silence and speech. And it insists that healing must be felt, not just thought.

We live in a culture that often mistrusts feeling, exalts efficiency, forgets that the body holds memory and that the soul grows quiet when rushed. But ritual interrupts that forgetting. It says. "Slow down. Come home. Feel. Listen. Bless what aches. Tend what's tender." This is the medicine. To reclaim ritual is to reclaim communication, not performance, not perfection. But access. Access to the deeper intelligence that lives inside you. Access to the sacred.

When we gather in ritual, alone or together, we enter a field where something more than us can move through us. This is what our ancestors knew. That through ritual, we don't just heal ourselves; we also help reweave the world. And in this way, each act of healing, each moment of turning inward with care becomes not just a personal act but also a collective one. A ripple. A remembering. A return.

Every tear you shed along the way created its own quiet ripple, widening the field around you. This is the truth at the heart of your journey: tears are holy water. They soften what has hardened, reconnect what has split, and offer nourishment not only to you but also to every relationship and community your life touches. In tending to your own healing, you become a well for others, which is steady, life-giving, and quietly transformative. Trust what your tears reveal. Trust what they cleanse. Trust that each one changes more than just you.

Case Study
Elijah's Thread

Elijah, a fifty-six-year-old high school teacher and grandfather, came to therapy not because of an acute crisis, but because of an ache he couldn't name. "I'm not falling apart," he said. "But I feel like I've been holding my breath for decades." A child of immigrants, raised in a home where survival was prioritized over softness, Elijah had mastered the art of containment. He was reliable, respected, and rarely vulnerable. But beneath his calm exterior lived chronic muscle tension, a racing mind, and a quiet despair that he couldn't "logic" his way out of.

His sessions began with silence. Long stretches of stillness where words felt too sharp for what his body carried. Over time, Elijah learned to track sensation—to notice how his stomach clenched when he talked about his childhood, how his throat tightened when he mentioned his adult son, how tears burned just behind his eyes when he allowed himself to feel. Together, with his therapist, he practiced grounding and orienting. He used breath as an anchor. He returned, again and again, to the simple truth that his feelings were not dangerous. That they were sacred. That they were messengers.

What unfolded was slow, deliberate, and radical. Elijah stopped trying to "fix" his family and instead began tending to his own nervous system with reverence. He started to just let them "be" themselves as he began taking walks at sunrise, letting the colors of the sky soften his chest and ground him into his day. He practiced resting without guilt. He allowed tears to come when they came, sometimes while washing dishes, sometimes while reading to his granddaughter. He no longer rushed them away.

Then one day, something shifted.

His teenage grandson, usually guarded and sarcastic, came home after school and flopped onto the couch beside him without a word. After a few minutes, the boy leaned his head on Elijah's shoulder. Elijah didn't speak. He simply exhaled, softened, and placed a hand on the side of his grandson's head while leaning his own head to softly meet his grandson's.

That moment broke something open.

Over the weeks that followed, Elijah noticed subtle changes: his wife laughing more, his son calling just to check in, a student staying after class to say, "You make me feel safe." He hadn't given them a lecture. He hadn't read them this book. He had changed his way of being, and something around him had responded.

"This isn't magic," he said once in session. "But it feels like grace."

Elijah's story is not unique, but it is sacred. It is the story of what becomes possible when one person decides to stop bracing and start feeling. When one nervous system becomes a sanctuary, others find their way home too. Elijah became what this book invites all of us to become: a living transmission of safety, a quiet revolution, a sacred thread in the web of repair.

Journal and Reflection Prompts

1. **Where have I felt the "quiet magic" of healing in my relationships or surroundings?**

   Describe a time when your own inner regulation seemed to shift something in the field around you. What changed? How did it feel?

2. **What patterns or wounds am I choosing to end with me?**

   Reflect on generational, relational, or cultural pain that you are no longer willing to carry forward. What does that boundary feel like in your body?

3. **In what ways has my nervous system become more available for connection, safety, or presence?**

   Explore the subtle (or profound) ways your inner state has changed through this somatic journey. What do you notice now that you didn't before?

4. **What is sacred to me about feeling? About tears?**

   Consider the book's title, *Tears Are Holy Water*. How have your tears been part of your transformation? What have they softened, cleared, or revealed?

5. **What kind of ripple do I want to offer to the web of life?**

   Imagine your nervous system as a strand in a greater collective. What tone, rhythm, or medicine do you most want to contribute?

Final Somatic Ritual: Anointing the Sacred Body

This ritual is both a return and a blessing. It marks the completion of your journey through this book and the beginning of your journey beyond it. It is a way to honor the tears you've shed, the sensations you've survived, and the quiet magic you carry.

1. **Prepare your space.**

   Find a quiet place where you can be undisturbed for 15–30 minutes. Dim the lights or light a candle. If you like, gather a small bowl of water, a warm cloth, or an oil you love. This will be your holy water, your own sacred anointing.

2. **Orient to the moment.**

   Begin by gently turning your head and eyes to notice three things in your environment that feel safe or comforting. Let your gaze land. Let your body feel where you are in time and space. Whisper softly to yourself, "I am here now."

3. **Ground through the body.**

   Come to a comfortable seated or lying position. Feel your seat or spine rooted to the earth. Notice the contact between your body and the ground. Let your breath drop into your belly. With each exhale, allow something old to leave you. With each inhale, receive something new.

4. **Reflect and remember.**

   Place one hand on your heart and one on your belly. Take a few breaths here. Ask yourself the following:

   – What have I reclaimed in this journey?

   – What patterns have I softened?

   – What is my body teaching me now?

   Let the answers arise as images, sensations, or words. There's no right way, only your way.

5. **Anoint with intention.**

    Dip your fingers into the water or oil. Slowly, gently, touch your body as you speak aloud the following:
    - Touch your forehead: *May my mind be clear and kind.*
    - Touch your lips: *May my words be rooted in truth and care.*
    - Touch your heart: *May I love and be loved with presence.*
    - Touch your belly: *May I trust my intuition and rest in my being.*
    - Touch your feet: *May I walk the path of healing and return to the sacred in all things.*

6. **Seal the ritual.**

    Close your eyes and rest both hands wherever your body wants them. Breathe. Say silently or aloud the following:

    My tears are holy water.

    I am wonderfully alive.

    I am my own sacred medicine.

Let this be your final exhale from the book—and your first inhale into what comes next.

APPENDIX A

Nervous System Regulation Activities

Somatic Invitations for Activation and Settling

Our nervous systems fluctuate throughout the day. Some moments require grounding; others need energy. The following activities offer embodied ways to respond to your internal state, either by downregulating (settling the system) or upregulating (bringing in vitality).

Upregulating Activities (Energy, Alertness, Reconnection)	Downregulating Activities (Soothing, Grounding, Centering)
Cold shower	Deep belly breathing
Jumping jacks	Lying down with a weighted blanket
Dancing to fast music	Humming softly
Brisk walking	Taking a warm bath
Singing loudly	Slow mindful walking
Laughing	Progressive muscle relaxation
Bright light exposure	Listening to calming music
Chewing gum	Gazing at nature
Power poses	Gentle rocking
Fast-paced drumming	Sipping warm tea
Spinning in a chair	Guided meditation
Clapping hands	Yoga *nidra*

Upregulating Activities (Energy, Alertness, Reconnection)	Downregulating Activities (Soothing, Grounding, Centering)
Playing upbeat music	Visualization of a safe place
Skipping	Inhaling calming essential oils (lavender, frankincense)
Running in place	Petting a soft animal
Splashing cold water on your face	Holding a warm mug
Bouncing on a yoga ball	Listening to ocean or rain sounds
Breath of Fire (fast-paced breathwork)	Watching clouds drift or trees sway
Lively conversation	Swaying slowly
Marching	Coloring or slow mindful drawing
Playing an energetic game	Journaling by candlelight
Waving arms overhead	Wearing soft, comforting fabrics
Using a mini trampoline	Placing a hand on your heart or belly
Opening a window for fresh air	Breathing in a 4-7-8 pattern
Shaking out limbs vigorously	Curling into a blanket or quiet corner

Note: Your body may need different things on different days. There is no "right" way to regulate, only what works for you in this moment. Let this list be a starting point, not a prescription.

APPENDIX B

Core Belief Reframes

Negative Core Belief	Positive Belief with "Regardless"
I am not good enough.	I am enough, regardless of what I've been told.
I am unlovable.	I am lovable, regardless of who failed to love me.
I am broken.	I am whole, regardless of what I've endured.
I don't matter.	I matter, regardless of how others have treated me.
I am too much.	I am worthy of belonging, regardless of my bigness or intensity.
I am not enough.	I am enough, regardless of my past or present imperfections.
I am disgusting.	I am worthy of love and care, regardless of how I've felt about my body or story.
I am invisible.	I am seen and known, regardless of who overlooked me.
I am a burden.	I am allowed to receive, regardless of how much I've needed support.
I'm not safe.	I am safe now, regardless of how unsafe my past has been.
I can't trust anyone.	I can build trust, regardless of past betrayals.
I have to be in control.	I can let go, regardless of how much I've had to hold.
I am powerless.	I have power and agency, regardless of how powerless I once felt.
The world is dangerous.	I can find safe places, regardless of the world's chaos.
I can't protect myself.	I can protect and care for myself, regardless of what happened before.

Negative Core Belief	Positive Belief with "Regardless"
I'll never be safe.	I can feel safety in my body, regardless of how long I've lived without it.
It was my fault.	I did the best I could, regardless of what I was told.
I should have done something.	I forgive myself, regardless of what I didn't know then.
I can't be forgiven.	I am worthy of compassion, regardless of my mistakes.
I ruin everything.	I can grow and repair, regardless of past patterns.
I don't deserve to heal.	I am healing, regardless of what I've been taught to believe.
I always hurt people.	I am learning to relate with care, regardless of my history.
I'm responsible for others' pain.	I am responsible for myself, regardless of old family roles.
If I say no, I'm bad.	I can say no with love, regardless of how I was conditioned.
I must fix everyone.	I can be present without fixing, regardless of what I once believed was my job.

APPENDIX C

Uplifting Marginalized Voices in Somatic Healing

This book stands on the shoulders of many wisdom traditions—some celebrated, others long suppressed. While much of modern somatic psychology and neuroscience is documented through Western institutions, many of its foundational insights echo practices that have lived for generations in Indigenous, Black, Brown, queer, disabled, and diasporic communities, horrifically impacted by colonization.

These traditions have always known what science is only beginning to affirm: that the body is sacred. That healing is relational. That trauma cannot be divorced from systems of oppression. That memory lives in the blood, breath, and bone.

This appendix is offered in recognition and reverence for the teachers, scholars, poets, musicians, healers, and ancestors whose work may not always be cited in the academic texts of psychology and psychiatry but pulses at the heart of embodied healing. These voices remind us that knowledge is not only intellectual; it is also rhythmic, lived, ancestral, and communal.

The following works are offered as invitations for deeper exploration. They center historically marginalized voices in the fields of embodiment, trauma healing, disability justice, decolonial practice, spiritual reclamation, and ancestral nervous system wisdom. These theorists and artists do not merely describe healing; they also *embody* it. Their work offers living maps toward wholeness rooted in justice, community, the body's innate intelligence, and its deep relationship with the land that holds it.

In honoring these voices and practices, we also acknowledge the long history of appropriation in Western wellness spaces. True healing cannot come at the cost of erasure. This book seeks to name, not claim, and to amplify, not extract. Let this be a nonexhaustive living document. Add to it. Share from it. Let it stretch to hold the truths of your lineage and the voices that guide you home.

Nonfiction

adrienne maree brown. (2019). *Pleasure Activism: The Politics of Feeling Good.* **AK Press.** — A collection of essays exploring pleasure, embodiment, healing, and justice through a Black feminist lens

Rev. angel Kyodo williams, Lama Rod Owens, & Jasmine Syedullah. (2016). *Radical Dharma: Talking Race, Love, and Liberation.* **North Atlantic Books.** — An urgent dialogue on spirituality, embodiment, race, and transformation

Bayo Akomolafe. (forthcoming / various essays). *These Wilds Beyond Our Fences: Letters to My Daughter on Humanity's Search for Home.* **North Atlantic Books.** — A philosopher of the postactivist and decolonial body, Akomolafe's work challenges normative healing frameworks and invites poetic rupture.

bell hooks. (2000). *All About Love: New Visions.* **William Morrow.** — Explores love as an intentional embodied practice that fosters healing, belonging, and radical connection—emphasizing that "rarely, if ever, are any of us healed in isolation"

bell hooks. (2004). *Sisters of the Yam: Black Women and Self-Recovery.* **South End Press.** — Centers emotional health for Black women, linking personal healing with collective resistance and self-recovery

Erika L. Sánchez. (2022). *Crying in the Bathroom: A Memoir.* **Viking.** — A memoir/mixed-genre work exploring immigrant womanhood, emotional embodiment, and the body's geography of belonging, sorrow, and resilience

Gerald Vizenor. (1999). *Manifest Manners: Narratives on Postindian Survivance.* **Bison Books.** — This foundational theoretical work introduces the concept of *survivance*—a portmanteau of "survival" and "resistance"—to describe the embodied, narrative, and cultural continuance of Indigenous presence beyond victimry. Vizenor challenges dominant colonial scripts and reframes Native identity as active, generative, and deeply tied to land, body, and story.

John O'Donohue. (1998). *Anam Cara: A Book of Celtic Wisdom.* **Harper Perennial.** — A luminous integration of Irish mysticism, philosophical reflection, and spiritual psychology, *Anam Cara* (meaning "soul friend") offers a contemplative guide to intimacy, embodiment, and inner awakening. O'Donohue explores how the soul expresses itself through the body, through landscape, and through loving relationship, drawing from Celtic tradition and the deep well of poetic insight.

John O'Donohue. (2005). *Beauty: The Invisible Embrace.* **Harper Perennial.** — In this meditative work, O'Donohue explores beauty not as surface adornment, but as a vital animating presence that can heal, awaken, and transform. With philosophical depth and poetic cadence, he invites the reader to perceive beauty as a somatic experience—felt through the senses, lived in the body, and inseparable from the sacred.

Kimberle Crenshaw. (1991). "Mapping the Margins: Intersectionality, Identity Politics, and Violence Against Women of Color." *Stanford Law Review,* **43(6), 1241–1299.** — Though not somatic, this legal theory is foundational to understanding how trauma and healing are shaped by intersectionality.

Lama Rod Owens. (2020). *Love and Rage: The Path of Liberation Through Anger.* **North Atlantic Books.** — A deeply embodied and spiritual exploration of how rage can be a sacred teacher and transformative force

Leah Lakshmi Piepzna-Samarasinha. (2018). *Care Work: Dreaming Disability Justice.* **Arsenal Pulp Press.** — A groundbreaking exploration of care, interdependence, and disability justice rooted in queer and trans BIPOC experiences

Linda Tuhiwai Smith. (1999). *Decolonizing Methodologies: Research and Indigenous Peoples.* **Zed Books.** — A foundational critique of Western knowledge systems and an advocacy for Indigenous ways of knowing and healing

Malidoma Patrice Somé. (1994). *Of Water and the Spirit: Ritual, Magic, and Initiation in the Life of an African Shaman.* **G. P. Putnam's Sons.** — A memoir and guide to West African spiritual healing practices through the Dagara tradition

Manchán Magan. (2020). *Thirty-Two Words for Field: Lost Words of the Irish Landscape.* **Gill Books.** — This poetic and linguistically rich book explores the Irish language as a portal into ancestral ways of seeing, sensing, and belonging. Magan weaves etymology, ecology, and spirituality to illuminate how language once mirrored the body's intimacy with land and weather. A profound invitation to remember somatic, cultural, and ecological interconnectedness.

Manchán Magan. (2022). *Listen to the Land Speak: A Journey into the Wisdom of What Lies Beneath Us.* **Gill Books.** — In this companion volume, Magan deepens his exploration of Ireland's mythic, linguistic, and geomantic heritage. Drawing from folklore, land-based ritual, and embodied presence, he invites readers into a listening relationship with the land where body, place, and ancestral story converge as sources of wisdom and healing.

Manchán Magan. (2023). *Focail na mBan: Women's Words.* **Mayo Books Press.** — A reverent collection of interviews and mixed media reflections from Irish women who carry cultural memory, spiritual insight, and embodied wisdom. Centering women's relationships with their own bodies, this book explores the often-silenced language surrounding female anatomy while uncovering the historical, linguistic, and somatic resonance of body parts and the sacred stories they hold. Magan illuminates how reclaiming these words becomes an act of healing, empowerment, and cultural continuity.

Maria Yellow Horse Brave Heart. (1998). "The Return to the Sacred Path: Healing the Historical Trauma and Historical Unresolved Grief Response Among the Lakota Through a

Psychoeducational Group Intervention." *Smith College Studies in Social Work*, *68*(3), 287–305. — Seminal work introducing the concept of historical trauma from a Native American framework

Maya Angelou. (1969). *I Know Why the Caged Bird Sings.* **Random House.** — A landmark memoir that traces the trauma and triumph of Angelou's early life. Through visceral language and deep attention to the body's experience of fear, silencing, and eventual expression, Angelou's writing models the power of reclaiming one's voice and physical presence after trauma. Her poetry and performances, especially "Still I Rise" and "Phenomenal Woman," are enduring testaments to embodied resilience, dignity, and survival in the face of systemic violence.

Nairy Fstukh / SoftMoonRose. (2025). Available on Substack and Instagram @softmoonrose. — Nairy Fstukh, writing under the name SoftMoonRose, offers a body of work that explores the sacred in the sensory, the erotic in the everyday, and the soul's language through the body. Her writing invites embodied presence, radical honesty, and slow unfolding. Through poetic essays and meditations on the nonsexual erotic, embodiment, grief, ancestry, and longing, she speaks to the nervous system's deep need for beauty and to the body's role in spiritual awakening. She invites readers to claim their relentless passions and desires without apology and to be fully seen in the fullness of their being. Her work centers queer, diasporic, and neurodivergent perspectives and functions as a living archive of personal and collective healing.

Nikki Giovanni. (2017). *A Good Cry: What We Learn from Tears and Laughter.* **William Morrow.** — A powerful reflection on grief, joy, and the healing power of tears. It celebrates emotional release as nourishment for self and community.

Nikki Giovanni. (2025). *The New Book: Poems, Letters, Blurbs, and Things.* **HarperCollins.** — A protest and celebration that weaves together personal reflection, joy, and generational legacy. It is embodied resilience in poetic form.

Porochista Khakpour. (2018). *Sick: A Memoir.* **Harper Perennial.** — Interweaves chronic illness, identity, and bodily suffering with emotive somatic storytelling

Resmaa Menakem. (2017). *My Grandmother's Hands: Racialized Trauma and the Pathway to Mending Our Hearts and Bodies.* **Central Recovery Press.** — A powerful guide to somatic healing of racial trauma for Black, White, and police bodies

Robin Wall Kimmerer. (2013). *Braiding Sweetgrass: Indigenous Wisdom, Scientific Knowledge, and the Teachings of Plants.* **Milkweed Editions.** — An ecological and poetic homage to relational wisdom rooted in Potawatomi traditions

Sonya Renee Taylor. (2018). *The Body Is Not an Apology: The Power of Radical Self-Love.* **Berrett-Koehler Publishers.** — A foundational text on body liberation and disrupting systems of shame and oppression

Thema Bryant. (2022). *Homecoming: Overcome Fear and Trauma to Reclaim Your Whole, Authentic Self.* **TarcherPerigee.** — A healing guide that integrates psychology, spirituality, and trauma recovery with particular attention to systemic injustice

Tricia Hersey. (2022). *Rest Is Resistance: A Manifesto.* **Little, Brown Spark.** — A spiritual and political call to reclaim rest as an act of liberation from grind culture

Yolo Akili. (2013). *Dear Universe: Letters of Affirmation and Empowerment for All of Us.* **Michael Todd Books.** — A heart-centered collection of reflections that address emotional healing, mental health, and collective care

Fiction

Alice Walker. (1982). *The Color Purple.* **Harcourt Brace Jovanovich.** — A narrative of reclaiming voice and body through letters; a somatic and emotional journey of survival, self-reclamation, and relational healing.

Alice Walker. (1992). *Possessing the Secret of Joy.* **Harcourt Brace Jovanovich.** — Explores trauma, embodied resilience, and liberation through a visceral portrayal of bodily violation and healing

Arundhati Roy. (1997). *The God of Small Things.* **IndiaInk.** — A lush sensory novel tracing grief, caste, and forbidden love through the body's memory. Roy shows how trauma imprints across generations and how nature and tenderness open pathways to repair. Her prose traces grief and longing with a visceral intimacy, offering both rupture and the possibility of repair through memory, nature, and human connection.

Arundhati Roy. (2017). *The Ministry of Utmost Happiness.* **Hamish Hamilton.** — A sweeping narrative that maps bodies as sites of resistance, mourning, and transformation. Roy highlights marginalized voices, including queer, trans, Dalit, and

Kashmiri—inviting the reader to feel the costs of violence and the radical possibility of collective healing. Roy reminds us that the body is not only a witness to history but also its archive and its hope.

Carmen Maria Machado. (2017). *Her Body and Other Parties***. Graywolf Press.** — A haunting short story collection that places bodies at the center while exploring pain, desire, trauma, and collective transformation through physicality

Elizabeth Acevedo. (2018). *The Poet X***. Quill Tree Books.** — A visceral YA novel where body, breath, and voice are reclaimed through slam poetry, with poems emerging directly from embodied experience

Gabriel García Márquez. (1970). *One Hundred Years of Solitude***. Harper & Row.** — García Márquez's magical realism throbs with bodily cycles: births, deaths, fevers, and communal ritual. Traumas echo and healing pulses through generational cycles.

Gerald Vizenor. (1991). *The Heirs of Columbus***. Wesleyan University Press.** — A postmodern novel that blends tribal stories, genetic memory, and historical revision. Through speculative and mythic satire, Vizenor reclaims the Indigenous body as a site of origin, healing, and communal continuity. Survivance here becomes flesh—resilient, contradictory, and ever adaptive.

Gerald Vizenor. (1991). *Landfill Meditation: Crossblood Stories***. Wesleyan University Press.** — A collection of short stories that deconstructs American mythologies and reasserts Native presence through ironic body-based storytelling. The characters' physical and spiritual lives echo survivance as somatic subversion.

Goli Taraghi. (various). — Her narratives delve into internal emotional landscapes shaped by war and displacement, giving voice to embodied war trauma.

Isabel Allende. (1982). *The House of the Spirits.* **Plaza & Janés.** — Embraces magical realism rich with vivid sensory detail invoking touch, taste, ritual, and ancestral spirits while grounding collective healing in the flesh of memory

Julia Alvarez. (2020). *Afterlife.* **Algonquin Books.** — By blending grief, embodied sensation, and memory, Alvarez crafts a somatic reckoning with loss through maternal body awareness and intergenerational lineage.

Laura Esquivel. (1989). *Like Water for Chocolate.* **Doubleday.** — Culinary somatics in action: the body's emotions infuse food making and eating works as embodied ritual, collective healing, and intergenerational memory

Louise Erdrich. (1984). *Love Medicine.* **Holt, Rinehart & Winston.** — Erdrich's debut novel weaves multigenerational Ojibwe family sagas across time and place. Through an interwoven ensemble cast, she explores land, memory, and survivance—channeling ancestral wisdom and embodied kinship through story and ritual.

Louise Erdrich. (1988). *Tracks.* **Henry Holt.** — Set in the early twentieth century, *Tracks* tells the story of land loss, cultural erosion, and spiritual resistance through alternating narratives by Fleur Pillager and Nanapush. Deeply mythic and viscerally physical, the novel roots itself in the somatic legacy of grief, hunger, and transformation. Erdrich renders the land and the body as interconnected sites of power, ceremony, and survival.

Nastaran Makaremi. (various). — An Iranian writer whose fiction explores memory, trauma, displacement, and psychic embodiment in exile

Ocean Vuong. (2019). *On Earth We're Briefly Gorgeous.* **Penguin Press.** — A novel written as an epistolary letter from son to mother, this narrative reads like extended poetry. It offers a raw, intimate reflection on Vietnamese identity, intergenerational trauma, and the somatic experience of queer love and survival. Vuong invites the reader into the textures of memory held in the body via scars, aches, language, and yearning.

Saadi Shirazi. (thirteenth century). *The Bustan* and *The Gulistan.* — These classical Persian works offer embodied ethical teachings. His poem "Bani Adam" speaks to the body politic and empathetic connection among all humans.

Sandra Cisneros. (1984). *The House on Mango Street.* **Arte Público Press.** — A poetic mosaic capturing the bodily rhythms of everyday life, sensory snapshots, and the physical textures of home and identity

Sonia Sanchez. (2011, 2022). *Morning Haiku* and *This Is Not a Small Voice.* **Beacon Press.** — Offers tender sonic meditations that embody community care, spiritual resonance, and the healing power of lyrical presence

Toni Morrison. (1977). *Song of Solomon.* **Alfred A. Knopf.** — A soaring mythic novel that traces the journey of Milkman Dead as he unearths his ancestral past and reclaims his embodied identity. Morrison braids flight, memory, and longing into a powerful meditation on liberation that is personal, political, and spiritual. The body becomes a vessel for both inherited trauma and sacred transformation; and the act of remembering emerges as a somatic ritual of reclamation, rooted in Black lineage, land, and story.

Toni Morrison. (1987). *Beloved.* **Alfred A. Knopf.** — An immersive somatic confrontation with ancestral and collective trauma. The novel's "rememory" process is a profound act of communal healing and embodied reckoning.

Toni Morrison. (2012). *Home.* **Alfred A. Knopf.** — Centers communal and embodied care as a path to healing. Its characters' recovery is tenderly rooted in collective nurturing and somatic reconnection.

Zora Neale Hurston. (1934). *Jonah's Gourd Vine.* **J. B. Lippincott.** — Draws on African American folk culture and oral tradition to portray the embodied contradictions of love, faith, trauma, and transformation. A powerful study in inherited pain and the body's struggle to find spiritual grounding.

Zora Neale Hurston. (1937). *Their Eyes Were Watching God.* **J. B. Lippincott.** — A seminal novel of embodied Black womanhood, self-reclamation, and ancestral wisdom. Through Janie's journey—marked by love, loss, silence, and voice—Hurston explores the somatic landscape of freedom and healing.

Zora Neale Hurston. (1942). *Dust Tracks on a Road.* **J. B. Lippincott.** — A genre-blending autobiography reflecting on Hurston's physical and emotional journey through racism, sexism, and self-invention. A testament to self-possession, unapologetic vitality, and the healing power of rooted identity.

Poetry
Andrea Gibson

(2018). *Lord of the Butterflies*. Button Poetry. — This collection pulses with embodied emotion via the grief, rage, desire, and tenderness, carried in the sinews of queer love and resistance. Gibson's spoken word style translates powerfully to the page, inviting readers into a felt experience of gender, illness, heartbreak, and hope as sacred rites of passage.

(2021). *You Better Be Lightning*. Button Poetry. — A breathtaking journey through chronic illness, political grief, and spiritual reawakening. These poems hold space for nonlinear healing, trans joy, and somatic liberation—reminding us that the body is not a battleground, but a prayer.

(2023). *Things That Don't Suck*. Substack newsletter. — A love letter to life's fragile beauty. Written during their cancer treatment, Gibson's reflections on breath, sensation, and ordinary awe are meditations in nervous system attunement, presence, and aliveness.

Audre Lorde

(1973). *From a Land Where Other People Live*. Broadside Press. — This National Book Award finalist explores race, ancestry, maternal lineage and the complexity of Black womanhood through a deeply embodied poetic lens.

(1978). *The Black Unicorn*. W. W. Norton. — A foundational collection that weaves together myth, sensuality, and ancestral wisdom. Poems include seminal works on survival and queer embodiment.

Dao Strom

(2015). *We Were Meant to Be a Gentle People.* Press Otherwise (and Paperdoll Works). — A hybrid poetry/music project that merges sound, voice, and text to explore inherited silence, diasporic identity, and the body as both instrument and archive

(2020). "Traveler's Ode." Fonograf Editions. — A poetic invocation of grief, memory, and longing across landscapes of migration and ancestral rupture. Blends Vietnamese and American cultural memory through sensory language and emotional resonance.

Esther Belin

(1999). *From the Belly of My Beauty.* University of Arizona Press. — A groundbreaking collection that reclaims the colonized Diné (Navajo) female body with fierce lyricism and embodied political critique. Belin's work is a poetic act of survival, asserting Indigenous presence through voice, rhythm, and sensory memory.

(2017). *Of Cartography: Poems.* University of Arizona Press. — This recent collection deepens Belin's exploration of trauma, land, identity, and cultural memory through poetic form. Includes meditations on bodily survival and the ceremonial inheritance of Diné identity.

Gwendolyn Brooks

(1960). *The Bean Eaters.* Harper & Brothers. — A landmark collection that centers Black urban life through vivid, intimate portraits of ordinary people. With precision and tenderness, Brooks explores the somatic textures of poverty, motherhood, aging, and daily survival—locating dignity and lyricism in the body's smallest rituals and fiercest reckonings.

Hafiz (Hafez of Shiraz)

(fourteenth century). *I Heard God Laughing: Renderings of Hafiz*. Translated by Daniel Ladinsky. (1996). Penguin Compass. — A beloved modern rendering of Hafiz's ecstatic poetry—emphasizing joy, love, and embodied spiritual intimacy. Poems that invite readers to experience the body as a vessel for divine connection, sensual presence, and radical generosity.

John O'Donohue

(2008). *To Bless the Space Between Us: A Book of Blessings*. Doubleday. — This collection of poetic blessings invites readers into a space of quiet reverence, embodiment, and belonging. Featuring the widely beloved poem "Beannacht" ("Blessing"), O'Donohue offers somatic sanctuaries for threshold moments— grief, transition, birth, aging—each poem calling the body back to presence, dignity, and inner peace.

Joy Harjo

(1983). *She Had Some Horses*. Thunder's Mouth Press. — A seminal collection exploring Indigenous womanhood, fragmentation, and the journey toward integration. Poetry centering on powerful embodiment of trauma, spirit, contradiction, and reclamation in the female Native body.

(1994). *The Woman Who Fell from the Sky*. W. W. Norton. — A collection that weaves together myth, memory, and embodied spirituality. Poetic invocations of breath, ritual, and reconnection between body and land.

(2000). *A Map to the Next World*. W. W. Norton. — A poetic cartography of survival and transformation, blending environmental, ancestral, and bodily wisdom. Domestic ritual is centered as sacred and somatic space.

(2019). *An American Sunrise*. W. W. Norton. — A reclamation of Indigenous joy, survival, and historical memory through breath, music, and spiritual embodiment. Features both poems honoring the interweaving of grief, presence, and ancestral return.

Junauda Petrus

(2023). *Can We Please Give the Police Department to the Grandmothers?* Dutton Books for Young Readers. — A poetic manifesto that reimagines public safety through the lens of Black ancestral compassion and embodied care. This visionary prose-poem invites a return to community-rooted justice, sensual wisdom, and intergenerational tenderness.

June Jordan

(1980). *Passion: New Poems, 1977–1980*. Beacon Press. — A collection that embodies political clarity and emotional urgency, written in the wake of personal and collective grief. Poems that assert the body as both witness and instrument of resistance and language as a somatic tool for survival and justice.

(2002). *Directed by Desire: The Collected Poems of June Jordan.* Copper Canyon Press. — This definitive volume spans over three decades of Jordan's work, offering a fierce and tender blueprint for living in the body amid systems of oppression. Featuring many poems rooted in Black feminist thought, sensual presence, communal care, and unapologetic embodiment.

Keli Stewart

(2021). *Small Altars.* Bronzeville Books. — A powerful debut collection that traces the sacred and everyday rituals of Black girlhood, motherhood, and bodily survival. Stewart's poems honor the flesh as archive, altar, and prayer—mapping grief, transformation, and inherited wisdom onto the landscape of the body.

Kelly Norman Ellis, PhD

(2003). *Tougaloo Blues.* Third World Press. — A vibrant and reverent collection that centers Black Southern womanhood, ancestral wisdom, and embodied ritual. Poems that celebrate the body as a vessel of memory, cultural resilience, and generational knowledge passed through gesture, touch, and sensory presence.

Various publications — Recent works appear in anthologies, readings, and scholarly texts that foreground Black bodily sovereignty, collective care, and the ritual of justice through movement and voice.

Koleka Putuma

(2017). *Collective Amnesia.* uHlanga Press. — A groundbreaking debut that redefines contemporary South African poetry through embodied Black queer feminist voice, spiritual reckoning, and political clarity. Putuma's poems are fierce and fluid—using repetition, form, and breath to explore trauma, faith, intimacy, and collective survival in the body.

Laura Murphy

Various live performances; internet, chapbooks, and independent publications — A poet, educator, and somatic practitioner, Murphy explores the sacred imprint of intergenerational trauma and healing on the body. Her poems treat the body as a living archive, where blood, breath, scars, and silence carry ancestral memory and sacred transmission. She is also known for reviving and reframing *imbas forosnai*, an ancient Irish ritual of embodied knowledge, as a somatic practice that honors vision, voice, and nervous system attunement through breath, stillness, and spiritual invocation.

Layli Long Soldier

(2017). *Whereas*. Graywolf Press. — A formally innovative and politically searing collection that responds to the US government's 2009 "Apology to Native Peoples" with embodied counternarratives. Through breath-infused line breaks, spatial disruption, and intimate repetition, Long Soldier addresses the somatic impact of colonial language and the ways memory, grief, and kinship live in the body. Her work reclaims poetic form as an act of Indigenous presence, resistance, and reclamation.

Leslie Marmon Silko

(1974). *Laguna Woman: Poems.* Greenfield Review Press. — A poetic collection grounded in Pueblo cosmology, embodiment, and the sacred rhythms of land and memory. Silko's poems honor the body's participation in cycles of ceremony, migration, and myth, where language and breath are ancestral technologies.

(1977). *Ceremony.* Viking Press. — A foundational decolonial novel that blends prose and lyrical interludes to trace the embodied healing journey of a Laguna Pueblo war veteran. Through ritual, storytelling, and land-based memory, the novel explores trauma, survival, and the somatic inheritance of Indigenous identity.

(1981). *Storyteller.* Seaver Books. — A hybrid collection of poems, photographs, and short stories that illuminate the intimate relationship between body, landscape, and ancestral wisdom. Features poems that portray healing through gesture, memory, and the porous boundary between human and more-than-human worlds.

Louise Erdrich

(1984). *Jacklight.* Holt, Rinehart & Winston. — Her first poetry collection, blending Indigenous storytelling with lyric verse, natural imagery, and ancestral echoes. Erdrich's poems bridge oral history, body, and place.

(1990). *Baptism of Desire.* Harper Perennial. — This second volume traces desire, spirit, and identity through Native poetics. Her verse is intimate, sensory, and rooted in embodied belonging.

(2004). *Original Fire: Selected and New Poems.* Harper Perennial. — A curated collection combining standout pieces from *Jacklight* and *Baptism of Desire* with newer poems. Erdrich's distinct voice—weather-wise, ancestral, and elemental—blazes here, merging memory, myth, and body.

Lucille Clifton

(1980). *Two-Headed Woman.* BOA Editions. — A National Book Award finalist that boldly centers Black womanhood, sexuality, and the body's cycles as sites of spiritual and political power. Clifton writes with fierce clarity and reverence, reclaiming physicality as divine inheritance.

(1993). *The Book of Light.* Copper Canyon Press. — A luminous collection that honors personal and collective resilience through sparse, yet potent language. Poetic meditations on identity, survival, and the sacred transitions of the feminine body.

(2000). *Blessing the Boats: New and Selected Poems, 1988–2000.* BOA Editions. — A wide-reaching retrospective that affirms the grace and grit of embodied life. Includes a gentle invocation of courage, release, and somatic trust in the face of the unknown.

Lyla June

(2020–present). Digital releases, performances, and lectures — Her work often merges traditional Diné ceremony with contemporary ecological, political, and somatic concerns, offering prayerful embodied blueprints for collective healing and Indigenous resurgence.

(2021). *Flesh to Fire*. Independent release. — A spoken word and prayer-poem collection that fuses Indigenous spirituality, matrilineal wisdom, and embodied resistance. June's work calls listeners and readers into relationship with land, lineage, and body as interconnected vessels of healing and remembrance.

Mary Oliver

(1992). *New and Selected Poems, Volume One*. Beacon Press. — Oliver's nature poetry is a practice of sacred noticing. With quiet precision, she invites readers to reinhabit the rhythms of the earth and the intelligence of the body—making space for stillness, wonder, and grief.

(2004). *Why I Wake Early*. Beacon Press. — These poems are morning rituals for the spirit. Through birdsong, salt air, and light on water, Oliver maps how nature mirrors emotional states and provides a steadying anchor in times of loss and longing.

(2019). *Upstream: Selected Essays*. Penguin Books. — A tender prose meditation on creativity, solitude, and spiritual embodiment. Oliver reflects on her early life, her love of language, and her belief in attention as a form of devotion, modeling a somatic way of being in the world.

Maya Angelou

(1978). *And Still I Rise*. Random House. — A landmark collection of poems that center Black womanhood, embodied self-worth, and the reclamation of dignity. Her poetic work includes joyful declarations of sacred physical presence, resilience, and defiance in the face of historical oppression.

(1994). *The Complete Collected Poems of Maya Angelou*. Random House. — A sweeping volume that gathers decades of Angelou's poetic work—blending personal testimony, spiritual invocation, and collective memory. Poems that explore containment and transcendence, somatic metaphor, and the healing power of hope, voice, and vision.

Naomi Shihab Nye

(1994). *Words Under the Words: Selected Poems*. Eighth Mountain Press. — A beloved collection that spans themes of cultural identity, grief, generosity, and the somatic textures of everyday life. Poems that explore the body's role in compassion, connection, and quiet transformation.

(2008). *Honeybee*. Greenwillow Books. — A collection that blends poetry and prose with political tenderness, familial warmth, and embodied truth. Nye's work invites readers into a spacious ethics of presence—where food, gesture, and story become acts of healing and remembrance.

Nastaran Makaremi

Various publications and performances — A poet, anthropologist, and human rights scholar whose writing explores displacement, bodily dislocation, and the intergenerational echoes of trauma. Includes poems that meditate on migration, loss, and the body's role in carrying both rupture and resilience. Her work traces how memory lodges in flesh, breath, and silence while mapping a path of survival across language, land, and lineage.

Nikki Giovanni

(2007). *The Collected Poetry of Nikki Giovanni, 1968–1998*. William Morrow. — A sweeping collection of Giovanni's early and middle work. These poems celebrate Black identity, ancestral pride, and embodied power with boldness, humor, and devotion.

(2008). *Acolytes*. William Morrow. — Giovanni writes with tenderness and clarity about the body as a vessel of memory, joy, grief, and generational resilience. Her poems offer poetic testimony to Black life and love as sacred.

(2018). *A Good Cry: What We Learn from Tears and Laughter*. William Morrow. — A moving exploration of grief, vulnerability, and the somatic wisdom of tears. Giovanni reflects on aging, motherhood, and legacy with unflinching softness, inviting the reader into the sacred rituals of feeling.

N. Scott Momaday

(1969). *The Way to Rainy Mountain*. University of New Mexico Press. — A hybrid work of prose, poetry, and myth that journeys through Kiowa history, personal memory, and ancestral geography. Healing is found through physical movement across land and time, with the body acting as a bridge between past and present, myth and self.

(1976). *The Gourd Dancer*. Harper & Row. — A poetry collection steeped in Kiowa oral tradition, ancestral memory, and the sacred relationship between body and land. These poems trace identity through elemental imagery, sacred embodiment, and the storytelling body as a vessel of renewal.

(2009). *In the Presence of the Sun: Stories and Poems, 1961–1991.* University of New Mexico Press. — A collection of poems that explore ritual, transformation, and the body's intimate connection to ceremony and cultural continuity.

Ocean Vuong

(2016). *Night Sky with Exit Wounds.* Copper Canyon Press. — A luminous debut poetry collection that weaves together war memory, queer longing, and ancestral grief through the language of the body. Vuong's work embodies tenderness and rupture; landing where touch, silence, and desire live side by side with historical trauma.

Petra Kuppers

With Neil Marcus. (2008). *Cripple Poetics: A Love Story.* Homofactus Press. — A collaborative exploration of intimacy, disability, and performance. This lyrical and visual work centers the sacredness of disabled embodiment and love, challenging normative narratives of desire through poetic tenderness and lived truth.

(2021). *Gut Botany.* Wayne State University Press. — This hybrid collection of poetry, ritual, and performance maps the intersections of disability, trauma, queer ecology, and embodiment. Kuppers reclaims the body as both archive and oracle—honoring pain, desire, access, and interdependence through sensorial experimental language.

Rita Dove

(1983). *Museum.* Carnegie Mellon University Press. — Contains meditations on bodily transformation and self-discovery. Dove's lyricism captures the awkward sacred unfolding of the feminine body in a patriarchal world.

(1986). *Thomas and Beulah.* Carnegie Mellon University Press. — This Pulitzer Prize–winning collection tells the story of Dove's grandparents through linked poems that honor Black domestic life, labor, and memory. The body is portrayed as a vessel of endurance, ritual, sensuality, and lineage. Everyday acts—such as sweeping, dancing, and touching—become sacraments of survival and love.

(1996). *Mother Love.* W. W. Norton & Company. — A modern reimagining of the Persephone-Demeter myth, centering the somatic intensity of mother-daughter bonds. These poems explore grief, longing, and maternal embodiment, touching archetype and anatomy alike.

(2000). *On the Bus with Rosa Parks.* W. W. Norton & Company. — A richly layered collection offering embodied narratives of violence, resistance, and quiet selfhood. The poems evoke ancestral trauma and healing through intimate portrayals of breath, labor, and silence.

Rūmī (Jalāl ad-Dīn Muhammad Rūmī)

Translated by Coleman Barks. (1995). *The Essential Rumi.* HarperCollins. — Rūmī's poetry, rooted in thirteenth-century Sufi mysticism, continues to offer radical invitations into presence, embodiment, and love. His verse often frames the body as a sacred vessel of divine encounter—fluid, ecstatic, and wise. Rūmī's mystical poetry invites us to greet each emotion as a sacred guest and to return to breath as a path to presence and union. His work dissolves the boundaries between body and spirit, offering the somatic self as a site of transformation and divine intimacy.

Seamus Heaney

(1966). *Death of a Naturalist*. Faber & Faber. — Heaney traces his lineage through manual labor, linking the act of writing to the embodied gestures of farming. Poems that honor the body as both a tool and memory keeper.

(1975). *North*. Faber & Faber. — Poems that engage preserved ancient bodies to reflect on tribal violence, complicity, and the eroticized suffering of women. Heaney wrestles with embodiment, empathy, and political responsibility.

(1984). *Station Island*. Faber & Faber. — A confessional pilgrimage that traverses guilt, colonialism, and spiritual estrangement. The poems evoke bodily memory and penance, offering poetic witness to trauma and ancestral burden.

(1987). *The Haw Lantern*. Faber & Faber. — Includes the sonnet sequence "Clearances," written in memory of his mother. Through tactile domestic imagery, like peeling potatoes and folding linens, Heaney evokes tenderness, grief, and the quiet physical rituals of love and loss.

(1991). *The Cure at Troy: A Version of Sophocles' Philoctetes*. Farrar, Straus and Giroux. — A poetic adaptation exploring justice, injury, and hope through mythic and bodily metaphor. The wounded body becomes a site of insight, transformation, and collective healing.

Sonia Sanchez

(1984). *Homegirls and Handgrenades.* Thunder's Mouth Press. — These poems trace the textures of Black womanhood, political awakening, and ancestral fire through jazz-inflected rhythm, breath, and embodied resistance. The body becomes both an instrument and an altar.

(1997). *Does Your House Have Lions?* Beacon Press. — This book-length poem centers around the AIDS-related death of Sanchez's brother. It is a deeply intimate meditation on grief, family, and spiritual continuity through the body. Breath, pulse, and memory anchor the text in somatic truth.

(2000). *Shake Loose My Skin: New and Selected Poems.* Beacon Press. — These works reclaim bodily sovereignty, voice, and tenderness. Sanchez's language dances between sensuality and survival, grief and joy—always grounding the political in the physical.

(2011). *Morning Haiku.* Beacon Press. — A collection of minimalist poems that honor daily rituals, spiritual presence, and the sacredness of breath. Sanchez distills somatic awareness into small luminous forms that open space for reflection and inner stillness.

Tanaya Winder

(2015). *Words Like Love.* West End Press. — Poems that center the body as a site of decolonial identity and spiritual remembering.

Winder's voice invokes breath, love, and lineage as somatic anchors for survival and emergence.

(2017). *Why Storms Are Named After People and Bullets Remain Nameless*. CreateSpace Independent Publishing Platform. — These poems explore Indigenous womanhood, missing and murdered Indigenous women (MMIW), collective grief, and the sacred body as both witness and altar. Winder writes with a pulse of grief and grace, embodying reclamation as ritual.

Toi Derricotte

(1983). *Natural Birth*. Crossing Press. — A courageous poetic memoir chronicling pregnancy and childbirth. Derricotte reveals the spiritual, physical, and social complexities of becoming a mother—centering bodily truth as both raw and redemptive.

(1997). *Tender*. University of Pittsburgh Press. — This collection explores trauma, eroticism, racialized violence, and the somatic contradictions of living in a Black female body. Derricotte writes with quiet power about vulnerability as strength and the sacred in the wounded.

(1999). *The Black Notebooks: An Interior Journey*. W. W. Norton. — This work is a deeply personal meditation on racial passing, shame, and the quest for authenticity in language and the body alike.

(2011). *The Undertaker's Daughter*. University of Pittsburgh Press. — These poems confront the legacies of racism, invisibility, and survival through deeply embodied grief and recognition. The body becomes both evidence and elegy.

Warsan Shire

(2011). *Teaching My Mother How to Give Birth*. Flipped Eye Publishing. — These works explore the visceral terrain of migration, generational trauma, and feminine embodiment. The home becomes both sanctuary and wound, and the body carries the memory of what was lost and what survives.

(2022). *Bless the Daughter Raised by a Voice in Her Head*. Random House. — This book is a somatic and spiritual map of exile, girlhood, and inherited pain. Shire's language pulses with grief, sensuality, and ancestral resonance—naming the body as a sacred text of both violence and reclamation.

Music
Altai Kai

Altai Kabai (2013) – A powerful album preserving Tuvan throat singing and animist ritual, inviting listeners into ancient soundscapes of spiritual embodiment

Beautiful Chorus

Hymns of Spirit (2015) – A soothing invitation to reclaim the spirit and trust the body's timing as the album sonically rises with grief and joy

Awakening (2022) – Meditative mantras and harmonic layering designed to regulate the nervous system and cultivate inner settling

Buffy Sainte-Marie

Power in the Blood (2015) – A reclamation of Indigenous power, grief, and resistance through electric protest songs and poetic ballads

Medicine Songs (2017) – A compilation album blending activism, ancestral memory, and sonic healing

Clannad

Macalla (1985) – Celtic harmonies and ethereal soundscapes evoke ancestral connection and emotional resonance.

Lore (1996) – Deeply rooted in Irish mythos and landscape, this album weaves stories of spirit and survival.

Clare Sands

Clare Sands (2022) – Tracks emphasizing the nervous system's relationship to migration, memory, and welcome

Enya

Watermark (1988) – Known for its atmospheric serenity, this album offers melodic grounding and emotional release.

Shepherd Moons (1991) – Evokes dream states and body-based stillness through layered harmonies and lullaby pacing

Erykah Badu

Mama's Gun (2000) – A deeply introspective, soul-infused journey through self-love, grief, and embodied liberation

New Amerykah Part One (4ᵗʰ World War) (2007) – Fuses funk, politics, and somatic storytelling of Black futurism and resistance

Hozier

Hozier (2014) – This debut album weaves gospel, soul, blues, and Irish folk traditions into a body-based call to feeling, with songs like "Take Me to Church" and "Work Song," which confront systems of shame while reclaiming the sacredness of the erotic and the mournful.

Wasteland, Baby! (2019) – A lush apocalyptic meditation on love and survival in the Anthropocene

Unreal Unearth (2023) – A sonically rich and lyrically mythic descent into the underworld of grief, rage, and renewal. Written in the aftermath of global upheaval, this album explores ancestral trauma, Irish history, and the healing powers of both language and land—offering listeners a ritual of emotional excavation and emergence.

Huun-Huur-Tu

Ancestors Call (2010) – Deep earthy harmonics that root the body in the pulse of land and lineage

India.Arie

Voyage to India (2002) – Celebrates spiritual and physical self-love as sacred acts of healing

Worthy (2019) – A soul medicine album for nervous system restoration and embodied dignity

Indigie Femme

Grandmother Earth Grandfather Sky (2011) – Indigenous lesbian duo offering layered harmonies rooted in land, prayer, and resistance

Just to Be (2023) – Songs that blend Native, Latina, and queer identities with body-sung resilience

Liam Ó Maonlaí

Rian (2005) – A raw embodied reclamation of Irish language, song, and spirit through which the singer's breath becomes a vessel for ancestral memory and cultural liberation

Lyla June

All Nations Rise (2020) – A sonic invocation of Indigenous sovereignty and embodied leadership

1000 Ancestors (2021) – Spoken word piece set to music addressing intergenerational trauma, colonization, and sacred embodiment

Native Women (2024) – A fierce and prayerful anthem that honors Indigenous matriarchs as the heart of cultural survivance

Mic Jordan

#DearNativeYouth (2015) – A Lakota rapper exploring trauma, masculinity, and mental health in Native communities through raw body-aware lyricism

Mind Like Mine (2024) – Rhythmic resilience and reclaiming narratives through hip-hop as a healing practice

Rhiannon Giddens

Freedom Highway (2017) – Songs tracing the historical roots of embodied Black resistance and spiritual survival

They're Calling Me Home (2021) – A haunting meditation on death, grief, exile, and embodied longing

Sinéad O'Connor

Universal Mother (1994) – An achingly raw sonic pilgrimage through motherhood, loss, anger, and ancestral sorrow

Faith and Courage (2000) – An album of spiritual reckoning and embodied testimony from within personal and collective wounds

Soweto Gospel Choir

Grace (2009) – A sonic invocation of compassion, sacred rhythm, and shared breath

Freedom (2018) – A jubilant reverent album blending Zulu, Xhosa, and English songs that center collective grief, joy, and resistance

Sweet Honey in the Rock

Still The Same Me (2000) – Songs woven from Black spiritual, gospel, and activist lineages honoring the body as sacred site of resistance and renewal

Sacred Ground (1995) – A lush invocation of ancestral memory and community care through layered vocal harmonies

Tanaya Winder

Poetry readings of her work on intergenerational trauma and identity – Often set to music or heartbeat percussion, Winder's delivery is inherently somatic

Toshi Reagon

The Parable of the Sower: The Opera (2017) – Based on Octavia Butler's novel, this operatic adaptation is a futuristic body-centered meditation on survival, faith, and community.

Toshi (2002) – Blues, rock, and gospel fusion that channels grief, resistance, and healing through electrifying vocal presence

Valerie June

Pushin' Against a Stone (2013) – Invites embodied perseverance and somatic release through hypnotic rhythms and ancestral groove

The Moon and Stars: Prescriptions for Dreamers (2021) – A lush otherworldly album fusing folk, gospel, and Afrofuturist healing textures

Young Spirit

Love, Life, Round Dance (2019) – Cree round dance songs that uphold collective memory and healing through Indigenous vocal tradition

Ostesihtowin / Brotherhood (2024) – A sonic record of cultural survival and ceremonial embodiment

Zap Mama

Adventures in Afropea 1 (2007) – A mosaic of African diasporic vocal techniques and rhythms—rooting voice in breath, play, and ancestral power

Ancestry in Progress (2003) – Songs that evoke sensuality, movement, and matrilineal healing through multilingual harmonies and daily embodiment practices

Glossary

activation. The process by which the nervous system becomes mobilized in response to a perceived stimulus, preparing the body for action.

aliveness. A felt sense of vitality, presence, and engagement with life, often arising from a regulated nervous system.

ancestral. Relating to the wisdom, practices, and lived experiences of one's ancestors, often carried forward through cultural memory, tradition, and the body.

arousal. The level of activation in the nervous system, ranging from calm and relaxed to highly mobilized.

attachment. The emotional bond between individuals, especially between a caregiver and child, that shapes relational patterns and nervous system development.

attunement. The capacity to sense, understand, and respond appropriately to another person's emotional and physiological state.

boundaries. Limits that define what is and is not acceptable in relationships, supporting emotional and physical safety.

breathwork. The intentional use of breathing patterns to influence nervous system states, enhance awareness, and support healing.

capacity. The ability of an individual's nervous system to tolerate and process emotional, sensory, or relational experience without becoming overwhelmed.

catharsis. The release of pent-up emotional energy through expression, movement, or other somatic processes.

coherence/congruence. Alignment between internal states (thoughts, feelings, body sensations) and external expressions or actions.

collapse. A dorsal vagal response characterized by withdrawal, immobility, or shutting down to preserve energy during overwhelming threat.

core beliefs. Deeply held assumptions about self, others, and the world, often formed early in life and influencing behavior and perception.

creative life force. The innate generative energy that fuels self-expression, innovation, and the pursuit of meaning, often accessed through regulation and embodied presence.

default mode network. A brain network active during rest and self-referential thinking, linked to memory, imagination, and sense of self.

discharge. The completion and release of survival energy (shaking, trembling, sighing) that was mobilized during a stress response.

dorsal vagal. The branch of the parasympathetic nervous system associated with immobilization, shutdown, and conservation of energy.

downregulation. The process of shifting the nervous system from a heightened or hyperaroused state toward calm and balance.

dysregulation. A state in which the nervous system has difficulty returning to balance after stress or threat.

edge of distress. The threshold where a person is close to becoming overwhelmed but still has the capacity to remain present and engaged.

embodied. The state of being fully present and alive within one's body, attuned to sensations, emotions, and movement as sources of wisdom and truth. To be embodied is not merely to have a body but also to inhabit it with full awareness by allowing the nervous system, breath, and felt sense to guide experience. In somatic healing, embodiment is the practice of reclaiming the body as home—integrating mind, spirit, and sensation into a coherent whole.

embodied movement. The body's ancient language of gesture, rhythm, and sensation that expresses emotion and restores vitality. By moving with rather than suppressing feeling, embodied movement supports emotional healing and nervous system regulation, reconnecting us to presence and authenticity.

EMDR. An abbreviation for "eye movement desensitization and reprocessing." A psychotherapy approach that uses bilateral stimulation to process and integrate traumatic memories.

enmeshment. Also known as "entanglement." Blurred or fused relational boundaries where individuals lose a sense of separate identity and purpose.

expressive art. The use of creative processes (painting, dance, music) to access and integrate emotional or somatic experience.

fawn. Also known as "appease." A survival response involving appeasing, pleasing, or accommodating others to avoid conflict or harm.

felt sense. A bodily awareness of a situation, experience, or emotion that is often vague or intuitive at first but can be explored and articulated through mindful attention.

fight. A sympathetic nervous system response involving confrontation or aggression toward a perceived threat.

flight. A sympathetic nervous system response involving escape or avoidance of a perceived threat.

freeze. A survival response combining sympathetic arousal and parasympathetic immobilization, resulting in stillness without relaxation.

glimmers. Small cues of safety that shift the nervous system toward regulation and connection—a term coined by clinician Deb Dana.

hyperarousal. A state of excessive nervous system activation, often associated with anxiety, restlessness, or hypervigilance.

hypoarousal. A state of low nervous system activation, often associated with numbness, shutdown, or dissociation.

incoherence/incongruence. Misalignment between internal states and outward expression or behavior.

Indigenous. Referring to the original peoples of a land and their cultural traditions, languages, and lifeways, often rooted in deep ecological and spiritual connection to place.

inner child. The part of the self that holds memories, sensations, and emotions from early developmental experiences and unmet needs in childhood. Somatic work with the inner child integrates these experiences through the body, offering repair and nurturing.

integration. The process of connecting and harmonizing different parts of the self or nervous system responses.

interoception. The sense of the internal state of the body, including awareness of breath, heartbeat, hunger, and emotional sensations.

joining. Coming into connection with another person while maintaining one's own sense of self.

meaning. A sense of purpose or significance that shapes motivation, resilience, and engagement with life.

merging. Blending with another person's emotions or experience to the point of losing self-boundaries.

neural network. A system of interconnected neurons that communicate to process information, form memories, and generate responses.

neuroception. The nervous system's subconscious evaluation of safety, danger, or life threat.

neutral. A physiological and emotional state characterized by calm attentiveness without heightened arousal or shutdown.

orienting. The act of using the senses to gather information about the environment, often to assess safety and support nervous system regulation.

override. The suppression or bypassing of a natural physiological or emotional response.

parasympathetic arousal. Activation of the parasympathetic nervous system, supporting rest, digestion, and recovery.

pendulation. The natural rhythm of moving between states of activation and states of settling or regulation—a core principle in trauma healing.

pleasure. A sensory or emotional experience that brings enjoyment, comfort, or satisfaction.

polyvagal theory. A framework developed by Stephen Porges explaining how the vagus nerve mediates safety, connection, and survival responses.

PTSD. An abbreviation for "post-traumatic stress disorder." A condition resulting from exposure to trauma, involving intrusive memories, avoidance, hyperarousal, and other symptoms.

purpose. A guiding sense of meaning, direction, or intention in life—often tied to values, identity, and contribution to others.

reflection. The practice of mindful self-observation and meaning-making from one's experiences.

regulation. The ability to manage and balance one's emotional and physiological states.

relational field. The shared emotional, sensory, and energetic space that exists between people in connection, influenced by nervous system states, attachment patterns, and presence.

resilience. The capacity to recover and adapt after stress, adversity, or trauma.

ritual. A repeated intentional act or sequence of actions, often with symbolic meaning, that marks transitions, fosters connection, and supports nervous system regulation.

safety. A state in which the body and mind perceive no imminent threat, allowing for rest, connection, and healing.

sensorimotor psychotherapy. A therapeutic approach developed by Pat Ogden that integrates body awareness and movement into trauma treatment, blending somatic and psychodynamic techniques.

shift. A noticeable change in state, perspective, or nervous system regulation.

somatic. Relating to the body, particularly as experienced from within.

somatic experiencing (SE). A trauma therapy modality developed by Peter Levine that focuses on releasing stored survival energy and restoring regulation.

survival instinct/energy. The physiological and psychological drive to preserve life in the face of threat.

susto. A cultural concept of illness in Latin America, often translated as "soul loss" or "fright sickness." It occurs when trauma or shock dislodges the soul from the body, leading to PTSD-like symptoms, such as sadness, fatigue, insomnia, or emptiness. In Indigenous and folk healing traditions, *susto* is treated through ritual practices (prayer, ceremony, or cleansing) to call the soul back home. Somatically, *susto* reflects how trauma fragments body, spirit, and psyche—leaving disconnection until repair is possible.

sympathetic arousal. Activation of the sympathetic nervous system, mobilizing the body for fight or flight.

touch work. The intentional therapeutic use of touch in somatic therapies to support regulation and integration.

tracking. The skill of noticing and following sensations, emotions, movements, or shifts in the body over time, often used in somatic therapies to guide healing.

trauma. An experience or series of experiences that overwhelm the body's ability to cope, often resulting in lasting dysregulation.

titration. Gradually approaching and processing traumatic material in small manageable amounts.

upregulation. The process of increasing nervous system activation to bring someone out of a hypoaroused or shutdown state.

ventral vagal. The branch of the parasympathetic nervous system associated with social engagement, safety, and connection.

vitality. A sense of energy, vibrancy, and engagement with life.

window of tolerance. The optimal zone of nervous system arousal where a person can function effectively, process information, and engage in relationships without becoming overwhelmed or shut down.

References

Ampomah, K. (2014). An investigation into Adowa and Adzewa music and dance of the Akan people of Ghana. *International Journal of Humanities and Social Science, 4*(10), 117–124.

Anda, R. F., Felitti, V. J., Bremner, J. D., Walker, J. D., Whitfield, C., Perry, B. D., Dube, S. R., & Giles, W. H. (2006). The enduring effects of abuse and related adverse experiences in childhood. *European Archives of Psychiatry and Clinical Neuroscience, 256*(3), 174–186. https://doi.org/10.1007/s00406-005-0624-4

Andrews-Hanna, J. R., Smallwood, J., & Spreng, R. N. (2014). The default network and self-generated thought: Component processes, dynamic control, and clinical relevance. *Annals of the New York Academy of Sciences, 1316*(1), 29–52. https://doi.org/10.1111/nyas.12360

Apffel-Marglin, F. (Ed.). (2011). *Subversive spiritualities: How rituals enact the world.* Oxford University Press.

Awolalu, J. O., & Dopamu, P. A. (1979). *West African traditional religion.* Onibonoje Press.

Barrett, L. F. (2017). *How emotions are made: The secret life of the brain.* Houghton Mifflin Harcourt.

Beaty, R. E., Benedek, M., Kaufman, S. B., & Silvia, P. J. (2016). Default and executive network coupling supports creative idea production. *Scientific Reports*, 5, 10964. https://doi.org/10.1038/srep10964

Bowlby, J. (1988). *A secure base: Parent-child attachment and healthy human development*. Routledge.

Breasted, J. H. (1930). *The Edwin Smith surgical papyrus*. University of Chicago Press.

brown, a. m. (2019). *Pleasure activism: The politics of feeling good*. AK Press.

Brown, B. (2012). *Daring greatly: How the courage to be vulnerable transforms the way we live, love, parent, and lead*. Gotham Books.

Center on the Developing Child at Harvard University. (2007). *InBrief: The science of early childhood development*. https://developingchild.harvard.edu/resources/inbrief-science-of-ecd/

Christakis, D. A., Ramirez, J. S. B., Ferguson, S. M., Ravinder, S., & Ramirez, J. M. (2018). How early media exposure may affect cognitive function: A review of results from observations in humans and experiments in mice. *Proceedings of the National Academy of Sciences*, 115(40), 9851–9858. https://doi.org/10.1073/pnas.1711548115

Chrousos, G. P. (2009). Stress and disorders of the stress system. *Nature Reviews Endocrinology*, 5(7), 374–381. https://doi.org/10.1038/nrendo.2009.106

Coan, J. A., Schaefer, H. S., & Davidson, R. J. (2006). Lending a hand: Social regulation of the neural response to threat. *Psychological Science, 17*(12), 1032–1039. https://doi.org/10.1111/j.1467-9280.2006.01832.x

Cozolino, L. (2017). *The neuroscience of psychotherapy: Healing the social brain* (3rd ed.). W. W. Norton & Company.

Craig, A. D. (2002). How do you feel? Interoception: The sense of the physiological condition of the body. *Nature Reviews Neuroscience, 3*(8), 655–666. https://doi.org/10.1038/nrn894

Critchley, H. D., & Garfinkel, S. N. (2017). Interoception and emotion. *Current Opinion in Psychology, 17*, 7–14. https://doi.org/10.1016/j.copsyc.2017.04.020

Dana, D. (2018). *The polyvagal theory in therapy: Engaging the rhythm of regulation.* W. W. Norton & Company.

Dana, D. (2021). *Anchored: How to befriend your nervous system using polyvagal theory.* Sounds True.

Daniel, Y. (2005). *Dancing wisdom: Embodied knowledge in Haitian Vodou, Cuban Yoruba, and Bahian Candomblé.* University of Illinois Press.

Dilts, R. (1990). *Changing belief systems with NLP.* Meta Publications.

Dispenza, J. (2017). *Becoming supernatural: How common people are doing the uncommon.* Hay House.

Doidge, N. (2007). *The brain that changes itself: Stories of personal triumph from the frontiers of brain science.* Viking.

Dudeja, J. P. (2022). *Walking meditation: Techniques and benefits.* BlueRose Publishers.

Farb, N. A. S., Segal, Z. V., & Anderson, A. K. (2013). Attentional modulation of primary interoceptive and exteroceptive cortices. *Cerebral Cortex*, *23*(1), 114–126. https://doi.org/10.1093/cercor/bhr385

Felitti, V. J., Anda, R. F., Nordenberg, D., Williamson, D. F., Spitz, A. M., Edwards, V., Koss, M. P., & Marks, J. S. (1998). Relationship of childhood abuse and household dysfunction to many of the leading causes of death in adults. *American Journal of Preventive Medicine*, *14*(4), 245–258. https://doi.org/10.1016/S0749-3797(98)00017-8

Finger, S. (2001). *Origins of neuroscience: A history of explorations into brain function*. Oxford University Press.

Fisher, J. (2021). *Transforming the living legacy of trauma: A workbook for survivors and therapists*. PESI Publishing.

Frawley, D. (1997). *Ayurveda and the mind: The healing of consciousness*. Lotus Press.

Füstös, J., Gramann, K., Herbert, B. M., & Pollatos, O. (2013). On the embodiment of emotion regulation: Interoceptive awareness facilitates reappraisal. *Social Cognitive and Affective Neuroscience*, *8*(8), 911–917. https://doi.org/10.1093/scan/nss089

Garfinkel, S. N., Seth, A. K., Barrett, A. B., Suzuki, K., & Critchley, H. D. (2015). Knowing your own heart: Distinguishing interoceptive accuracy from interoceptive awareness. *Biological Psychology*, *104*, 65–74. https://doi.org/10.1016/j.biopsycho.2014.11.004

Gbadegesin, S. (1991). *African philosophy: Traditional Yoruba philosophy and contemporary African realities*. Peter Lang.

Gebirrebbi, S. (2025, June 8). *Prayer, peace, and the brain: The psychological and neurological impact of Islamic rituals.* Youth Neuropsychology Society. https://youthneuropsychology.com/2025/06/13/prayer-peace-and-the-brain-the-psychological-and-neurological-impact-of-islamic-rituals/

Glazer, M., Baer, R. D., Weller, S. C., de Alba, J. E. G., & Liebowitz, S. W. (2004). Susto and soul loss in Mexicans and Mexican Americans. *Cross-Cultural Research, 38*(3), 270–288. https://doi.org/10.1177/1069397104264277

Gottman, J., & Silver, N. (2015). *The seven principles for making marriage work: A practical guide from the country's foremost relationship expert.* Harmony Books.

Guffey, R. V., & Kaewkaen, A. (2017). Historical practices and modern interpretations: Understanding the Wai Khru ceremony as a Thai educational and cultural tradition. *Journal of Educational Leadership in Action, 5*(1), article 3. https://doi.org/10.62608/2164-1102.1049

Handy, E. S. C., & Pukui, M. K. (1999). *The Polynesian family system in Ka'ū, Hawai'i.* Mutual Publishing.

Hari, J. (2018). *Lost connections: Uncovering the real causes of depression—and the unexpected solutions.* Bloomsbury Publishing.

Haskie, M. J. (2023). Living holistically: Practicing the Navajo principles of Hózhǫ́ and K'é. *Holistic Education Review, 3*(1). https://her.journals.publicknowledgeproject.org/index.php/her/article/view/2662/2498

Heller, D. P. (2019). *The power of attachment: How to create deep and lasting intimate relationships.* Sounds True.

Helminski, K. (2000). *The knowing heart: A Sufi path of transformation*. Shambhala Publications.

Hersey, T. (2022). *Rest is resistance: A manifesto*. Little, Brown Spark.

Hölzel, B. K., Carmody, J., Vangel, M., Congleton, C., Yerramsetti, S. M., Gard, T., & Lazar, S. W. (2011). Mindfulness practice leads to increases in regional brain gray matter density. *Psychiatry Research: Neuroimaging, 191*(1), 36–43. https://doi.org/10.1016/j.pscychresns.2010.08.006

hooks, b. (2000). *All about love: New visions*. William Morrow.

Johnstone, K. (1981). *Impro: Improvisation and the theatre*. Methuen.

Kabat-Zinn, J. (2005). *Coming to our senses: Healing ourselves and the world through mindfulness*. Hyperion.

Kahn-John (Diné), M., & Koithan, M. (2015). Living in health, harmony, and beauty: The Diné (Navajo) Hózhó wellness philosophy. *Global Advances in Integrative Medicine and Health, 4*(3), 24–30. https://doi.org/10.7453/gahmj.2015.044

Kaptchuk, T. J. (2000). *The web that has no weaver: Understanding Chinese medicine*. McGraw-Hill.

Kashdan, T. B., Barrett, L. F., & McKnight, P. E. (2015). Unpacking emotion differentiation: Transforming unpleasant experience by perceiving distinctions in negativity. *Current Directions in Psychological Science, 24*(1), 10–16. https://doi.org/10.1177/0963721414550708

Ke, S., Guimond, A.-J., Tworoger, S. S., Huang, T., Chan, A. T., Liu, Y.-Y., & Kubzansky, L. D. (2023). Gut feelings: Associations of emotions and emotion regulation with the gut microbiome in women. *Psychological Medicine, 53*(15), 7151–7160. https://doi.org/10.1017/S0033291723000612

Kimmerer, R. W. (2013). *Braiding sweetgrass: Indigenous wisdom, scientific knowledge, and the teachings of plants.* Milkweed Editions.

Kosslyn, S. M., Ganis, G., & Thompson, W. L. (2001). Neural foundations of imagery. *Nature Reviews Neuroscience, 2*(9), 635–642. https://doi.org/10.1038/35090055

Leech, K., Stapleton, P., & Patching, A. (2024). *A roadmap to understanding interoceptive awareness and post-traumatic stress disorder: A scoping review. Frontiers in Psychiatry, 15,* 1355442. https://doi.org/10.3389/fpsyt.2024.1355442

Lerner, H. (2014). *The dance of anger: A woman's guide to changing the patterns of intimate relationships.* William Morrow Paperbacks.

Levine, P. A. (2010). *In an unspoken voice: How the body releases trauma and restores goodness.* North Atlantic Books.

Lewton, E. L., & Bydone, V. (2000). Identity and healing in three Navajo religious traditions: Sa'ah Naagháí Bik'eh Hózho. *Medical Anthropology Quarterly, 14*(4), 476–497. https://doi.org/10.1525/maq.2000.14.4.476

Lieberman, M. D., Eisenberger, N. I., Crockett, M. J., Tom, S. M., Pfeifer, J. H., & Way, B. M. (2007). Putting feelings into words: Affect labeling disrupts amygdala activity in response to affective stimuli. *Psychological Science, 18*(5), 421–428. https://doi.org/10.1111/j.1467-9280.2007.01916.x

Maezumi, H. T., & Glassman, B. (2002). *On Zen practice: Body, breath, mind.* Wisdom Publications.

Malchiodi, C. A. (2007). *The art therapy sourcebook*. McGraw-Hill.

Martínez-Radl, F. B., Hinton, D. E., & Stangier, U. (2023). *Susto* as a cultural conceptualization of distress: Existing research and aspects to consider for future investigations. *Transcultural Psychiatry, 60*(4), 690–702. https://doi.org/10.1177/13634615231163986

Maté, G., & Maté, D. (2022). *The myth of normal: Trauma, illness, and healing in a toxic culture*. Avery.

McEwen, B. S., & Sapolsky, R. M. (1995). Stress and cognitive function. *Current Opinion in Neurobiology, 5*(2), 205–216. https://doi.org/10.1016/0959-4388(95)80028-x

McGuire, M. B. (2003). Why bodies matter: A sociological reflection on spirituality and materiality. *Spiritus: A Journal of Christian Spirituality, 3*(1), 1–18. https://doi.org/10.1353/scs.2003.0017

Mead, H. M. (2003). *Tikanga Māori: Living by Māori values*. Huia Publishers.

Mehling, W. E., Price, C., Daubenmier, J. J., Acree, M., Bartmess, E., & Stewart, A. (2012). The multidimensional assessment of interoceptive awareness (MAIA). *PLoS ONE, 7*(11), e48230. https://doi.org/10.1371/journal.pone.0048230

Meisner, S., & Longwell, D. (1987). *Sanford Meisner on acting*. Vintage.

Neff, K. D. (2003). The development and validation of a scale to measure self-compassion. *Self and Identity, 2*(3), 223–250. https://doi.org/10.1080/15298860309027

Ogden, P., & Fisher, J. (2015). *Sensorimotor psychotherapy: Interventions for trauma and attachment.* W. W. Norton & Company.

Ogden, P., Minton, K., & Pain, C. (2006). *Trauma and the body: A sensorimotor approach to psychotherapy.* W. W. Norton & Company.

Ó Madagáin, B. (1985). The keening tradition in Ireland and Scotland. Éigse: *A Journal of Irish Studies, 21*, 225–252.

Perry, B. D., & Szalavitz, M. (2006). *The boy who was raised as a dog and other stories from a child psychiatrist's notebook: What traumatized children can teach us about loss, love, and healing.* Basic Books.

Perry, B. D., & Winfrey, O. (2021). *What happened to you? Conversations on trauma, resilience, and healing.* Flatiron Books.

Phromrekha, K. (2019, April 19). Rites of passage. *The Nation Weekend.* https://www.nationthailand.com/thai-destination/30367983

Pidokrajit, N. (2011). Thai traditional music in the Wai Khru ceremony. *Fine Arts International Journal: Srinakharinwirot University, 15*(1), 10–20. https://so01.tci-thaijo.org/index.php/jfofa/article/view/93002

Pollatos, O., & Schandry, R. (2008). Emotional processing and emotional memory are modulated by interoceptive awareness. *Cognition and Emotion, 22*(2), 272–287. https://doi.org/10.1080/02699930701357535

Porges, S. W. (2011). *The polyvagal theory: Neurophysiological foundations of emotions, attachment, communication, and self-regulation.* W. W. Norton & Company.

Rizzolatti, G., & Craighero, L. (2004). The mirror-neuron system. *Annual Review of Neuroscience, 27,* 169–192. https://doi.org/10.1146/annurev.neuro.27.070203.144230

Sakakeeny, M. (2013). *Roll with it: Brass bands in the streets of New Orleans.* Duke University Press.

Sapolsky, R. M. (2004). *Why zebras don't get ulcers: The acclaimed guide to stress, stress-related diseases, and coping* (3rd ed.). Henry Holt.

Saraswati, S. N. (2009). *Prana and pranayama.* Yoga Publications Trust.

Scaer, R. C. (2005). *The trauma spectrum: Hidden wounds and human resiliency.* W. W. Norton & Company.

Schore, A. N. (2012). *The science of the art of psychotherapy.* W. W. Norton & Company.

Schwartz, J. M., & Begley, S. (2003). *The mind and the brain: Neuroplasticity and the power of mental force.* Harper Perennial.

Shapiro, F. (2017). *Eye movement desensitization and reprocessing (EMDR) therapy: Basic principles, protocols, and procedures* (3rd ed.). Guilford Press.

Sheldrake, R. (2009). *Morphic resonance: The nature of formative causation* (4th ed.). Park Street Press.

Shepherd, G. M. (1991). *Foundations of the neuron doctrine.* Oxford University Press.

Siegel, D. J. (1999). *The developing mind: Toward a neurobiology of interpersonal experience.* Guilford Press.

Siegel, D. J. (2010). *The mindful therapist: A clinician's guide to mindsight and neural integration.* W. W. Norton & Company.

Siegel, D. J. (2020). *The developing mind: How relationships and the brain interact to shape who we are* (3rd ed.). Guilford Press.

Somé, M. P. (1994). *Of water and the spirit: Ritual, magic, and initiation in the life of an African shaman.* Penguin Books.

Taylor, J. B. (2008). *My stroke of insight: A brain scientist's personal journey.* Viking.

Taylor, S. E., Dickerson, C., Lewis, B. P., & Gruenewald, T. L. (2000). Feminine power: A male bias in social psychology and a possible way out. *Psychology of Women Quarterly, 24*(2), 212–216.

Thompson, R. F. (2005). *Tango: The art history of love.* Pantheon.

van der Kolk, B. (2014). *The body keeps the score: Brain, mind, and body in the healing of trauma.* Viking.

Walker, P. (2013). *Complex PTSD: From surviving to thriving.* Azure Coyote.

Wikeepa, J. (2023, July 5). The sacred hā (breath): Nurturing wairua and cultivating growth. *Hā Habit.* https://www.hahabitnz.com/en-us/blogs/news/the-sacred-ha-breath-nurturing-wairua-and-cultivating-growth

Winkelman, M. (2010). *Shamanism: A biopsychosocial paradigm of consciousness and healing.* Praeger.

Wyman, L. C. (2017). *Blessingway: With three versions of the myth recorded and translated from the Navajo by father Berard Haile, OFM.* University of Arizona Press.

About the Author

Rose Rita James, LCSW, MSW, MAT, (she/her) is a trauma therapist, somatic practitioner, special educator, artist, and ritualist whose debut work bridges neuroscience, ancestral wisdom, and poetic storytelling. Trained in EMDR, somatic experiencing, polyvagal theory, child development, family systems and constellations, and Reiki, she has spent over a decade guiding artists, therapists, students, and seekers through the sacred work of nervous system repair.

Her approach is tender, embodied, and unapologetically rooted in the belief that healing is not a destination; it is a daily practice of returning to oneself.

When she's not writing or working with clients, you can find her sculpting and painting in her office/studio or dancing and singing in her kitchen. In her free time, she takes to the streets of her community to protest with hand-painted signs or to parade in handmade costumes, depending on the needs of the day. She is most enlivened while traveling with her family, soaking in the awe and wonder of the earth's bounty. A good day for her includes breathless, table-slapping laughter and a few long hugs. *Tears Are Holy Water* is her first book.

Photo by Russell Ingram